New Perspectives on Power and Political Representation
from Ancient History to the Present Day

Radboud Studies in Humanities

Series Editor

Sophie Levie (*Radboud University*)

Editorial Board

Paul Bakker (*Radboud University*)
André Lardinois (*Radboud University*)
Daniela Müller (*Radboud University*)
Glenn Most (*Scuola Normale Superiore, Pisa*)
Peter Raedts (*Radboud University*)
Johan Tollebeek (*KU Leuven*)
Marc Slors (*Radboud University*)
Claudia Swan (*Northwestern University Evanston*)

VOLUME 9

The titles published in this series are listed at *brill.com/rsh*

New Perspectives on Power and Political Representation from Ancient History to the Present Day

Repertoires of Representation

Edited by

Harm Kaal
Daniëlle Slootjes

BRILL

LEIDEN | BOSTON

This is an open access title distributed under the terms of the CC-BY-NC 4.0 License, which permits any non-commercial use, distribution, and reproduction in any medium, provided no alterations are made and the original author(s) and source are credited.

Cover illustrations: A relief of the so-called Arch of Constantine depicting the emperor among senators, but clearly in a superior position. Source: H.P. L'Orange and A. von Gerkan, *Der spätantike Bildschmuck des Konstantinsbogens* (Berlin 1939), Taf 5.a. (top). Parliamentary duel in The House. Source: Photo by: Erich Salomon, in *Het Leven*, February 29, 1936 (bottom).

The Library of Congress Cataloging-in-Publication Data is available online at http://catalog.loc.gov
LC record available at http://lccn.loc.gov/2019015897

Typeface for the Latin, Greek, and Cyrillic scripts: "Brill". See and download: brill.com/brill-typeface.

ISSN 2213-9729
ISBN 978-90-04-29195-9 (hardback)
ISBN 978-90-04-29196-6 (e-book)

Copyright 2019 by the Author(s). Published by Koninklijke Brill NV, Leiden, The Netherlands.
Koninklijke Brill NV incorporates the imprints Brill, Brill Hes & De Graaf, Brill Nijhoff, Brill Rodopi, Brill Sense, Hotei Publishing, mentis Verlag, Verlag Ferdinand Schöningh and Wilhelm Fink Verlag.
Koninklijke Brill NV reserves the right to protect the publication against unauthorized use and to authorize dissemination by means of offprints, legitimate photocopies, microform editions, reprints, translations, and secondary information sources, such as abstracting and indexing services including databases. Requests for commercial re-use, use of parts of the publication, and/or translations must be addressed to Koninklijke Brill NV.

This book is printed on acid-free paper and produced in a sustainable manner.

Contents

Acknowledgements   VII
List of Figures   VIII
Contributors   X

1   Introduction: Repertoires of Representation   1
    Harm Kaal and Daniëlle Slootjes

2   Emperors and Councillors: Imperial Representation between Republic
    and Empire   11
    Olivier Hekster

3   Politics of Access at the Court of the Caliph   26
    Maaike van Berkel

4   Representative Bodies in Medieval Religious Orders: A Discarded
    Legacy?   37
    Bert Roest

5   The Political Rhetoric of Capitals: Rome and Versailles in the Baroque
    Period, or the "Power of Place"   56
    Peter Rietbergen

6   Repertoires of Access in Princely Courts, 1400-1750   78
    Dries Raeymaekers and Sebastiaan Derks

7   The Image of Prime Minister Colijn: Public Visualisation of Political
    Leadership in the 1930s   94
    Marij Leenders and Joris Gijsenbergh

8   Postwar Popular Politics: Integrating the Voice of the People in Postwar
    Political History   124
    Harm Kaal and Vincent van de Griend

9   Majdan: Presence and Political Representation in Post-Communist
    Ukraine   144
    Wim van Meurs and Olga Morozova

10 Regulation without Representation? Independent Regulatory Authorities
and Representative Claim-Making in the Netherlands, 1997-now   171
Adriejan van Veen

Index   202

Acknowledgements

Repertoires of Representation was the title of a lecture series hosted by the editors in 2014 and 2015 at The Institute for Historical, Literary and Cultural Studies of Radboud University. It was an attempt on our part to draw connections between the research that is carried out by our colleagues at the departments of ancient, medieval, cultural and political history. We would like to thank all participants for their contributions and the animated discussions at our monthly meetings.

Figures

2.1   A Clipeus virtutis (26 BC) showcasing the honours bestowed upon Augustus by the Senate   14

2.2   Augustus being depicted alongside senators in a sacrificial procession on the so-called Ara Pacis   21

2.3   The Decennalia base showing the emperor sacrificing in the presence of the Genius 'divine spirit' of the Senate   21

2.4   A relief of the so-called Arch of Constantine depicting the emperor among senators, but clearly in a superior position   22

5.1   Portrait of Pope Sixtus V (r. 1575-1580). Published by Nicolaus van Aelst (Flemish, Brussels 1526-1613 Rome)   63

5.2   Versailles, during the first building campaign. Pierre Patel, ca. 1670   69

5.3   Versailles, after the last building campaign. Pierre-Denis Martin, ca. 1720   69

6.1   A view of the palace of Versailles (after Jacques Rigaud)   86

6.2   Charles-Alexandre of Croÿ (1581-1624)   89

7.1   'Colijn speaks!'   99

7.2   Parliamentary duel in The House   101

7.3   'After 6 years on the breakers...'   102

7.4   'Antipodes, Colijn having a friendly chat with the leader of the Communist Party Mr. de Visser with that other 'extremist', NSB's Mr. Woudenberg standing behind'   105

7.5   'Third Tuesday in September. Hunting season is opened...'   106

7.6a   'Primary 2 at politics school' November 1933. Boys: 'Sir, please ban Mussert. We are all scared of him!' December 1933. Schoolmaster: Get lost you spoilsport! Or they will all leave me!   107

7.6b   'January 1934. Schoolmaster and teachers (together): 'Right boys, the danger has passed! He's gone!'   107

7.7   'Even more feelers?'   108

7.8   Traditional staging of a statesman   111

7.9   Private and public within politics   114

7.10   'The third Tuesday in September: 'Get to work!'. PM/School Master H. Colijn, calls the playing MPs/school children to attention, on the opening day of the parliamentary year   115

7.11   Captain of the Ship of State   116

7.12   'Hold that course!'   117

9.1   Euromajdan in Kyiv on 1 December 2013   147

FIGURES

IX

9.2 The headquarters of Euromajdan in January 2014, a prominent portrait of Stepan Bandera at the front entrance   164

10.1 The representative claim framework (RCF)   175

10.2 OPTA depicts its constituency in its annual report   185

10.3 NZa corporate logo   187

Contributors

Maaike van Berkel
is Professor of Medieval History at the Institute for Historical, Literary and Cultural Studies, Radboud University Nijmegen.

Sebastiaan Derks
is Head of the Department of Digital Data Management at the Huygens Institute for the History of the Netherlands.

Joris Gijsenbergh
is a political historian and guest researcher at the Philipps-Universität in Marburg, Germany

Vincent van de Griend
is Junior Researcher at the Institute for Historical, Literary and Cultural Studies, Radboud University Nijmegen.

Olivier Hekster
is Professor of Ancient History at the Institute for Historical, Literary and Cultural Studies, Radboud University Nijmegen.

Harm Kaal
is Associate Professor of Political History at the Institute for Historical, Literary and Cultural Studies, Radboud University Nijmegen.

Marij Leenders
is Associate Professor of Political History at the Institute for Historical, Literary and Cultural Studies, Radboud University Nijmegen.

Wim van Meurs
is Professor of European Political History at the Institute for Historical, Literary and Cultural Studies, Radboud University Nijmegen.

Olga Morozova
studied History at Radboud University Nijmegen and Russian and Eurasian Studies at Leiden University.

CONTRIBUTORS

Dries Raeymaekers

is Associate Professor of Political History at the Institute for Historical, Literary and Cultural Studies, Radboud University Nijmegen.

Peter Rietbergen

is Emeritus Professor of Cultural History at the Institute for Historical, Literary and Cultural Studies, Radboud University Nijmegen.

Bert Roest

is Associate Professor of Medieval History at the Institute for Historical, Literary and Cultural Studies, Radboud University Nijmegen.

Daniëlle Slootjes

is Associate Professor of Ancient History at the Institute for Historical, Literary and Cultural Studies, Radboud University Nijmegen

Adriejan van Veen

is Associate Professor of Political History at the Institute for Historical, Literary and Cultural Studies, Radboud University Nijmegen

CHAPTER 1

Introduction: Repertoires of Representation

Harm Kaal and Daniëlle Slootjes

From classical societies to our modern age, ruling classes and their subjects have sought ways to communicate their rights and expectations to each other. Rulers have pursued avenues for legitimising and consolidating their position of power. Subjects in turn have looked for ways to express their loyalty or make known their discontent about their leaders. Over time and in different political systems, both leaders and those being led have developed and reshaped various modes of political communication to do so, be it oral, written, or material.[1] This volume examines these various modes of political communication between rules and ruled from antiquity to the present day by the application of the concept of representation. This concept has proven its value in studies that explore the functioning of power relations.[2]

According to recent studies and public debate, political representation is in a state of crisis. The authority of the key institute of political representation – parliament – and its members is subject to a fierce debate and the same goes for the status of political parties as the competent and trustworthy intermediaries between government and the people.[3] Initiatives have been launched to develop alternative forms of political representation.[4] Moreover, political scientists and philosophers have tried to come to terms with the recent historical trajectory of political representation.[5] These studies have been added to an already vast body of scholarship on political representation that stretches out into the disciplines of political philosophy, political science, art history, cultural history and, of course, political history. Most of these studies are oriented towards the "formal" aspects of political representation, treating it as a status that results from particular political procedures and constitutional arrangements, and research is dedicated to an investigation of how representatives take up their role.

In a thought-provoking article on political representation, Michael Saward takes issue with such interpretations. Saward invites us to move away from a

---

1 Craig (1999) 119-161; Carey (2009).
2 Hall (1997); Pitkin (1967); Weber (2003).
3 Crouch (2004); Mair (2013).
4 Van Reybrouck (2013). Excerpts in English available via Van Reybrouck (2014).
5 Manin (1997); Rosanvallon (2008); Saward (2005).

© HARM KAAL AND DANIËLLE SLOOTJES, 2019 | DOI:10.1163/9789004291966_002
This is an open access chapter distributed under the terms of the CC-BY-NC 4.0 License.

focus on "forms" of representation (such as trustees or delegates) and to ask ourselves the question, "what is going on *in* representation?" His answers revolve around the notion of claim making: what is going on in representation is that political actors are claiming to be representative. Rather than mirroring reality (*mimesis*), representation thus is constructed through the making of representative claims. He sees political representation as a "dynamic relationship" and stresses its "performative" and "aesthetic" aspects: "representing is performing [...] and the performance [...] adds up to a claim that someone is or can be 'representative.'"[6]

Saward's main contribution to the historiography of modern political representation is that he offers a theoretical reflection that underpins recent deconstructions of political representation in the wake of the cultural and linguistic turn. For political historians, Saward's approach to political representation indeed sounds familiar.[7] Since the 1980s, a broad body of scholarship has emerged on the impact and meaning of the language and culture of politics in explaining the formation of political identities and constituencies, starting with Gareth Stedman Jones's work on the Chartist movement and Lynn Hunt's and Keith Michael Baker's studies on eighteenth century French political culture.[8] Political constituencies, Jon Lawrence has argued, should not be treated as "pre-established social blocs awaiting representation," but seen as "painstakingly constructed [...] alliances." Political parties in turn were not the "passive beneficiaries of structural divisions within society," but "dynamic organizations actively involved in the definition of political interests and the construction of political alliances" through political discourse.[9] The performative power of the language and culture of politics has also been taken up by German political historians such as Willibald Steinmetz and Thomas Mergel in explorations of both extremist and democratic politics.[10]

In this volume, building on Saward, we employ the concept of representation as an instrument that assists us in understanding the "dynamic relationship" between elites and the people which is shaped by the following two discursive practices. First of all, constructions of self-representation are being employed in the search for public display of one's power, be it of the individual ruler or of the collective of subjects. We define a variety of material and immaterial instruments that have been used to achieve and promote

---

6   Saward (2006) 302.
7   Saward does not seem to acknowledge this: he does not refer to any of the major historical studies on political representation mentioned in the notes below.
8   Stedman Jones (1983); Hunt (1984); Baker (1987); Baker (1990).
9   Lawrence (1993) 630-31.
10   Steinmetz (2011); Mergel (2010).

INTRODUCTION

self-representation, ranging from statues, coins, dress, manifestations to speeches, biographies, and interviews. Throughout the centuries these instruments have been at the heart of constructions of self-representation or *Selbstdarstellung*.[11] Nevertheless, we also witness the emergence of new media or the abandonment of certain instruments that are no longer being regarded as effective (see for instance the chapters by Hekster, and Gijsenbergh and Leenders). In our effort to examine these constructions of self-representation and position them into a larger repertoire, it is important to consider their reception as well as contested or alternative constructions. Both rulers and subjects are agents and receptors within these constructions of self-representation. Furthermore, accessibility to rulers offers valuable insights into the representative relations between rulers and ruled. This requires us to take into account the various practices through which accessibility of rulers was shaped, expressed, and represented, which includes the visual and material culture that surrounded those in power (see the chapters by Van Berkel, Rietbergen, and Raeymaekers and Derks).

Second, representative claims are verbal acts through which political actors and institutions present themselves as representatives of others. Political actors such as politicians, leaders of social movements, or even "ordinary" citizens claim that they represent a particular group of people, that they speak on behalf of others (see the chapters by Van Meurs and Morozova, Kaal and Van der Griend). The same is applicable to institutions, ranging from parliament to less obvious institutions such as medieval religious orders (see the chapter by Roest) and present-day independent regulatory agencies (see the chapter by Van Veen). Deconstruction helps us to appreciate that through these claims people are in fact invited to understand themselves as a group that is being represented. This thus calls for an analysis of political communication, because here we find how a broad range of political actors define the nature and identity of those they claim to represent.[12]

Representative claims are "read back," that is, they are not merely imposed on a passive audience, but they are received and possibly also contested in various ways. We should therefore also explore political representation *in interaction* between the makers and recipients of representative claims (see the chapters by Van Meurs and Morozova, and Kaal and Van der Griend). Moreover, representative claims potentially have a "silencing effect": turning those who are claimed to be represented into a passive audience that is expected to put its trust into their representative.[13]

---

11   Weber (2003).

12   Saward (2006) 313-14. See for a more extensive account also Saward (2010).

13   Saward (2006) 303-04.

Building on these two discursive practices, we aim to move away from normative and essentialist notions of political representation, as well as from limited, reductionist associations of political representation with the formal aspects of modern, democratic, electoral, and parliamentarian politics. In this volume, we bring together work on political representation conducted by scholars of Radboud University working on ancient, medieval, early modern, and modern political history. The research conducted by the political historians of the modern era on representative claim-making and self-representation acted as a starting point for a discussion with colleagues working on earlier eras. To what extent were the concepts that are at the heart of modern theories of political representation – such as representative claims and repertoires of representation – also applicable to earlier political systems and contexts? And to what extent are acts of (self-)representation built around similar practices and discourses throughout the ages? This set-up enabled us to integrate recent work by ancient, medieval, and early modern political historians, and the research conducted within the field of political science and communication, political philosophy, and modern political history. The latter includes innovative studies on deliberative democracy, on the interaction between formal and informal politics, and on practices of democracy, such as the recent work on petitioning by political scientist Dan Carpenter.[14] The former have introduced new methods to explore the history of political representation from a constructivist, cultural perspective. This has, among others, resulted in new perspectives on the concept of political power through research on how Roman emperors, medieval kings, and the pope *publicly represented themselves* as a way of *performing power*. Such studies have drawn attention to the semiotics of representation in the form of symbols, rituals, festivities, dress, speech acts (and so forth).[15] This invites us to also explore these elements of political representation for the modern era. But it also works the other way around: what has been argued for modern representative claims is also significant for scholars working on earlier eras. The public performance of power through a range of media like statues, parades, dress, coins, and architecture, for instance, also involved a negotiation of the reception of these representations of the political and again show that political representation is in essence a dynamic process.

Our volume does not offer a full-fledged diachronic overview, but we do aim to inspire scholars to delve deeper into the continuities (and breaks) at play in political representation. Chapters collected in this volume at least provide

---

14 Rollison (2010); Carpenter (in press); Kruke and Kufferath (2018); Landemore (2012); Fishkin (1995).

15 Braungart (2012).

INTRODUCTION 5

enough evidence to suggest that this is a path worth pursuing. Moreover, although the majority of the chapters focus on the European context, the chapter by medievalist Maaike van Berkel on the accessibility of Abbasid rulers at their courts shows striking similarities with Western repertoires of representation. She makes clear that it is also worthwhile for future researchers to widen their geographical scope and study political representation cross-culturally, exploring similarities and differences in practices and discourses of political representation not only across time, but also across space.

We contend that the construction of political representation involves a set of discourses, practices, and mechanisms that, although they have been applied and appropriated in various ways in a range of historical contexts, has stood the test of time. As a consequence, the contributions in our volume will demonstrate that, due to the continuity in certain customs and constructions of self-representation, the artificial boundaries between Antiquity, the Middle Ages or the Renaissance, and the modern era should be lifted. One can think, for instance, of the ceremonial surrounding the inauguration of Queen Elizabeth II of England in 1952 or that of King Willem Alexander of the Netherlands in 2013 to see the strong resemblance with the ceremonies of Roman or Karolingian emperors and kings. Modern kings and queens stand in a long tradition that we will fail to understand if we continue to apply artificial chronological boundaries.[16] Moreover, our perspective allows us to connect the assemblies of the people and representative claims as they emerged in the early Roman Republic with those in the Middle Ages and later eras when parliaments arose. Indeed, the determination of the Roman tribune of the plebs Tiberius Gracchus to make the Roman people aware of their potential power shows similarities with later expressions throughout the states of Europe of popular leaders who offered to represent citizens within politics.

The contributions in this volume, which are presented in a chronological order, originate from a series of seminars in which the members of the Institute for Historical, Literary, and Cultural Studies at Radboud University reflected on the meaning of the concept of political representation in their field. In his chapter, Olivier Hekster shows that, in their representation of power, Roman emperors had to deal with institutionally and deeply entrenched senatorial elites. Hekster analyses imperial Roman representation in order to explore how the institutional basis of councillors surrounding a monarch influences and shapes competing representative claims of rulers and the circles revolving around them. Early emperors had to uphold the republican ideal that their extraordinary position was based on senatorial acclamation. Architecture,

---

16   Stollberg-Rilinger (2013).

images, coins, and other visual sources are studied and show a mixed message of a superior senator annex monarch visible throughout Rome. The notion of Roman emperorship as tempered by senatorial advice remained strong, but the balance increasingly shifted towards councillors as supporting actors who belonged to the monarch. Although the distance between reality and representative claim had widened enormously over the centuries, the representative claim by senatorial councillors was maintained. Roman emperors continued to rule in a senatorial world, at least symbolically.

In her contribution, Maaike van Berkel focuses on the accessibility of rulers by analysing how access to the Abbasid Caliph was represented in (near)contemporary writings on the reign of Al-Muqtadir (r. 906-932). Van Berkel approaches access as a gradual and differentiated phenomenon shaped by cultural representations. Accessibility and simplicity were the ideal example of early Islam as epitomised by Mohammed himself, but were gradually replaced by the more hierarchical social models of the cultures the Muslims conquered. Although access to the Abbasid court became increasingly regulated, the seemingly contradictory discourses on the accessible yet distant ruler remained dominant. Al-Muqtadir's rule is an exception, as he is virtually solely represented as an inaccessible, distant Iranian ruler. In this case, representations of power closely resembled Al-Muqtadir who came to power at a young age and was dependent on his relatives and courtiers to rule. This perceived relationship of dependence resulted in ideals of accessible rulers being projected on the vizier, rather than his caliph.

The political nature of medieval religious orders is at the heart of Bert Roest's chapter. Roest argues that, in the historiography of medieval political thought and religious orders, the representative organisation in religious orders is often neglected. He demonstrates that religious orders were powerful, multinational organisations that played many roles within medieval society and influenced secular governance. Classical texts on political thought therefore need to be re-examined from this angle, as they were shaped by familiarity with religious modes of representation and delegation. Roest discusses Franciscan thought on and practices of representative government and urges historians to take it seriously. Franciscan ideals of evangelical equality gradually evolved in a balanced hierarchical administrative system. Later changes reinforced the executive power of provincial ministers and the minister general, but did not undermine the central tenets of the representative elements and priority attached to the legislative power of the general chapter. Franciscans played important roles in secular and ecclesiastical government, and their expertise, especially in technical matters, was drawn upon and applied in local representative government.

INTRODUCTION

In his contribution to this volume Peter Rietbergen analyses and compares the built environments of Rome and Versailles and their representations in print as rhetorical texts that proclaim a message of supreme power. Although Rome and Versailles are perceived as the prime embodiments of religious and secular monarchy, the distinctions were less clear-cut than often assumed. Both French and papal rulers' power representations were intimately shaped by conceptualisations of cosmic order and hierarchy legitimating their rule. Popes very much represented themselves with all the trappings of temporal monarchs, while the kings of France never ceased to present themselves in a religious, transcendental context as well. Both Rome and Versailles were constructed to face political challenges, respectively the Reformation and Humanism and power claims by urban elites and aristocrats. Both popes and kings exploited all aspects of visual propaganda, from religious iconology to print publications, thereby elevating the political rhetoric of capitals to a new height.

The issue of access is again taken up by Dries Raeymaekers and Sebastiaan Derks. Much like Van Berkel, they approach access primarily form a cultural perspective. Whereas previous historical research on the *politics of access* focused on physical access and its regulation to monarchs, their chapter widens the scope for future research by including the interconnected and complex practices in which the idea of access itself was shaped, expressed, and represented: the *culture of access*. Access was firstly a process of negotiation – a constant interplay of spaces, strategies, personalities, rituals, artefacts, and events – which was presented and visualised in varied ways and enacted through diverse repertoires of performances. By focusing on its representation, the manifold nature of arrangements characterising courtly life can be approached better in context, and its structures laid bare. Raeymaekers and Derks discuss four repertoires to study this: the articulation of space; the regulation of space; monopolising access; and visualising access, as in day-to-day practices, rituals, the visual and material culture of courts, architecture, and the politics of access are expressed.

Marij Leenders and Joris Gijsenbergh invite us to consider the modern era with their chapter on the ways in which the Dutch Prime Minister Hendrikus Colijn (1869-1944) has been depicted in photographs and cartoons. They show how the relationship between leaders and "the people" was a recurring theme in interwar debates on the system of political representation. Leenders and Gijsenbergh argue that visual sources offer insights into the ideals of political representation as they were presented to voters. Photographers, caricaturists, and (newspaper) editors influenced the reputation and representation of politics and attempted to legitimise and delegitimise certain types of leadership. Two repertoires of representing idealised leadership stand out: deliberative leadership, with leaders holding courteous, constructive discussions with MPs, and authoritative leadership or disciplined democracy, in which leaders largely ignored Parliament. The 1930s witnessed an important shift in representing representative politics: deliberative parliamentarianism did not disappear, but a strong leader now represented the nation, and photographs and caricatures delivered an important contribution to this image. Although some perceived this shift in the representation of political leadership as a threat to democracy, the vast majority, so Leenders and Gijsenbergh argue, welcomed it as an improvement of the system of parliamentary democracy.

Harm Kaal and Vincent van de Griend offer a critical examination of the current discourse of a crisis of political representation in both research and public debate. This discourse suffers from a lack of reflection on the multifaceted ways in which politicians and the people they represent interact. Historians, so they argue, must ask what went on *in* representation and explore the repertoires of communicative practices to study the interaction between the formal and informal worlds of politics. The authors identify four practices to explore popular perceptions of political representation and "the political": letters; television; opinion polls; and popular culture. They introduce a case study of letters written to the Dutch social-democratic party in the second half of the 1960s. These letters offer insight into how people experienced and responded to party developments, how they conceived themselves as political subjects, but also how the party itself responded to the "voice of the people." They claim that in order to incorporate the voice of the people in post-war political history, historians must study the communicative practices and media through which citizens have voiced their political opinions.

The chapter by Wim van Meurs and Olga Morozova concentrates on contemporary practices of representative claim-making in post-communist Ukraine. Van Meurs and Morozova compellingly show that representation in the sense of claiming to act on the behalf of others rests on legitimation. In 2014, opposition leader Julia Tymošenko, just released from prison, went to Majdan, Kyiv's main square in an attempt to turn herself into the leader of the popular revolt that had broken out. The crowd, however, failed to accept her claim that she would defend their interests. The protesters, as the authors argue, "refused to be 'led' or 'represented'" and instead embraced the romantic ideal of popular sovereignty. Van Meurs and Morozova do not approach democratic representation or street politics through a normative lens, but instead explore explicit references and acknowledged role models by actors themselves in the dynamics of political contestation. The authors zoom in on Majdan square as a site of political contestation to study its layers of meanings and how actors diachronically link their repertoires of action and representative

INTRODUCTION

claims to the past. They argue that "Majdan" signifies a fundamental rejection of existing representative institutions and show how street politics acts as part of a repertoire with which "the people" contest politicians' representative claims.

In the final part of this volume Adriejan van Veen explores the representative claims of Independent Regulatory Authorities (IRA). Van Veen takes issues with the characterisation of IRAS as "unrepresentative" unelected bodies and goes on to show that they should be considered non-electoral representative claimants that wield considerable competences today. He offers an examination of four Dutch IRAS by applying Michael Saward's framework of representative claims. These IRAS have been instituted as independent bodies that are to represent economic and non-economic "public" interests in marketised and liberalised domains. Van Veen shows that the IRAS themselves increasingly claim to represent public and consumer activities in their public self-representation. Moreover, through their interaction with representatives of sectoral interests, IRAS are also confronted with a host of representative claims. Far from being unrepresentative, IRAS, thus, are representative claimants – and facilitators of representative claims. Independent market regulation involves the construction and reception of representative claims just as much as the traditional electoral sphere.

Bibliography

Baker, K.M., *Inventing the French Revolution. Essays on French Political Culture in the Eighteenth Century* (Cambridge, Eng., 1990).

Baker, K.M., (ed.), *The French Revolution and the Creation of Modern Political Culture*, vol. I, *The Political Culture of the Old Regime* (Oxford, 1987).

Braungart, W., *Ästhetik der Politik, Ästhetik des Politischen: Ein Versuch in Thesen* (Göttingen, 2012).

Carey, J.W., "A cultural approach to communication," in J.W. Carey (ed.), *Communication as Culture: Essays on Media and Society* (New York, 2009), 11-28.

Carpenter, D., *Visions of the Republic: Petitions, Associations and Elections in Early America* (in press).

Craig, R.T., "Communication Theory as a Field," in *Communication Theory* 9 (1999), 119-161.

Crouch, C., *Post-Democracy* (Cambridge, Eng., 2004).

Fishkin, J.S., *The Voice of the People: Public Opinion and Democracy* (New Haven and London, 1995).

Hall, S., (ed.), *Cultural Representations and Signifying Practices* (London, 1997).

Hunt, L., *Politics, Culture and Class in the French Revolution* (Berkeley, 1984).

Kruke, A. and P. Kufferath, "Einleitung: Krisendiagnosen, Meistererzählungen und Alltagspraktiken. Aktuelle Forschungen und Narrationen zur Demokratiegeschichte in Westeuropa," in *Archiv für Sozialgeschichte* 58 (2018), 3-20.

Landemore, H., *Democratic Reason. Politics, Collective Intelligence, and the Rule of the Many* (Princeton and Oxford, 2012).

Mair, P., *Ruling the Void. The Hollowing of Western Democracy* (London, 2013).

Manin, B., *The Principles of Representative Government* (Cambridge, Eng., 1997).

Mergel, T., *Propaganda nach Hitler: Eine Kulturgeschichte des Wahlkampfs in der Bundesrepublik 1949-1990* (Göttingen, 2010).

Pitkin, H.F., *The Concept of Representation* (Berkely, 1967).

Reybrouck, D. van, "Against Elections," *Policy Network*, 23 October 2014, [accessed online 25.11.2018: <http://www.policy-network.net/pno_detail.aspx?ID=4760&title=Against-elections>].

Reybrouck, D. van, *Tegen verkiezingen* (Amsterdam, 2013).

Rollison, D.A., *Commonwealth of the People: Popular Politics and England's Long Social Revolution, 1066-1649* (Cambridge, Eng., 2010).

Rosanvallon, P., *Counter-Democracy. Politics in an Age of Distrust* (Cambridge, Eng., 2008).

Saward, M., *The Representative Claim* (Oxford, 2010).

Saward, M., "The Representative Claim," in *Contemporary Political Theory* 5 (2006), 297-318.

Saward, M., "Governance and the Transformation of Political Representation," in J. Newman (ed.), *Remaking Governance: Peoples, Politics and the Public Sphere* (Bristol, 2005), 179-196.

Stedman Jones, G., *Languages of Class. Studies in English Working Class History (1832-1982)* (Cambridge, Eng., 1983).

Steinmetz, W., (ed.), *Political Languages in the Age of Extremes* (Oxford, 2011).

Stollberg-Rillinger, B., *Rituale* (Frankfurt am Main/New York, 2013).

Weber, G. and M. Zimmermann (eds.), *Propaganda – Selbstdarstellung – Repräsentation in römischen Kaiserreich des 1. Jhs. n. Chr.* (Stuttgart, 2003).

CHAPTER 2

Emperors and Councillors: Imperial Representation between Republic and Empire

Olivier Hekster

Introduction: Rulers and Ruling Circles

No monarch rules on his own. Even the most unmitigated autocrat needs people to undertake administrative roles, sit as judges, command armies, and support the pomp and splendour with which rulers surround themselves. Yet, the status that these supporting actors have can vary wildly. On one end of the spectrum are people who wholly belong to the monarch and depend on his whims for their position. The most eloquent description of that extreme is probably in Kapuscinski's semi-documentary description of the court of Haile Sellasie:

> The faction of 'personal people' was a peculiarity of our regime, created by the Emperor himself. His Supreme Majesty, a partisan of a strong state and centralised power, had to lead a cunning and skilful fight against the aristocratic faction, which wanted to rule in the provinces and have a weak, pliable Emperor. But he could not fight the aristocracy with his own hands, so he always promoted into his circle, as representatives of the people, bright young men from the lowest orders, chosen from the lowest ranks of the plebeians, picked often on little more than a hunch from the mobs that surrounded his majesty whenever he went among the people. These 'personal people' of the emperor, dragged straight from our desperate and miserable provinces into the salons of the highest courtiers – where they met the undisguised hatred of the long-established aristocrats – served the emperor with an almost indescribable eagerness, indeed a passion, for they had quickly tasted the splendours of the Palace and the evident charms of power, and they knew that they had arrived there, come within reach of the highest state dignities, only through the will of His Highness. It was to them that the Emperor would entrust the positions requiring greatest confidence.[1]

---

1 Kapuscinski (1978) 30.

© OLIVIER HEKSTER, 2019 | DOI:10.1163/9789004291966_003

This is an open access chapter distributed under the terms of the CC-BY-NC 4.0 License.

At the other side of the spectrum is, by implication, a monarch interacting with a much more self-contained group of advisors, who hold their position by long-established patterns. Examples of weak rulers effectively outranked by powerful aristocratic courtiers are abound throughout history. Yet, not only weak rulers are confronted by self-sufficient surrounding circles. How does one deal with a situation in which both ruler and advisors have a strong institutional embedding? How then does one present the ruler and aristocracy? In other words, how does the institutional basis of the people surrounding a monarch influence the representations of the monarch and his advisors? If, as argued in the introduction to this volume, representation is constructed through making representative claims, rather than mirroring a reality, surely the importance of embedding would feature such claims. This chapter looks at imperial Roman representation, as a case study to explore competing claims of representation of rulers and the circles surrounding them.

Absent Emperorship in a Senatorial World

There were no Roman emperors and yet the emperor formed the centre of the world. When Roman sole rule was shaped under the first emperor Augustus, he had the negative example of his adoptive father Caesar in mind. The latter was assassinated for being too openly monarchical, so his adoptive son formulated his position of sole rule over a long trajectory in which he accumulated various honours and powers step-by-step. Important in this process was that he did not seem to acquire these powers actively (to avoid appearing monarchical) but that they were bestowed upon him by existing (Republican) institutions.[2] As stated in the much-cited *Res Gestae Divi Augusti*, 'the accomplishments of the deified Augustus', which were inscribed in bronze and marble throughout the empire after the emperor's death in 14 AD:

> In my sixth and seventh consulships [28 and 27 BC], after I had put an end to civil wars, although by everyone's agreement I had power over everything (*potens rerum omnium*), I transferred the state from my power into the control of the Roman senate and people. For this service, I was named Augustus by senatorial decree, and the doorposts of my house were publicly clothed with laurels, and a civic crown was fastened upon my doorway, and a golden shield was set up in the Julian senate house; through an inscription on this shield the fact was declared that the Roman senate

---

2 Hodgson (2016) 264-65.

EMPERORS AND COUNCILLORS

and people were giving it to me because of my valour, clemency, justice and piety. After this time, I excelled everyone in influence (*auctoritas*), but I had no more power (*potestas*) than the others who were my colleagues in each magistracy.[3]

The passage is much discussed, with most attention going to the accuracy of the *auctoritas/potestas* statement, and the meaning of *auctoritas* in this context.[4] Yet equally striking is the emphasis in the passage on the ruler as a passive figure. All the powers were given to him, and in the list of honours the golden shield in the senate house took pride of place (see Figure 2.1). The senate house itself was renamed after Julius Caesar (who rebuilt it after it was demolished by fire) showing the continuous ambiguity of Augustus's representation. In the heart of Republican institutions, renamed after the founder of what would become an imperial dynasty, a golden shield marked that one person now outshone everyone else. But that same shield formulated what the new ruler also proclaimed elsewhere: that his extraordinary position was based on senatorial acclamation. He was "simply" a more prominent member of the elite. Yet, as one of the foremost scholars on imperial history remarked over thirty years ago with wonderful irony, most people in Rome were "probably not clever enough to read it as a senatorial document."[5]

The mixed message that the new ruler was just a superior senator (the 'first senator', or *princeps*), but at the same time a recognisable monarch, was visible throughout Rome.[6] A massive mausoleum celebrated the new-founded dynasty, but made references to republican precedents. A new monumental Forum celebrated the young monarch, by placing him in a line with a number of senatorial heroes. And even the imperial residence showed these two facets of imperial representation. Augustus extended an existing senatorial house on the Palatine – the location of many of the elite residences – to his purpose, and his second-century biographer Suetonius emphasised the modesty of this new house. To an extent, Augustus's house seems to only have appeared modest in retrospect, but its more monumental aspects could all be argued away by pointing at precedents, and because the most ornamental parts were dedicated to various Roman gods.[7] Augustus's house was linked to a new shining temple for Apollo, near the historical hut of Rome's founder Romulus, and in

---

3 *RGDA* 34, trans. Cooley (2009) 98-99, with commentary on 256-72.
4 Rowe (2005) 80-84.
5 Millar (1984).
6 Hekster (2011) 111-24.
7 Raimondi Cominesi (2018); Hekster (2006).

FIGURE 2.1　A Clipeus virtutis (26 BC) showcasing the honours bestowed upon Augustus by the Senate. *Source*: Wikimedia commons, photo by Maarjaara (CC BY 2.0). [accessed online 28.02.2019: <https://commons.wikimedia.org/wiki/File:Clipeus_virtutis_-_Augusto_-_Arles.jpg>].

the vicinity of a famous temple to Magna Mater.[8] This showed the emperor's near-divine prominence, but could be presented as honourable links to Rome's famous past and present. Many senators were Augustus's neighbours, and some of them lived in houses which were strictly speaking comparable. But the overall impression of his house was very different from theirs.

Representation is more than words, images, and buildings. At a performative level, too, the ambiguous position of the Roman ruler as simultaneously a representative but superior senator and a near omnipotent emperor becomes clear. An important aspect of Roman Republican social interaction consisted of fairly formalised series of meetings, of which formal dinner and the morning reception (*salutatio*) were the more important ones. At the *salutatio*, clients could pay respect to their (senatorial) patron and ask his advice or support. Houses were set up for the ceremony, with sufficient room in the *atrium* or *vestibulum* for groups of clients to wait, whilst more prominent clients or

---

8　On the Apollo temple as a "golden temple" see Zink (2009). On the link between Augustus's house and the temple, see still Zanker (1987) 59-60.

EMPERORS AND COUNCILLORS

friends (*amici*) were being received. As any senator, the emperor would receive his clients, but amongst his "friends" were increasing numbers of prominent senators. This increasingly made the imperial salutation into a social and political ritual, which distinguished people's rank and relationship to the emperor.[9] The performance also became more complex: rather than the earlier handshake, it became possible to kiss the emperor on hand, chest, or knee, or be embraced by him. Different reactions reflected a different relationship, and court officials (*admissionales*) were appointed to manage the event.

Likewise, being invited to official dinners became a sign of status, and the dinners themselves varied widely in scale and ostentatiousness. Being invited to a more intimate dinner bestowed prestige. So, although the imperial events were similar to senatorial events, the scale and consequences were very different. The result was the increasing institutionalisation of access to the court for so-called imperial friends (*amici*), rather than for advisors in their role of senator.[10] Importantly, those who for whatever reasons were personally close to individual emperors could increasingly gain systematic influence.

Yet, whilst such institutionalised social gatherings highlighted the superior position of the emperor, it also suggested the importance of regular meetings with councillors. Though the form of meetings made clear who held social prestige, the very fact of those meetings showed that the ruler was still held by the convention to listen to his advisors. This concept of the Roman emperor as a sort of superior servant, who was present for his advisors and even had to listen to his subjects at large continued for a long time, and is illustrated by a famous anecdote: the third-century senator and historian Cassius Dio writes how the emperor Hadrian (117-138) was approached on a journey by a woman who asked him a question. When the emperor replied that he did not have time, the woman stated "then stop being emperor." One of the main roles of the Roman emperor was to respond to petitions, and "administrate" the Empire like senators had done before.[11] An emperor could, at his own peril, ignore a random passer-by. Formal councillors and other (more or less) official members of the court could not be ignored at all. Senior senators and a range of magistrates were part of the court through their function. Emperors could, of course, execute and exile such senators and magistrates, and so face constraints which court-life imposed on them, but they would then need to be re-

---

9   Winterling (1999) 117-44.
10 Winterling (1999) 161-91.
11 Dio, 69.6.3. On the Roman emperor as a responsive figure, see the monumental book by Millar (1992).

placed by other, similar, councillors.[12] The emperor needed to publicly interact with his councillors, and show them due reference.

One final form of representation that is indicative for the powerful position of elite councillors in the Roman world is that of literary reflections on individual emperors and on emperorship. Succinctly put: emperors explicitly ruling *with* senators were described positively, those explicitly ruling *over* senators were portrayed in negative terms. This, again, shows the strong institutional basis of those senators. Roman historiography, moreover, was systematically written by the Roman elite, mostly by senators. It is unexpected that their texts have a strong senatorial basis.[13] Yet, it was not only senators who described a form of emperorship in which the relation between the ruler and his councillors was a benchmark for good rule. Other authors, too, saw "aristocratic rule" as the best way to guarantee successful emperorship.[14]

Even emperors themselves seem to have often incorporated such a point of view and interpreted their basis of power in similar light. The famous *Meditations* of Marcus Aurelius (r. 160-180) include a number of passages in which the emperor reminds himself not to aim for too exalted a status, to "take care that you are not made into a Caesar, that you are not dyed with this dye; for such things happen" (6.30), to "speak both in the senate and to every man, whoever he may be, appropriately" (8.30), and to "stop and take the best advisers [...] if you do not see clear" (10.12). Similarly, the wonderful *Caesares* by the emperor Julian the Apostate (r. 361-363), a satirical account of the election of the best emperor by the gods, is ironical about much, but not about the exalted status of the ultimate winner Marcus Aurelius, whose temperance and philosophical way of life are praised. It also praises the very pro-senatorial Nerva (r. 96-98): "Very mild were his manners, most just his dealings" (311g). Augustus is praised for the role he played in legislation, with explicit reference to the way he was advised to administer an empire (325-c-d).

In contrast, emperors who ruled openly monarchical were inevitably described as monsters. Prime examples are Caligula, Nero, Domitian, Commodus and Elagabalus. All of whom are blamed for excessive behaviour, inevitably including ridiculing senators and appointing unsuited advisors. Famously, Caligula threatened to appoint his horse Incitatus to the consulship.[15] Commodus is said to have considered someone a close friend because he had "a penis larger than even most animals,"[16] and he made the freedman M. Aurelius Cle-

---

12 Michel (2015) 195-232.

13 Kraus (1997); Scheithauer (1987) 21-58.

14 See Herodian, 2.3.10, 8.7.5, with Kuhn-Chen (2002) 303-05.

15 Suetonius 55; Dio, 59.14.

16 Historia Augusta, *Life of Commodus*, 10.9.

EMPERORS AND COUNCILLORS

ander one of the more powerful people in the empire, outranking senatorial advisors. Nero's downward path is almost inevitably heralded in by the dismissal of his senatorial advisor Seneca, who is then forced to commit suicide. So dominant is this view, that later authors have often accepted it at face value. Prime of place goes to a famous statement by Edward Gibbon (1737-1794), who describes the years "from the death of Domitian to the accession of Commodus" (96-180) as the "most happy and prosperous" period in history, mainly because:

> The forms of the civil administration were carefully preserved by Nerva, Trajan, Hadrian and the Antonines, who delighted in the image of liberty, and were pleased with considering themselves as the accountable ministers of the laws. Such princes deserved the honour of restoring the republic had the Romans of their days been capable of enjoying a rational freedom.[17]

Though recent literature has firmly argued against easy acceptance of this point of view, popular perception has not really changed: ignoring the senatorial elite would have dire consequences for imperial reputations.

Councillors in an Imperial World

Emperors could not easily ignore senators. At the same time, senatorial roles as councillors and magistrates changed markedly during the empire. Though senators remained important in the administration and organisation of the Empire (as governors, priest, holders of various Roman magistracies, and generals), they increasingly did so under the direct command of the emperor. At an informal level, it was clear that disobeying an emperor who held the monopoly of violence could be dangerous, but at a formal level too, important posts were regularly bestowed upon individuals by imperial appointment Before there was an emperor, senatorial considerations carried much authority. If senators reached consensus, their advice was invariably followed by the peoples' assemblies who technically decided on laws. After the reign of Augustus, senatorial decrees formally took on legal status, but this boost of their formal powers was only minor compensation for the loss of informal authority.[18] In the Republic, senators' status was so clear, that formal powers were

---

17   Gibbon (1776) chapter 4.
18   Talbert (1996) 324-37.

less important. Under the emperors, the role of the senate become more prescribed. The senate still represented an institution of great power, and at occasions, for instance when emperors were away from Rome for longer periods of time, they even seemed to represent supreme power. Yet, it had become rapidly clear that senators could no longer rule without an emperor – from early in the Empire on, the question at the death of an emperor was not if but by who he would be replaced.[19]

So how could senators retain their standing, and increase their influence? The most important way, as suggested above, was by proximity to the ruler. Much of this could be at the whim of the monarch and at an informal level. Here too, however, some sort of institutionalisation took place. From the early empire onwards, emperors made use of a so-called *concilium principis* 'council of the emperor', much like family councils had been normal in the Republic, as had been the practice by senior magistrates to ask advice on judicial questions from a *concilium*.[20] At the beginning of imperial rule, the council consisted of senators drawn by lot, but appointments to this council by the emperor rapidly established itself as the norm. Rather than being a permanent body, the council could be called together by the emperor at a case-by-case basis. Membership could shift from one council to the next, depending on specific expertise. [21] Already during the reign of Tiberius (r. 14-37), non-senators were asked to be part of an imperial *consilium*. This was a problem for senators, who lost easy access to the emperor and status and in this way. Increasingly, discussing matters in *consilium principis* came to represent the way in which emperors could show that they listened to their councillors, effectively sidestepping the senate as a body. "Good" emperors still filled their councils with senior senators and high-ranking other members of the elite, but nothing stopped an emperor from excluding senators from his advisory board.[22] That was one way for him to represent himself as an emperor who listened to his councillor whilst picking his advisors himself. This, then, seriously weakened the institutional basis of the senate as representatives of power.

It was easier for an emperor to exclude senators from his councils when he was traveling in the provinces than when he was in Rome. He could simply argue that there were fewer senators at hand, and that members of the local

---

19   Wiedemann (1996) 198-209.

20   Aulus Gellius, *NA* 17.21; Valerius Maximus. 5.9.1; Seneca, *Clem.* 1.15; Cicero, *Att.* 4.2.5.

21   Eck (2000) 195-213; Crook (1955) 26, 105.

22   Cf. for instance the *consilium principis* of Marcus Aurelius (r. 161-180) in 177, which included five former consuls, with the one of his son Commodus in 186/7, which does not mention any senators, but includes a freedman: Eck (1997) 7-8, 13.

EMPERORS AND COUNCILLORS

(non-senatorial) elite had more local expertise.[23] At the same time, the senate could more easily be represented as body of supreme power when the emperor was in the provinces for a longer period of time. A travelling emperor, in this way, both limited and enhanced the position and status of the senate. But even when the senate as an institution had relative leeway, individual senators who made up that institution were still beholden to the emperor. By the second century AD, its composition had also changed markedly, with a far larger number of senators from outside the Italian peninsula, increasingly from the Eastern part of the Empire; a closer reflection of the composition of the empire.[24] Good news for some, of course, but not quite so good for those Roman senatorial families who for generations had dominated the senate, but were now pushed towards the periphery of power.

All these elements together show that though the notion of Roman emperorship as tempered by senatorial advice remains strong, the balance increasingly shifted towards advisors as supporting actors who belonged to the monarch. Yet, they were still represented as having status and power in their own right. Here, we see the same process as we saw above with senatorial recommendations: when the authority of the senate diminished, senatorial edicts formally became law. Likewise, the role of the *consilium principis* became formalised when emperorship became more openly monarchical. From the reign of Constantine (r. 306-337) onwards the council was renamed as *consistorium*. Its procedures became formalised as was, to an extent, its membership. There were now *ex officio* members, but that only marginally hid the fact that the emperor could (and did) still co-opt anyone he wanted.[25] At the same time, Constantine created a new Senate in Constantinople, and increased the number of senators enormously, raising it from about six hundred to, ultimately, some two thousand.[26] This is likely to have diminished the entry threshold to the senate, and with it senatorial standing. It may be more than coincidental that the sole surviving letter of Constantine to the senate, addressed it as 'his own senate' (*senatui suo*). The possessive pronoun is telling.[27] Notwithstanding the diminished status of individual senators, the term "*consistorium*," like "senate" and to a lesser extent "*concilium*," would for a long time retain the aura of power, and be used by popes and princes to denote institutionalised advi-

---

23   On the Roman emperor as a travelling ruler, see still Halfmann (1986).
24   Halfmann (1979).
25   Ammianus Marcellinus, 15.5, 16.7-8, 30.6.2, with the commentary of Boeft (2015) 140-41; Codex Justinianus 1.14.8.
26   Näf (1995) 13-14.
27   Millar (1992) 354 n. 94. Cf. *CIL* 6.1873.

sors. Yet, often, as in Rome, the presumed power of these institutions was a representative claim, rather than mirroring a reality.

Emperors, Councillors, and Imagery

Roman emperors, it appears, were on a tightrope as to whether they represented themselves as dependent on their councillors or superior to them. Over time, political status of senators, the most institutionalised type of councillors, diminished. Yet, political support by these senators remained important. Senatorial acclamation was still an expected element of taking up the purple. In the third century, during substantial parts of which the Roman empire was under great military pressure, this practice was not always upheld. The more important acclamation in this period was by the troops. Military success was the surest base of power. Even so, only few rulers ignored the possibility to be acclaimed by senators. That senators had little choice in the matter does not diminish the symbolic importance of their role. Legitimacy was still bestowed upon a ruler by senatorial supports. Senators therefore retained an important role in imperial display. They were, for instance, the first group following the imperial family at emperors' funerary processions.[28]

Monumental art also continued to show emperors surrounded by senatorial advisors. In one of the more famous historical reliefs from ancient Rome, the so-called Ara Pacis, Augustus is depicted alongside senators in a sacrificial procession (see Figure 2.2). The emperor is taller than those surrounding him and followed by a group of priests (the *flamines*) but he does not particularly stand out. Three centuries later, the similarities and differences with another well-known monument are striking. The so-called Decennalia base, which was erected in 303 AD, when the emperor Diocletianus visited Rome for the first time in twenty years of rule (r. 284-305), also shows a procession of Roman senators. The emperor, however, is on another side of the base, sacrificing in the presence of the *Genius* (divine spirit) of the Senate (see Figure 2.3). The link to senatorial councillors is retained, but the emperor is secluded at the same time. Likewise, on the near-contemporary reliefs of the so-called Arch of Constantine (dedicated in 315 AD), the emperor is explicitly depicted among senators, but clearly holds a superior position (see Figure 2.4). Noticeably, some of the *spolia* (reused sculpture, in this case from the second century AD) on the same arch show emperor and senators in a more egalitarian context.

---

28   Zanker (2004) 16-56.

EMPERORS AND COUNCILLORS

FIGURE 2.2 Augustus being depicted alongside senators in a sacrificial procession on the so-called Ara Pacis.
PHOTO BY THE AUTHOR.

FIGURE 2.3 The Decennalia base showing the emperor sacrificing in the presence of the Genius (divine spirit) of the Senate. *Source*: DAI Rom: 35.357.

FIGURE 2.4 A relief of the so-called Arch of Constantine depicting the emperor among senators, but clearly in a superior position. *Source*: H.P. L'Orange and A. von Gerkan, *Der spätantike Bildschmuck des Konstantinsbogens* (Berlin 1939), Taf 5.a.

EMPERORS AND COUNCILLORS

Finally, the ambiguous and shifting relation between emperor and senators also becomes clear from the way they are represented on coins. As late as 324 AD, Constantine is regularly depicted wearing the senatorial toga, and small togate figures are still shown next to emperors on coins that are dated between AD 367-375.[29] Yet, clear numismatic depictions of senators or references to the senate in coin legends peter out after the late second century AD.[30] From the third century onwards, the emperor is numismatically increasingly depicted in a military guise.[31] Senatorial standing of the emperor can still be expressed by showing him wearing the toga, but senators are no longer visible on perhaps the most potent visual medium of antiquity.

The later period of the Roman Empire, from the late third century AD onwards, is sometimes described as the Dominate, from *dominus* 'master'. It is contrasted with the earlier period, called the Principate, from *princeps* 'first man' – the imperial form of address that denoted the emperor as most important senator. Yet, not even the emperors in the later Roman Empire ruled on their own. Nor could they wholly depend on their "personal people" in the way that a ruler like Haile Sellasie seems to have done. Even when senators had lost much of their actual power, the senate retained a potent symbolical function. Councillors may have been convened in a *consistorium* that was handpicked by the ruler and may have mainly rubberstamped imperial decision, but it was still important for the emperor to appear to consult his councillors, and to be shown in the senatorial toga. The distance between reality and representative claim had widened enormously over the centuries, but the representative claim was maintained. Roman emperors continued to rule in a senatorial world, at least symbolically.

Bibliography

Agamben, G., *State of Exception* (Chicago, 2005).
Boeft, J. den, J.W. Drijvers, D. den Hengst, and H. Teitler, *Philological and Historical Commentary on Ammianus Marcellinus XXX* (Leiden, 2015).
CIL – *Corpus Inscriptionum Latinarum* (1893-).

---

29 *RIC* VII, Antioch, nos. 39-41, 46; *RIC* IX, Antioch, nos. 20a-f.
30 *RIC* III Commodus, nos. 194, 538, 549 for the emperor clasping hands with a senator/ genius of the Senate; a coin from AD 213, from the reign of Caracalla, is the last to show the legend GENIO SENATVS with an image of the genius of the Senate: *RIC* IV Caracalla, no. 234.
31 Manders (2012) 63-94.

Cooley, A., *Res Gestae Divi Augusti: Text, Translation, and Commentary* (Cambridge, Eng., 2009).

Crook, J., *Consilium Principis. Imperial Councils and Counsellors from Augustus to Diocletian* (Cambridge, Eng., 1955).

Eck, W., "The Emperor and his Advisers," in A. Bowman, P. Garnsey, and D. Rathbone (eds.), *The Cambridge Ancient History* 11, 2nd ed. (Cambridge, Eng., 2000), 195-213.

Eck, W., "Der Kaiser, die Führungsgeschichten, und die Administration des Reiches," in W. Eck (ed.), *Die Verwaltung des römischen Reiches in der hohen Kaiserzeit*, vol. 2, (Basel, 1997), 3-145.

Gibbon, E., *The History of the Decline and Fall of the Roman Empire*, vol. 1 (London, 1776).

Halfmann, H., *Itinera* principum: *Geschichte und Typologie der Kaiserreisen im römischen Reich* (Stuttgart, 1986).

Halfmann, H., *Die Senatoren aus dem östlichen Teil des Imperium Romanum bis zum Ende des 2. Jh. n. Chr.* (Göttingen, 1979).

Hekster, O., "Imagining power. Reality gaps in the Roman Empire," in *BABESCH* 86 (2011), 111-124.

Hekster, O., and W. Rich, "Octavian and the Thunderbolt: The Temple of Apollo Palatinus and Roman Traditions of Temple Building," in *The Classical Quarterly* 56 (2006), 149-168.

Hodgson, L., *Res Publica and the Roman Republic: 'Without Body or Form'* (Oxford, 2016).

Kapuscinski, R., *The Emperor. The Downfall of an Autocrat* (New York, 1978).

Kraus, C., and A. Woodman, *Latin Historians* (Oxford, 1997).

Kuhn-Chen, B., *Geschichtskonzeptionen griechischer Historiker im 2. und 3. Jahrhundert n. Chr.* (Frankfurt am Main, 2002).

Manders, E., *Coining Images of Power. Patterns in Representation of Roman Emperors on Imperial Coinage, AD 193-284* (Leiden, 2012).

Michel, A-C., *La cour sous l'empereur Claude: les enjeux d'un lieu de pouvoir* (Rennes, 2015).

Millar, F., *The Emperor in the Roman World, 31 BC – AD 337*, 2nd ed. (London, 1992).

Millar, F., "State and Subject: The Impact of Monarchy," in F. Millar and E. Segal (eds.), *Caesar Augustus. Seven Aspects* (Oxford, 1984), 37-60.

Näf, B., *Senatorisches Standesbewusstsein in spätrömischer Zeit* (Freiburg, 1995).

Raimondi Cominesi, A., "Augustus in the Making. A Reappraisal of the Ideology behind Octavian's Palatine Residence through its Interior Decoration and Topographical Context," in *Latomus* 77 (2018), 704-735.

Rowe, G., "Reconsidering the Auctoritas of Augustus," in *Journal of Roman Studies* 103 (2013), 1-15.

Scheithauer, A., *Kaiserbild und literarisches Programm. Untersuchungen zur Tendenz der Historia Augusta* (Frankfurt am Main, 1987).

RIC = *Roman Imperial Coinage* (1923-).

Talbert, R., "The Senate and Senatorial and Equestrian Posts," in A. Bowman, E. Champlin, and A. Lintott (eds.), *The Cambridge Ancient History*, vol. 10, 2nd ed. (Cambridge, Eng., 1996), 324-343.

Wiedemann, T., "Tiberius to Nero," in A. Bowman, E. Champlin, and A. Lintott (eds.), *The Cambridge Ancient History*, vol. 10, 2nd ed. (Cambridge, Eng., 1996), 198-255.

Winterling, A., Aula Caesaris. *Studien zur Institutionalisierung des römischen Kaiserhofes in der Zeit von Augustus bis Commodus (31 v. Chr. – 192 n. Chr.)* (Munich, 1999).

Zanker, P., *Die Apotheose der römischen Kaiser* (Munich, 2004).

Zanker, P., *Augustus und die Macht der Bilder* (Munich, 1987).

Zink, S., and H. Piening, "*Haec aurea templa*: the Palatine temple of Apollo and its Polychromy," in *Journal of Roman Archaeology* 22 (2009), 109-122.

CHAPTER 3

Politics of Access at the Court of the Caliph

Maaike van Berkel

Introduction

In the Abbasid Empire (eighth-tenth centuries), the caliph's ear was the key to power. Anyone seeking political power at the highest level had to gain access to the caliph in some way or another, through personal interaction or intermediaries. Narratives describing the functioning of the court of the caliph pay lengthy attention to the rules and regulations orchestrating the accessibility of the ruler.

Court studies increasingly pursue questions on the accessibility of the pre-modern ruler. Most of these studies analyse European court cultures, discussing topics such as the balance between the prince's seclusion and his public display, the rituals related to the various forms of access, and the relations between ideas on access and the spatial arrangements of the palace.[1] For the pre-modern Middle East, most studies covering these topics focus on the Ottoman rulers and their court culture.[2] However, miscellaneous studies also deal with earlier eras. The accessibility of the Abbasid caliphs has so far received most attention in studies on the position of courtiers regulating access, especially chamberlains and eunuchs.[3]

Contemporary narratives on the politics of accessibility at the Abbasid court convey two seemingly contradictory messages. On the one hand, (ideal) descriptions of court life emphasise the numerous impediments outsiders encounter while trying to approach the caliph. They stress the spatial segregations within the palace, between the inhabitants of the palace and the outside world, and the role of the court attendants protecting the caliph from the world outside his private chambers. The ruler's inaccessibility and the selectness of the group of favourites able to approach him are pivotal elements in these narratives. However, a second discourse stresses (the ideal of) the accessible ruler who is personally dealing with the redress of wrongs and therefore

---

1 See, for example, Adamson (1999); Raeymaekers (2016); Starkey (1987); Weiser (2003).
2 See, for example, Necipoglu (1991); Sievert (2011); Talbot (2016).
3 See, for example, El Cheikh (2013); El Cheikh (2005).

© MAAIKE VAN BERKEL, 2019 | DOI:10.1163/9789004291966_004

This is an open access chapter distributed under the terms of the CC-BY-NC 4.0 License.

constantly approachable for his people and the world outside his palace. Both discourses will be discussed in more detail in the first part of this chapter.

Whereas both discourses receive equal attention in contemporary characterisations of the politics of most Abbasid caliphs, the narratives on the eighteenth Abbasid caliph, al-Muqtadir (r. 906-932), focus almost exclusively on one ideal. Al-Muqtadir is presented as being protected by barriers and staff and almost inaccessible for any outsider. Is the ideal of the approachable caliph in decline in his age, an era characterised by political fragmentations and financial troubles? By analysing and contextualising the narratives on caliph al-Muqtadir's (in)accessibility and the messages they try to convey, the second part of this chapter will argue that the model of accessible rulership did not disappear, but was transferred to members of the caliph's entourage.

Models of Accessible and Distant Leadership

In his article on the court of the Prophet Muhammad, "Did the Prophet Keep Court," Michael Cook argues that on the basis of the account of Ibn Hisham (d. 833), historian and biographer of the Prophet Muhammad, we may draw the conclusion that Muhammad did not want to regulate or restrict access to him.[4] There were no gate-keepers stopping and screening people at the entrance to the Medina mosque, there was no one guiding visitors and regulating access to the Prophet, Muhammad did not distinguish himself from the rest of the people in the mosque (in dressing or in seating), and no elaborate protocol existed to approach him. This style of open, accessible, leadership, Cook argues, is compatible with the style attributed to Muhammad in other (later) narratives and might thus seem plausible. On the other hand, Cook warns that there is reason for caution since "the tradition may not be innocent of conveying an appealing image of prophetic simplicity" as a way to criticise later court culture.[5]

If accessibility and simplicity were the ideal example of early Islam, how then did later rulers legitimise their pomp and inaccessibility and from where did our second model, the unapproachable majestic ruler, emanate? In her book on hierarchy and egalitarianism in Islamic thought, Louise Marlow demonstrates the co-existence in Islamic societies of, on the one hand, the egalitarian ideals associated with the Qur'an and the tribal past of the early Muslim community, and, on the other hand, the more hierarchical social models of the

---

4   Cook (2011) 23-29.
5   Cook (2011) 26. See also Morris (2017).

cultures the Muslims conquered, especially the Iranian court culture of gate-keeping, screening, regulating access, and protocol.[6] According to Marlow, the Iranian hierarchical models entered the Muslim literature from the late Umayyad period (the second quarter of the eighth century) onwards.

Corroborating Marlow's argument, the Buyid secretary Hilal al-Sabi' (d. 1056) attests in his *Rusum dar al-khilafa* 'The Rules and Regulations of the Caliphal Court' to the decline of the accessibility of the caliph in the course of the first centuries of Islam. According to al-Sabi', this was due to the dramatic increase of protocol. Unfortunately, he remains rather ambiguous on when these developments took off and why. In the second chapter of the *Rusum*, discussing the rules of attendance at the caliphal court, he mentions that:

> It was not the practice of old for a military leader, a vizier or a high dignitary to kiss the ground when he entered the presence of the caliph. But when he entered and saw the caliph, he would address him in the second person singular saying: Peace be upon you, O Commander of the Faithful, and may the mercy and blessings of God be upon you. [...] In the past it was the practice of the caliph to sometimes offer his hand, covered with his sleeve, to a military leader or vizier to kiss. [...] This practice has now been replaced by kissing the ground, and to this rule all people now comply. In the past the crown princes from among the sons of the caliphs, and members of the Hashemite House, the judges, jurists, ascetics, and readers of the Qur'ān kissed neither the hand nor the ground. They merely saluted, as we mentioned above.[7]

Despite Marlow's argument that from the late Umayyad period onwards the egalitarian model was "increasingly postponed to the next world," many later sources continue to emphasise the ideal of direct accessibility.[8] Both models – of the accessible and distant ruler – continue to find expression in a wide variety of sources – historical annals, advice literature, and other literary texts – written from diverse perspectives and either presenting the models as such or describing the behaviour of actual historical situations and rulers as examples of good and bad governance. In one of the best-known mirrors for princes by the Saljuq vizier Nizam al-Mulk (d. 1092), for example, both ideals smoothly co-exist in the characterisations of good governance. The first quota-

---

6 Marlow (1997) 174-77.

7 Al-Sabi' (1964) 38-39; trans. Elie Salem with some modifications in wording: al-Sabi' (1977) 29.

8 Marlow (1997) 174.

tion emphasises the ideal of the accessible ruler personally dealing with complaints and inexhaustibly redressing wrongs:

> It is absolutely necessary that on two days in the week the ruler should sit for the redress of wrongs, to extract recompense from the oppressor, to give justice and to listen to the words of his people with his own ears, without any intermediary. It is fitting that some written petitions should also be submitted if they are relatively important, and he should give a ruling on each one. For when word spreads throughout the kingdom that, on two days in the week, The Master of the World summons complainants and petitioners before him and listens to their words, all oppressors will be afraid and curb their activities, and no one will dare to practise injustice or extortion for fear of punishment.[9]

Similarly, at another instance Nizam al-Mulk argues that:

> When the ruler is difficult of access the affairs of the people are put into suspense, evil-doers are encouraged, facts remain concealed, the army suffers harm and the peasants fall into trouble. There is no better rule for a ruler than to hold frequent audiences.[10]

Although Nizam al-Mulk seems to put more emphasis on the accessibility of the ruler and the disadvantages of having to deal with these matters through intermediaries, at other instances he focuses more on the necessary protocol, gatekeeping, and courtiers distancing the ruler from the ordinary people. An example of the latter is the description of the conduct of audiences:

> It is necessary to have an organized system for giving audiences. First of all the relatives [of the ruler] come in, after them distinguished members of his entourage, then other classes of people. If they all come in at once, [the correct] distinction between humble and noble is not observed. Raising of the curtain is the sign that an audience is in progress; when the curtain is lowered it indicates that there is no admittance, except for persons who are summoned.[11]

---

9   Nizam al-Mulk (2006) 13-14.
10 Ibid. 118.
11 Ibid. 117-18.

While Nizam al-Mulk's focus is more on the accessible ruler, the historian Hilal al-Sabi' highlights aspects of the distant type of ruler, a monarch surrounded by screens, barriers, pomp, and servants. By emphasising the vast dimensions of the residence, the number of servants and security personnel, and the detailed rules of attendance, he projects the image of an almost unapproachable ruler. According to al-Sabi', in the presence of the caliph, one should be dressed in clean cloths, perfumed with scents the ruler likes, appear with clean teeth, refrain from speaking without having been asked, avoid laughing, and avoid asking for clarifications or turning your back towards the caliph.[12] In addition, he emphasises the role of the chamberlain in regulating access:

> On procession days, the chief chamberlain comes fully attired in black robe and black turban, wearing sword and belt. With the chamberlains and their lieutenants marching in front of him, he sits in the corridor behind the screen. Then comes the vizier, the commander of the army and all those who are supposed to attend the procession. When all are in their places, the chief chamberlain sends a note to the caliph to that effect. If the caliph wishes to give a general audience, he sends his private servant in charge of correspondence to bring the chief chamberlain. The latter enters alone, stand in the courtyard, and kisses the ground. He is then ordered to admit the people according to their respective ranks. [...][13]

And he describes the elevated, and thus distant, position of the caliph: "it has been the tradition for the caliph to sit on an elevated seat on a throne covered with pure Armenian silk, or with silk and wool."[14]

Noticeably, these two seemingly contradictory discourses on the accessible and distant ruler remain dominant in advice texts after the demise of the Abbasids. In fact, they are not restricted to Islamic political thought. They appear in numerous characterisations of ideal governance, whether Chinese, Middle Eastern, or European.[15] However, despite the striking similarities in discourse, the precise application of these models, the ways in which they are deployed to legitimise, promote, discredit, or disparage a specific ruler can best be understood from rather specific historical contexts. The second part of this

---

12   Al-Sabi' (1964) 38-46.
13   Al-Sabi' (1964) 107-08; trans. Elie Salem with some modifications in wording: al-Sabi' (1977) 63.
14   Al-Ṣābi' (1964) 125; trans. Elie Salem with some modifications in wording: al-Sabi' (1977) 75.
15   See, for example, van Berkel (2018).

POLITICS OF ACCESS AT THE COURT OF THE CALIPH 31

chapter will analyse the historical circumstances under which al-Muqtadir's court operated and how his (in)accessibility was represented by (near-)contemporaries.

The Inaccessibility of Caliph al-Muqtadir

According to Charlemagne's biographer, Einhard, the great Carolingian Emperor often invited nobles, friends, and bodyguards to bathe with him at his palace in Aachen, thus creating the smallest possible distance between himself and those around him.[16] Other sources tell us how the Byzantine envoys who arrived at Charlemagne's court could not distinguish the emperor from his entourage since court ritual did not emphasise his elevated position; on the contrary, ritual emphasised his approachability.[17] Nothing could be more removed from the stories told about al-Muqtadir and the Byzantine envoys arriving at his court.

In the year 917, a Byzantine delegation visited the Abbasid court of caliph al-Muqtadir in Baghdad to negotiate a truce and discuss the exchange of prisoners of war. The description of this embassy is well-known. Almost all contemporary and near-contemporary sources describe the events taking place in vivid detail. While each author emphasises different aspects of the ceremonial pomp surrounding it, the message they try to convey is identical. All the narratives glorify the grandeur of the Abbasid court and the power of its main inhabitant, the caliph. Moreover, the most conspicuous elements of the caliph's majesty in these narratives is his inaccessibility.

Al-Muqtadir's lack of approachability is displayed in a series of physical and psychological barriers raised by his entourage, the dimensions and sublime decorations of his palace, and the immenseness of his retinue. When the Byzantine envoys reach Baghdad they are housed in the splendidly decorated palace of Sa'id ibn Makhlad in the neighbourhood of the caliphal palace. When they request an audience with the caliph to deliver the letter they brought from the Byzantine emperor, they are told, according to the tenth century chronicler Miskawayh, that:

> this was a matter of great difficulty, only possible after a meeting with the caliph's vizier, informing the latter of their design, arranging the matter

---

16   Nelson (1987) 156.
17   Nelson (1987) 171.

with him and requesting him to facilitate the granting of the audience and to advise the caliph to accord their request.[18]

The vizier Ibn al-Furat indeed grants the envoys an audience, but our source, Miskawayh, makes it very clear that it is the vizier who is orchestrating the meeting and that the envoys are at his mercy. On the day of their meeting with the caliph the Byzantines are led through the streets of Baghdad and the alleys of the palace, in which a series of ceremonies take place showing off the court's grandeur. Civil and military officials of all ranks line up the streets to the palace, the cavalry on horseback and in full armour. Inside the palace the chamberlains guide the envoys through endless numbers of courtyards, vestibules, and passageways, all crowded with retainers and servants and all richly decorated with draperies, tapestries, curtains, and luxurious objects.

Finally, the envoys are brought in the presence of the caliph in the so-called Palace of the Crown. There the caliph is seated on an ebony throne covered with brocade. The vizier Ibn al-Furat and the highest military leader of the caliphate, Mu'nis, stand next to him. The caliph's sons sit in front of him. Lined up in this audience room are also the various military officers, all according to their rank. The envoys kiss the ground in front of the caliph and they are instructed to stand at a certain distance from him. Only the caliph's family, the vizier, and the military chief are allowed to be in his immediate presence, and, although the envoys are now in the same room as the caliph, they are not allowed to directly communicate with him. Interaction with al-Muqtadir is the exclusive preserve of the same small group of favourites. After the envoys have delivered their message through an interpreter, it is the vizier who answers them on the caliph's behalf. While here the caliph is described as visible at an elevated position, at other instances al-Muqtadir is said to have attended meetings from behind a curtain.

Obviously, the narratives on the Byzantine embassy to Baghdad – all written by or based on sources close to the Abbasid court – had an interest in exaggerating the grandeur of the palace buildings, its decorations, and the majesty of its main inhabitant, the caliph. Yet, the message they try to convey is clear: access to al-Muqtadir is extremely well-guarded, it is a privilege enjoyed by a happy few who, by the time they enter in his presence, will be completely overwhelmed by his sublimity and superiority. Whereas the narratives on the Byzantine embassy are the most vivid, detailed, and outspoken in presenting the image of al-Muqtadir as a distant ruler, numerous other characterisations of this caliph corroborate his inaccessibility. Indeed, there exists hardly any story

---

18   Miskawayh (1920-21) 1:53.

on his approachability. This caliph is definitely portrayed as the Persian style inaccessible, majestic ruler and not as the approachable tribal leader of early Islam.

Yet while stories on al-Muqtadir's accessibility are missing, these anecdotes do exist for some of his immediate predecessors. Stories abound on how al-Muqtadir's father, caliph al-Muʿtadid (r. 892-902), directly interacted with his lower officials and even the populace. These narratives range from his personal inspection and assignment of each low-ranking member of the cavalry to the summoning of a common cotton merchant to his palace.[19] The same can be said about other immediate predecessors of al-Muqtadir.

Traditionally, historians analysed access in a binary way. Rulers were either seen as easily accessible or as distant and unapproachable. However, recent scholarship on pre-modern Europe has argued that it might be much more fruitful to approach accessibility as a nuanced and perhaps more gradual and differentiated phenomenon.[20] The narratives on Islamic rulers, most of which represent both models of access, endorse a more gradual and less binary approach. The one-sided focus on al-Muqtadir's inaccessibility seems to have been the exception rather than the rule. Then how can we explain al-Muqtadir's exceptional position? What message do authors describing the culture of access at his court try to convey? Do they seek to discredit a caliph, who, no longer represents the early Islamic ideals of accessible leadership, while at the same time glorifying the grandeur of his court? Or does this mean that the model of the egalitarian ruler had become less prominent?

A Young Caliph and His Approachable Representatives

Although there is virtually no narrative on al-Muqtadir as a public and approachable figure, the discourse on accessibility is vividly present in the sources. During the long reign of caliph al-Muqtadir, the ideal of accessible leadership seems to have been transferred to the caliph's main representative, the vizier. It is the vizier who is presented as talking directly to the people, listening to complaints and dispensing justice upon them. So, while al-Muqtadir is presented as a distant Iranian ruler, his vizier is often characterised as the more accessible early Islamic ruler.

Anecdotes on viziers who take it upon themselves to deal with public requests abound. These narratives cover both formal settings – such as the

---

19   See, for example, al-Tanukhi, (1971-73), 1:326-28, 2:248; See also Marmer (1994) 36-41.
20   See, for example, Weiser (2003) 13.

vizier's chairmanship of the petition procedures – and informal contexts such as the ways in which he is approached by passers-by in the street. Hilal al-Sabi', for example, narrates on how a small estate-holder from Baghdad's hinterland, wrote a petition to Ibn al-Furat, al-Muqtadir's famous vizier, complaining about an excessive tax assessment of his estates. When after an investigation in the archives by some of the scribes of the administration, his case is dropped, the man continues to show up at the vizier's office and even buttonholes him in the streets. In the end, the vizier investigates the matter himself, discovers that the petitioner is right, and restores justice upon him. Despite the obvious fictional elements in this narrative, it nevertheless depicts a situation in which the ideal of the accessible ruler is projected on the vizier, the main representative of the caliph. It is the vizier who needs to be available to the public, it is the vizier who directly restores justice upon the people.[21] Similar anecdotes are told about al-Muqtadir's other viziers, riding the streets of Baghdad, talking to people, receiving gifts and repaying them generously.

A final question that needs to be pursued is why contemporary historians transferred the ideology of the accessible ruler from the caliph to the vizier. What was the precise historical context in which such a transfer was acceptable for their readership? Caliph al-Muqtadir was only thirteen years old when he ascended the throne in 908. The uncertain conditions surrounding his accession – his succession was controversial, and the young prince was first installed, then dethroned and then installed again – and his young age initiated a political power strife at his court during the early years of his reign. Unlike his immediate predecessors, his father and brother, he missed administrative and military experience and a personal bond with the military. Therefore, he seems to have depended more than his predecessors on court officials and family members. His mother and aunts, for example, became very prominent and powerful figures at his court. And so did his viziers. Particularly Ibn al-Furat, the first vizier after al-Muqtadir's re-instalment to the caliphate, was said to have operated as a kind of father-figure to the young caliph. Many contemporary authors mention a story on how al-Muqtadir's mother invited the vizier to call the young caliph "his son" and take him on his lap during meetings.[22] Whether fictional or not, these anecdotes demonstrate that the perceived relationship between the young caliph and his vizier was one of dependence. It is therefore also not surprising that the ideal of the accessible ruler talking to his subjects and dispensing justice upon them was also projected on the caliph's vizier rather than on this young boy himself.

---

21   Al-Sabi' (1904) 163-64.
22   Miskawayh (1920-21) 1:13; al-Sabi' (1904) 117.

POLITICS OF ACCESS AT THE COURT OF THE CALIPH

We may thus conclude that the two models of good leadership – the distant and majestic monarch and the more approachable and egalitarian ruler – were still both highly valued in the days of caliph al-Muqtadir. The ideal of accessible leadership did not disappear, but was transferred from the caliph to his main representative, the vizier. The image which remained for the caliph himself was one of an inaccessible, highly distant, and remote ruler protected by palace walls, luxury, servants, soldiers, chamberlains, and his vizier. This transfer might have been rather convenient for those surrounding and representing him, especially for the vizier. It should not surprise us that the vizier Ibn al-Furat is said to have commented upon al-Muqtadir's accession to the throne:

> For God's sake do not appoint to the post a man who knows the house of one, the fortune of another, the gardens of a third, the slave girls of a fourth, the estate of a fifth and the horse of a sixth; nor one who has mixed with the people, has had experience of affairs, has gone through his apprenticeship and made calculations of people's fortunes. [...] Why should you appoint a man who will govern, who knows our resources, who will administer affairs himself and regard himself as independent? Why do you not entrust this matter to someone who will leave you to manage it?[23]

Bibliography

Adamson, J., *The Princely Courts of Europe: Ritual, Politics and Culture under the Ancien Régime, 1500-1750* (London, 1999).

al-Tanukhi, *Nishwar al-Muhhadara wa-Akhbar al-Mudhakara*, 8 vols., ed. 'A. al-Shaliji (Beirut, 1971-1973).

Berkel, M. van and J. Duindam (eds.), *Prince, Pen and Sword. Eurasian Perspectives* (Leiden, 2018).

Berkel, M. van, N.M. El Cheikh, H. Kennedy, and L. Osti, *Crisis and Continuity at the Abbasid Court. Formal and Informal Politics in the Caliphate of al-Muqtadir (295-320/908-32)* (Leiden, 2013)

Cheikh, N.M. El, "The Chamberlains," in M. van Berkel, N.M. El Cheikh, H. Kennedy, and L.Osti, *Crisis and Continuity at the Abbasid Court* (Leiden, 2013), 145-164.

Cheikh, N.M. El, "Servants at the Gate: Eunuchs at the Court of al-Muqtadir," in *Journal of the Economic and Social History of the Orient* 48 (2005), 234-252.

---

23 Miskawayh (1920-21) 1:3; trans. Hugh Kennedy in Van Berkel (2013) 18.

Cook, M., "Did the Prophet Muhammad Keep Court," in A. Fuess and J. Hartung (eds.), *Court Cultures in the Muslim World. Seventh to Nineteenth Centuries* (London, 2011), 23-29.

Hilal al-Sabi', *Rusum Dar al-Khilafa (The Rules and Regulations of the Abbasid Court)*, trans. E.A. Salem (Beirut, 1977).

Hilal al-Sabi', *Rusum Dar al-Khilafa*, ed. Mikhàil 'Awwad (Baghdad, 1964).

Hilal al-Sabi', *Tuḥfat al-Umarà fi Tàrikh al-Wuzarà. The Historical Remains of Hilal al-Ṣabi' 1st Part of his Kitab al-wuzara (Gotha Ms. 1756) and Fragment of his History 389-393 A.H. (B.M. Ms, add. 19360)*, ed. H.F. Amedroz (Beirut, 1904).

Marlow, L., *Hierarchy and Egalitarianism in Islamic Thought* (Cambridge, Eng., 1997).

Marmer, D., "The Political Culture of the 'Abbasid Court, 279-324 (A.H.)," PhD Diss., (Princeton University, 1994).

Miskawayh, *Tajarib al-Umam. The Eclipse of the Abbasid Caliphate* 1, ed. H.F. Amedroz, trans. D.S. Margoliouth (Oxford, 1920-1921).

Morris, I.D., "Hajib," in K. Fleet, G. Krämer, D. Matringe, J. Nawas, and E. Rowson (eds.), *Encyclopaedia of Islam, THREE* (Leiden, 2017).

Necipoglu, G., *Architecture, Ceremonial, and Power. The Topkapi Palace in the Fifteenth and Sixteenth Centuries* (Cambridge, Mass., 1991).

Nelson, J.L., "The Lord's Anointed and the People's Choice: Carolingian Royal Ritual," in D. Cannadine and S. Price (eds.), *Rituals of Royalty. Power and Ceremonial in Traditional Societies* (Cambridge, Eng., 1987), 137-180.

Nizam al-Mulk, *The Book of Government or Rules for Kings. The Siyar al-muluk or Siyasat-nama of Nizam al-Mulk*, trans. H. Darke (Abingdon, 2006).

Raeymaekers, D., and S. Derks (eds.), *The Key to Power? The Culture of Access in Princely Courts, 1400-1750* (Leiden, 2016).

Sievert, H., "Favouritism at the Ottoman court in the eighteenth century," in A. Fuess and J. Hartung (eds.), *Court Cultures in the Muslim World Seventh to Nineteenth Centuries* (London, 2011), 273-292.

Starkey, D. (ed.), *The English Court form the Wars of the Roses to the Civil War* (London, 1987).

Talbot, M., "Accessing the Shadow of God: Spatial and Performative Ceremonial at the Ottoman Court," in D. Raeymaekers and S. Derks (eds.), *The Key to Power? The Culture of Access in Princely Courts, 1400-1750* (Leiden, 2016), 103-123.

Weiser, B., *Charles II and the Politics of Access* (Woodbridge, 2003).

CHAPTER 4

Representative Bodies in Medieval Religious Orders: A Discarded Legacy?

Bert Roest

Introduction

The study of representation and representative bodies in later medieval and renaissance studies is frequently framed in a vocabulary of political thought and then more often than not connected with concepts in Roman and canon law and with the reception of Aristotle's *Politics*, and how the latter played out in the works of late medieval political theorists.[1] Beyond this theoretical approach, most scholars who study medieval forms of representation "in practice" focus by and large on representation in "secular" political bodies, such as Spanish and Italian towns and communes, the Republic of Venice, and the emerging parliaments and estates general in larger territorial entities, such as England, Catalonia, Scotland, and the Low Countries.

It is less common for historians of political thought and later medieval parliamentary developments to integrate in these discussions the tradition of representative government in Europe's medieval religious orders, which often predated and continued to develop alongside representative developments in the secular world. This tradition within religious orders probably provided viable examples of efficacious representative procedures, and as such might have been of primordial importance for shaping late medieval concepts of political representation to begin with. This essay therefore tries to address this issue, by evaluating how scholars of medieval political thought and the origins of parliamentarism have ignored representative government in medieval orders, notwithstanding the availability of studies by specialists of order history, and by discussing the role of representative government in the Franciscan order, and its possible implications for the wider socio-political world in which the friars were active.

---

1 A standard treatment in this regard is provided in Quillet (1988).

© BERT ROEST, 2019 | DOI:10.1163/9789004291966_005
This is an open access chapter distributed under the terms of the CC-BY-NC 4.0 License.

Representation in Religious Orders within the History of Political Thought

Within modern scholarship concerning the history of political representation, representative developments in religious orders normally do not figure prominently. Insofar as these developments are mentioned, they are signalled without analysing their properties or their possible consequences for the proliferation of representative institutions. A case in point is Arthur Monahan's *Consent, Coercion, and Limit: The Medieval Origins of Parliamentary Democracy* from 1986. This work devotes six pages to representative bodies within the Dominican order, charting in a not completely correct and coherent manner the role of elections and representation at the level of order provinces and at the level of the Dominican general chapter. Yet it does not come to terms with the possible revolutionary nature of this form of representative organisation.[2]

In fact, Monahan is more generous than most of his colleagues. In Wim Blockman's allegedly encompassing 1978 typology of representative institutions in late medieval Europe, religious institutions are conspicuously absent.[3] Likewise, James M. Blythe's influential *Ideal Government and the Mixed Constitution in the Middle Ages* does not have much to say about the development of checks and balances and forms of representation in religious orders. It is fifteenth-century conciliarism that is portrayed as the ecclesiastical pendant to (proto-) parliamentary developments in the secular realm, and the focus is squarely on the legacy of classical legal and political concepts and their recasting by political thinkers from the mid-thirteenth century onwards, again in the wake of the reception of Aristotle's *Politics*.

This tendency is confirmed in more recent studies on medieval forms of representative government. It shows in Hwa-Yong Lee's popular *Political Representation in the Later Middle Ages: Marsilius in Context* from 2008. In its introductory chapter on the medieval understanding of political representation it succinctly refers to Gratian's *Decretum* in the context of episcopal elections, without displaying a profound understanding of the text in question, but it does not provide a proper analysis of the highly developed systems of election and representation in the medieval church and the religious orders, and does not ponder their possible long-term implications.[4]

Oakley's *The Watershed of Modern Politics* from 2015, which also focuses on the origin of political representation, devotes a full chapter to fifteenth-

---

2   Monahan (1987) 142-148.
3   Blockmans (1978).
4   Lee (2008) 39.

century conciliarism. It also alludes to developments in late medieval ecclesiology leading up to conciliarist positions in the context of the pope-emperor struggles of the fourteenth century, to outline some formative influences on "the emerging tradition of constitutionalism in the West," and the "process whereby the practices of representation and consent in the European kingdoms came gradually to be theorized."[5] Oakley builds in that regard on the work of Brian Tierney, who probably has done most to put conciliar theory in the crosshairs of modern scholars of medieval political thought,[6] and on the more recent studies of Anthony Black, which also interpret ecclesiastical constitutionalism and ecclesiological reflections on mixed government and representation first and foremost as the legacy of conciliarism.[7] Yet this lip service to conciliarism notwithstanding, both in the works of Oakley and Black, and in a large number of other studies, the real move towards forms of representative government is nearly always connected with the nature of Europe's fragmented political landscape, the peculiar character of urban communal development, and the complex nature of late medieval state formation.

In slightly different terms, this is precisely the argument in the sweeping 2016 article on representation and consent by David Stasavage, which seems to be a sketchy preliminary study for a forthcoming monograph. For him the question concerning the rise of mechanisms of consent and representation in Western Europe, as opposed to the supposed failure of such mechanisms to evolve in Byzantium, imperial China, or the Islamic world, can be explained in terms of the emergence of "small and fragmented policies" after the decline of the Roman Empire in the West, "where it was feasible to organize representation and also desirable for rulers to do so."[8]

Beyond attention to fifteenth-century conciliarism, references to the *Decretum* and other prominent canon law texts, and to the theoretical statements made by prominent medieval political theorists in the context of the struggles between papal and royal and/or imperial power that seem to prefigure full-blown conciliarist thought, most scholars of medieval political thought do not deal with the ubiquitous representative organs in other parts of the medieval church and especially within the religious orders. Nor do they analyse the electoral concepts and techniques developed within precisely these circles between the eleventh and the thirteenth century.

---

5 Oakley (2015) 210.
6 Tierney (1956; 1983); cf. Congar (1958) and Pennington (2004).
7 Black (1979; 1992).
8 Stasavage (2016) 162.

There are possibly good reasons for this apparent neglect. One that immediately comes to mind has to do with the fact that, for a variety of reasons, the writings of the most well-known medieval political theorists, including Thomas Aquinas, John of Paris, Aegidius Romanus, Marsilius of Padua, William of Ockham, and Bartolo of Sassoferrato, were prone to provide authoritative references to "universal" legal and philosophical principles, in line with scholastic modes of academic reasoning in which they had been trained. Intellectual historians, or rather historians of ideas following the great chain of high-brow political thought in the later middle ages all the way up to Machiavelli, will not quickly find in the works of these authors overt references to actual representative procedures in religious orders and the validity of such functioning systems in religious corporations to underpin their theoretical arguments. History of political thought in that sense frequently amounts to not much more than echoing the debates of academically trained medieval controversialists, quite a few of whom wrote in particular polemical contexts, and charting the way in which the protagonists in question developed philosophically convincing arguments based on uncontestable foundations of divine and natural law and fashionable (Aristotelian) notions of human nature, ethics, and politics. This tendency also has facilitated modern scholars to approach medieval representation predominantly as a secular political phenomenon, and even as part and parcel of the growth of later medieval secularism.[9]

The Long-term Availability of Specialist Studies

Nevertheless, the overall neglect of highly developed forms of representative government in Europe's medieval religious orders by most scholars of medieval political thought remains puzzling. After all, over the years several specialists of order history signaled the importance of this phenomenon and its possible impact on theories and especially on practices of representation in the late medieval secular world. As early as the late 1840s, the French erudite Victor Leclerc pointed out the significance of 'general chapters' – *ces grandes assemblées déliberantes* – and election procedures in medieval religious orders, starting with the Cistercians, and called for studies on this phenomenon.[10]

---

9   One could argue that this is in part the legacy of John W. Allen and George de Lagarde. Cf. Allen (1923) and de Lagarde (1934-1963; 1937). Their works still seem to shape the research questions of most scholars of medieval political thought, either unconsciously or consciously, as in the case of Nederman (1995).

10   See, for instance, Leclerc (1849).

REPRESENTATIVE BODIES IN MEDIEVAL RELIGIOUS ORDERS

The issue was dealt with more systematically with regard to the Dominican order in the 1913 monograph of Ernest Barker. This work outlines in considerable detail the emergence of representative assemblies and the election of offices within the order, and tries to reconstruct the influences behind these developments. It makes a case for the inspiration and influence of these mechanisms in the Dominican order on comparable mechanisms introduced in thirteenth-century English episcopal synodal procedures under the friar-Archbishops Robert Kilwardby (a Dominican) and John Pecham (a Franciscan), as well as on assemblies called for by the English kings, and on the emergence of specific mechanisms of representative convocation that came to define the English parliamentary system from the late thirteenth century onwards.[11]

For whatever reason, Barker's work never made much of an impact. During the following decades, the issue of representative bodies in religious institutions was only raised in passing, without much elaboration, most often in the context of studying majority principles in political assemblies.[12] Yet in the 1950s, the Belgian sociologist-historian Leo Moulin devoted at least three seminal articles to the government of religious communities and their representational aspects. He argued for the primacy of religious institutions in developing forms of representative government and modern techniques of voting and majority formation. Starting from the view that matters of representation and consent built on very old principles within the early church, and as such were codified in twelfth-century canon law, Moulin distinguished a quick development in representative government and election procedures during and after the twelfth century, first in the Cistercian order, and subsequently in orders of regular canons, Benedictine congregations, the Carthusians, and in the budding mendicant orders, concomitant with the adoption of provincial and general chapters with legislative powers. This went hand in hand with an increase in canon law regulations concerning chapter representation and election procedures in religious corporations, all of which were codified in decrees issued by the third and fourth Lateran Councils (held in 1179 and 1215 respectively).[13]

Much later, in 1983, Moulin once more addressed the issue, but now from a different angle, suggesting that Marsilius of Padua's famous *Defensor pacis* (1324), which figures prominently in many studies on the development of late

---

11   Barker (1913). Not all of Barker's inferences and interpretations have withstood the test of time, of course. The main importance of this work was its emphasis not to isolate church and state, but to recognise that the development of representation in church and state developed side by side and that there was considerable interaction between the two realms in this development.

12   See the dispersed remarks in Stawski (1920) and in Avondo (1927).

13   Moulin (1951; 1952; 1953).

medieval political thought, was indeed inspired by systems of representation and governmental organisation in Europe's main religious orders. This would have been visible in Marsilius's depiction of the *universitas civium* and its powers, in his depiction of the principles of *potestas delegata*, and also in his treatment of election procedures and qualified majority principles. Due to his own conflicts with the papacy at the time, Moulin argued, Marsilius would never have openly acknowledged this debt, and it is clear that most modern scholars have never looked in this direction, trying instead to establish with limited success how Marsilius's system compares to the theories outlined in the *Politics* of Aristotle.[14]

The question is not so much as to whether Moulin is right, but that, just like the interpretation put forward in the older work of Barker, Moulin's call to take representative bodies in religious orders seriously hardly seems to have registered among later scholars of medieval political thought. It is probably not a coincidence that the previously-mentioned monograph of Hwa-Yong Lee on the historical context of the *Defensor pacis* from 2008 does not broach this possibility, not even to deny it, and that the author, if his bibliographical references are any indication, is largely unaware of this angle of scholarship, which as late as 1979 had seen a significant additional contribution. In that year, the French law historian Jean Gaudemet issued with three colleagues a book-length study on the development of election procedures and representative systems within all types of medieval religious institutions and at different levels of the ecclesiastical hierarchy. One is hard put to find this work in bibliographies of subsequent publications on medieval political thought that in one way or another deal with medieval concepts of representation.[15]

Due to peculiar cultural divisions in both the world of medieval studies and in the sub-fields of history of political thought and parliament studies, the suggestions of Barker, Moulin, Gaudemet, and others have not made much of an impact beyond specialists in the history of medieval religious orders and their institutional setup. Aside from the monograph of Arthur Monahan mentioned earlier, which pays lipservice to Moulin's articles from the 1950s, most specialists of medieval political thought and political organisations do not deal at length with religious orders as age-old multinational playing grounds for functioning systems of representation in their own discussions of participation of stakeholders within various types of corporate government. As said before, only in the context of the early fourteenth-century conflict between pope and emperor – the background against which scholars normally discuss political

---

14   Moulin (1983).
15   Gaudemet (1979).

representation in the works of Ockham, Marsilius of Padua, and others – and in the context of the fifteenth-century conciliar movement do they include the church and the general council in their discussion of political representation.

Since the later 1990s a group of predominantly French and Italian scholars has asked attention for the compatibility between the Franciscan project of evangelical pacification of society and the unfolding commercial urban body politics in Italy and Catalonia. Counter to much earlier research, which saw an intrinsic discrepancy between the Franciscan ideals of poverty and the proto-capitalist transformation of urban society, these scholars have pointed out that the friars were willing to accept the dynamics of the market economy and the entrepreneurial spirit of urban merchants, as long as acquired wealth and economic power could be made to benefit the *bonum commune*. In the course of time, as has been argued in particular by Giacomo Todeschini, Paolo Evangelisti, and their disciples, this enabled Franciscan friars to develop encompassing visions of urban and territorial socio-economic and political development within overarching evangelical parameters, geared towards the realisation of an economically and politically flourishing *civitas christiana*.[16] But even in this rather innovative type of scholarship, issues of representation and related topics concerning corporate government structures advocated by Franciscan spokesmen such as Francesc Eiximenis (d. 1409) and fifteenth-century Italian Observant friars are to my knowledge not analysed in depth. It remains somewhat of a blind spot within historical research on medieval political thought.[17]

Questions of influence aside, the emergence of representative bodies within Europe's major religious orders from at least the twelfth century onwards in and of itself provides more than sufficient grounds to incorporate it in the history of medieval political thought. After all, we are talking about huge and rather powerful multinational corporations that played a variety of roles within medieval society. That alone should suffice to include the study of medieval religious orders in discussions on the rise of representative bodies and the

---

16   See, for example, Todeschini (2008); Evangelisti (1996; 2006); Cacciotti and Melli (2011).

17   Beyond this, most scholars interested in Franciscan or more general mendicant political theory are either interested in the ecclesiological consequences of Franciscan concepts of evangelical poverty, which Ockham exploited to deny the church the right to exercise power over secular affairs, or in the way concepts of natural law and Aristotle's *Ethics* and *Politics* shaped mendicant mirrors of princes and scholastic treatises on royal and papal power. Alongside of additional contributions within the tradition of Todeschini and Evangelisi, these are central themes in several contributions to the volumes *Etica e politica: Le teorie dei frati mendicanti nel due e trecento. Atti del XXVI Convegno internazionale, Assisi, 15-17 ottobre 1998*, Atti dei Convegni della Società internazionale di studi francescani e del Centro interuniversitario di studi francescani, Nuova serie, 9 (Spoleto: Centro Italiano di studi sull'alto medioevo, 1999), and Musco (2007).

technical apparatus that facilitated its fruition. Luckily, thanks to much recent scholarly investment in the institutional setup of medieval religious institutions across the board, it is now much easier than before to access details on the representative systems developed in various orders.[18]

Mechanisms of Political Representation in the Franciscan Order

I would like to exemplify this with a short analysis of government structures within the Franciscan order, or the order of friars Minor, which in its set-up followed both Cistercian and Dominican examples,[19] and which, as the research of Todeschini *cum suis* indicates, is increasingly being scrutinised for its importance in late medieval socio-economic and political life. The Franciscan order has as added relevance its relative size and impressive geographical distribution. Established as a canonically recognised order by 1209 or thereabouts, it quickly became the largest mendicant order by far. By the early 1330s it had more than 1376 convents, divided over 34 European order provinces and a number of additional vicariates in European border regions and far beyond, with missionary stations as far away as Central Asia and Mongol China.[20]

Whereas Dominicans quickly fleshed out a streamlined and hierarchical system of representation between 1216 and the 1230s, in line with the latest canonical guidelines, but with a deliberately more democratic streak than the representative systems in the Cistercian order and within most orders of regular canons, the early Franciscans came to a comparable setup somewhat reluctantly. At first, the order was subject to the overwhelming charismatic authority of Francis of Assisi, and at the same time seemed to have coveted ideas of a divinely inspired form of direct democracy.[21] This was part and parcel of the original utopian vision of the functioning of the Franciscan fraternity. It was conceived as a fully evangelical community where all could live the perfect imitation of Christ on Earth without hierarchies and distinction between

---

18 See for instance Hoffmann (2000); Cygler (2001); Waddell (2002); Freeman, (2002); Andenna and Melville (2005); Cygler (2007); Sykes (2008); Cygler (2009); Grélois (2016).

19 On the Cistercians, see several studies mentioned in the previous note. On the Dominicans, see aside from Barker also Galbraith (1925), Cygler (2014), as well as the in-depth articles of Tugwell: "The evolution of dominican structures of government", *Archivum Fratrum Praedicatorum* 69 (1999), 5-60; 70 (2000), 111-242; 71 (2001), 5-182; 72 (2002), 26-159; 75 (2005), 29-79, which provide much additional nuances, especially with regard to the way Dominican general chapters and provincial chapters held the "executive branch" of order government to account.

20 Golubovich (1913); Moorman (1983); Eubel (1892).

21 Desbonnets (1986).

members. Those in charge were nothing more than ministers, that is to say the servants of those they were guiding. Whatever the subsequent stages in order development, that name with its biblical connotations was to stay. In contrast with the nomenclature we find in other orders, the Franciscan order would continue to have ministers, guardians, and custodians, not priors, abbots, superiors, or magisters general.[22]

This initial vision also meant that in principle all friars were to take part in the deliberations during the annual general chapter meetings at Assisi. The rapid numerical and geographical expansion of the order after its first papal recognition in 1209 ensured that this situation soon became untenable. This became clear at the famous general chapter *delle stuoie*, held around 1220, in which according to some sources no less than 5000 friars would have taken part.[23] Two or three years prior to that event, a first structure of order provinces and custodies emerged, to streamline communication and the efficacious deployment of friars in the quickly growing order. Yet at that juncture the Franciscan order did not even have a properly recognised rule, nor proper procedures for decision making and internal appointments.

The Franciscan rule of 1221 and the papally approved Franciscan rule of 1223 circumscribe to some extent the functions of guardians (in charge of an individual convent), custodians (administrators of custodies, or sub-provincial networks of friaries), provincial ministers (administrators of individual order provinces), and the minister general of the order, but they are not strong in details. They provide some information about the convocation and the participants of provincial and general chapters (probably also to curb the number of friars present). Moreover, the rule of 1223 does indicate that at the general chapter the collected custodians and provincial ministers together were to choose and in principle also could depose the minister general. These texts remain silent about the length of tenure of the minister general, or about the question how the custodians and provincial ministers were selected. In practice, Francis of Assisi and his immediate successors as minister general

---

22   Cf. Dalarun (1999) 34-38, 48-49. While working on this essay, I came across yet another, more recent work by Jacques Dalarun, which from a slightly different angle makes a case for looking at monastic and mendicant forms of government as an inspiration for thinking about democracy. Instead of focusing on issues and technicalities of representation, it proposes first and foremost a perusal of monastic and mendicant concepts of service (*ministerium*) in the context of community and order government, thus to provide an alternative vision on leadership and the exercise of power. See: Dalarun (2012).

23   *Legenda Perusina seu Compilatio Assisiensis*, in E. Menestò and S. Brufani (eds.), *Fontes franciscani*, Testi, 2 (Assisi, 1995), 1471-1690, no. 114.; cf. Desbonnets (1986) 9.

frequently appointed provincial ministers to their liking, and this could undermine the chapter's control over the order's executive branch.

Shortly before his death in 1226, Francis had issued a testament, which tried to fixate the interpretation of the rule for once and for all. It soon became apparent that this blocked constitutional developments, and in 1230 the Franciscan general chapter decided to appeal to Pope Gregory IX. The resulting bull *Quo elongati* not only denied the legal validity of Francis's testament but also established that from henceforth each order province should dispatch to the order's general chapter its provincial minister, as well as one custodian, to be selected by all custodians from the province. From this moment onwards, a clear principle of representation guided the makeup of the Franciscan general chapter.[24] Yet the convocation of the general chapter remained at the whim of the minister general. Hence the young order retained an authoritarian streak that distinguished it from its Dominican counterpart.

This would change, however, in response to ongoing expansion and continuing unrest under minister generals Giovanni Parenti (1227-1232) and especially Elias of Cortona (1232-1239). The latter was accused of authoritarian behavior, especially for his appointment of provincial ministers and officials empowered to perform visitations of individual provinces and friaries, and for his refusal to convoke a general chapter. He was deposed in 1239 in an extraordinary general chapter meeting called for by his opponents, who had obtained the backing of Pope Gregory IX. These events more or less forced the order to take its institutionalisation seriously. This led to a body of legislation in and after 1239, all of which was streamlined in the so-called Narbonne Constitutions from 1260, and their revision during the general chapters of Assisi (1279) and Paris (1292).[25]

---

24   *Quo elongati*, in: *Bullarium Franciscanum* I, 70 (no. 56). See also Gregory IX, "Die Bulle 'Quo elongati' Papst Gregors IX," H. Grundmann (ed.), *Archivum Franciscanum Historicum* 54 (1961), 20-25.

25   The statutes of Narbonne, Assisi and Paris received their first critical and synoptic edition as *Statuta Generalis Ordinis edita in Capitulis Generalibus celebratis Narbone an. 1260, Assisii an. 1279 atque Parisiis an. 1292 (Editio critica et synoptica)*, ed. M. Bihl, *Archivum Franciscanum Historicum* 34 (1941), 13-94; 284-358. They, as well as the constitutions of 1239, and fragments of intermediate texts are now also accessible in Cenci and Mailleux (2007). For a long time, historians thought that none of the constitutions prior to 1260 had survived, and some scholars assumed that the 1260 Narbonne constitutions were in fact the oldest ones ever made. This was disproven for once and for all when Cesare Cenci discovered fragments of the 1239 constitutions and compared them with the Narbonne text in *De fratrum Minorum Constitutionibus Praenarbonensibus*, ed. C. Cenci, *Archivum Fratrum Historicum* 83 (1990), 50-95. The following paragraphs are based on my reading of the *Constitutiones praenarbonenses* in: Cenci and Mailleux (2007) 69-75, and the secondary literature listed in note 26.

REPRESENTATIVE BODIES IN MEDIEVAL RELIGIOUS ORDERS

These documents reveal that a more balanced hierarchical system of order administration came into being, which gave due attention to the frequency of provincial and general chapter meetings, the way in which representatives for these bodies were chosen, the procedures concerning which matters were first to be discussed and approved at the provincial level prior to forwarding them to the general chapter, the transfer of authority by these bodies onto the executive officials on the provincial and the general levels for specific time periods, and the way in which these officials were held to account. This went hand in hand with the creation of formal procedures to codify and distribute decisions of the provincial and general chapters.

From 1239 onwards, general chapters were to be held every three years, and the representatives consisted of the body of provincial ministers from all Franciscan order provinces, with in addition from each order province one custodian elected by the custodians from the province in question, as well as a *frater discretus* representing all other friars within each province. This *frater discretus*, the representative of the rank and file, was elected by friars from the province (or by their representatives sent from individual friaries) during the preceding provincial chapter meeting. At the general chapter, which after 1239 on average would have consisted of circa 140 persons, a number of *definitori* was elected from the gathered *fratri discreti* and provincial ministers. This separately selected group was made responsible for the management of the general chapter itself. It was also supposed to gather and read the sealed missives and requests from provincial chapters and individual houses brought toward the general chapter, and to help prepare the text of the general chapter decisions.

Each triennial general chapter was to begin on the day of Pentecost, the day that commemorated the apostles' infusion with the Holy Spirit. The first act of the chapter was to judge the performance of the existing minister general. He was to ask forgiveness for his mistakes and leave the convocation hall, after which the gathered provincial ministers and custodians, assisted by the *definitori*, evaluated the performance of the minister general since the previous general chapter, taking into account the comments and complaints sent in by individual provinces and religious houses. Following this evaluation, a subsequent vote by the attending provincial ministers and custodians determined the fate of the minister general by absolute majority. This could mean the deposition of the minister general, and in that case his successor was to be elected the next day. When the provincial ministers and custodians eligible to vote on this matter did not succeed to choose a candidate by majority vote, the decision was handed over to a committee of three or five wise friars, who could act on behalf of everybody.

Once the vote concerning the minister general had passed, the general chapter – the provincial ministers and the *fratri discreti*, minus the custodians – began discussing the dossiers and wishes brought forward from the various provincial chapters, as well as the assignment of students and lectors to the order's *studia generalia*, and the appointment of important public preachers with license to preach in one or more order provinces. The general chapter also appointed *visitatores* to check on the religious life and rule observance within each order province, it made decisions concerning the dispatch of missions *apud infideles*, the creation of new order provinces and related matters, ending with deciding upon the venue for the next general chapter meeting.

At the provincial level a provincial chapter was to be held each year. This chapter was in principle open to the custodians of the provincial custodies and all friars of the province in question, although it was from nearly the outset rather common for friaries to send only a few representatives. Each friary in the province had one vote in the assembly, to be voiced by a *frater discretus* deputised for that task by his respective community. At the provincial chapter a body of four *definitori* was elected, with a spare one in case of a tied vote, which was to evaluate the performance of the sitting provincial minister, and which together with him was responsible for determining the chapter's agenda and the organisation of its orderly proceeding. Following the evaluation of the provincial minister's performance, the provincial chapter voted on the appointment and dismissal of the provincial minister, with voting rights given to the custodians of the individual custodies and to the *fratri discreti* sent by the friaries of the province. In the same way the provincial chapter decided on the designation of custodians (something that later reverted back to the discretion of the provincial minister), the appointment of convent lectors, the assignment of students within provincial and custodial schools, and discussed topics brought forward in writing by the representatives of individual friaries. The provincial chapter came to decisions by majority vote, and only those matters that had been discussed and decided upon with a majority vote in the provincial chapter were to be submitted in sealed documents to the upcoming general chapter.[26]

This basic structure of representative government, pushed through at the general chapter of 1239, met with some resistance and would undergo several emendations in the course of the thirteenth century, which on average tend to reinforce the executive power of the provincial ministers and the minister

---

26   See on all this also the analyses in Mapelli (2003) 21-24; Barone (1999) 87-98; Dalarun (1999) 73-102; Etzi, (2005) 36-74. Among the older studies, still valuable are Neukirchen (1952) and Brooke (1959).

general. Yet none of the major legislative texts accepted at important general chapter meetings, including those of Narbonne (1260), Assisi (1279), and Paris (1292), undermined the central tenets of the representative elements and the priority attached to the legislative power of the general chapter. These texts also detailed voting procedures for provincial and general chapters, which followed in principle the instructions put forward in canon 24 of the Fourth Lateran Council. Both in line with these instructions, and on the basis of practical experience, the constitutions of Narbonne and later installments likewise included additional procedures in case of the sudden death of provincial ministers or the minister general, and in case of other extraordinary circumstances, such as the forced abdication of order superiors due to heresy. In this way, the whole representative system was able to cope with specific crisis situations.[27]

Possible Repercussions of Representative Practices in Religious Orders

Hence, like their colleagues in other major religious orders, all clerical friars active within the Franciscan order from the late 1230s onwards, would have become thoroughly acculturated by the practices of representation, deliberation, and voting in their order's provincial and general chapter meetings. Many of these friars would go out in the world, to act as public preachers, to perform as counsellors of rulers and city councils. A significant number of them would also end up in high ecclesiastical positions as bishops, archbishops, and the like, and as such presided over provincial synods and acted as personal advisors to kings. A case in point is Archbishop John Pecham in England, who figures alongside of his Dominican predecessor Robert Kilwardby in the aforementioned study of Barker. It has also been documented that from early on mendicant friars acted as arbiters and guarantors within Italian, Spanish, French, and Flemish communes during all kinds of legal and economic transactions, and were used by these communes as impartial officials to oversee and confirm local elections, just as their friaries were used as communal meeting points for urban council meetings, and as archival depositories for important communal documents and guild statutes.[28] In this context it should also be noted that quite a few Franciscan friars (like some of their Dominican

---

27   Cf. Mapelli (2003) 29-34.
28   For an initial overview of the activities of Franciscan (and other mendicant) friars as peace brokers in and between communes, as election officers, and as communal embassadors, see da Campagnola (1999) 65-118; Artifoni (1995) 163-164; Bartoli Langeli (1985) 91-99; Vauchez, (1966).

counterparts) were directly involved with drawing up new communal statutes. This phenomenon, which already started early in the order's history, surged during the fifteenth century, when Franciscan Observant preachers were asked to draw up a number of governing statutes for towns such as Perugia (1425), Terni (1444), and Trevi (1487).[29]

Considering the embeddedness of the mendicant friars in the urban landscape and their presence at European courts, the question can be asked whether their intra-order government experience would have been brought to bear on the way in which they acted as preachers, counsellors, and even co-legislators between the thirteenth and the late fifteenth century. It is not easy to answer this question. Jacques Dalarun, who in 1999 issued an influential study on the issue of power in the Franciscan order during the thirteenth century, has been inclined to answer negatively: according to him there is not much evidence to support the thesis that the friars actively tried to export directly aspects of their own stratified representative system to communes for which they acted as counsellors or even as co-legislators.[30]

Dalarun's interpretation might be correct in so far as friars normally did not impose their representative systems on the communities for which they acted in some kind of legislative capacity. Yet this verdict needs careful verification, with attention to more technical aspects, as the friars did apply their expertise with regard to voting procedures, codification, and confirmation practices when they acted on behalf of communes, and the fact alone that they were asked in these capacities might indicate the acknowledged expertise of the mendicants in such matters. Moreover, as both Dalarun and Barone have signalled with recourse to the Franciscan friar Salimbene of Parma, the mendicants were often proud of their representative structures, judging them to be superior to some of the more fledging communal structures they encountered in the secular realm.[31]

It might not have been a coincidence that Franciscan friars, as well as their Dominican and Augustinian colleagues, produced texts of political theory that habitually discussed matters of sovereignty, delegation, and representation. After all, Thomas Aquinas, William of Ockham, John of Paris, and Bonagratia of Bergamo, to name but a few, were all mendicant friars. As explained, many of their texts were produced in specific polemical contexts. At the same time, these academically trained authors expounded their arguments on ideal forms

---

29   See aside from the studies mentioned in the previous note also Bonmann (1965) and Evangelisti (2013).

30   Dalarun (1999) 131-134.

31   Barone (1999) 59, 68-70; Dalarun (1999) 131-132. With reference to Salimbene of Parma, *Cronica*, ed. G. Scalia, 2 vols. (Bari: Laterza, 1966) I, 230.

of government, or their expositions for or against the *plenitudo potestatis* of pope or king/emperor in universalist terms. Historians of political thought have not considered as to whether underlying implicit assumptions in these texts might have been informed by a thorough familiarity with modes of representation and delegation within their own religious life. It might be worthwhile to re-investigate some of these texts from this specific angle.

Likewise, scholars who, in the wake of the ground-breaking work of Todeschini and Lambertini, focus on the Franciscans as strong proponents of a program of religious, social, and economic pacification of Christian society that even allowed for the development of economically flourishing urban communities within strict evangelical parameters, might also want to include this perspective in their discussions. After all, Franciscan experiences of order government might have impacted their vision of the ideal organisation of the communes and the larger realms in which they were active. Only a thorough re-reading of the available sources will bear this out.

Finally, the very example of the government organisation of large religious orders, such as the Cistercians, the Carthusians, various orders of regular canons, the Dominicans, and the Franciscans, might have influenced outsiders. The enduring representative elements present in these multinational entities provided ample evidence for the feasibility of representative processes and carefully imposed checks and balances between legislative and executive levels of corporate government. Outsiders must have noticed the institutional strength these orders were able to display in the face of changing historical circumstances, and that much of this strength was bound up with the way in which these orders had organised their internal government structures. That alone might have been an incentive to emulate some of their most successful practices, overtly or in silence.

Whatever the actual influence of representative bodies within religious orders on the secular world, it is a mistake to ignore them when discussing the emergence of representative institutions during the medieval period. The mere size and omnipresence of these orders, as well as their stature as near-independent international organisations make that an untenable option.

Bibliography

Allen, J.W., "Marsiglio of Padua and Medieval Secularism," in F.J.C. Hearnshaw (ed.), *The Social and Political Ideas of Some Great Medieval Thinkers* (London, 1923), 167-191.

Andenna, C. and G. Melville (eds.), *Regulae-Consuetudines-Statuta. Studi sulle fonti normative degli ordini religiosi nei secoli centrali del Medioevo* (Münster, 2005).

Artifoni, E., "Gli uomini dell'assemblea. L'oratoria civile, i concionatori e i predicatori nella società communale," in *La predicazione dei frati dalla metà del '200 alla fine del '300. Atti del XXII convegno internazionale, Assisi, 13-15 ottobre 1994* (Spoleto, 1995), 143-188.

Avondo, E.R., *I sistemi di deliberazione collettiva nel medioevo italiano* (Turin, 1927).

Barker, E., *The Dominican Order and Convocation. A Study of the Growth of Representation in the Church during the Thirteenth Century* (Oxford, 1913).

Barone, G., *Da frate Elia agli Spirituali* (Milan,1999).

Bartoli Langeli, A., "Comuni e frati minori," in *Il francescanesimo nell'Umbria meridionale nei secoli XIII-XIV. Atti del V convegno di studio, Narni-Amelia-Alviano, 23-25 maggio 1982* (Narni, 1985), 91-99.

Black, A., *Council and Commune: The Conciliar Movement and the Fifteenth Century Heritage* (London, 1979).

Black, A., *Political Thought in Europe, 1250-1450* (Cambridge, Eng., 1992).

Blockmans, W., "A Typology of Representative Institutions in Late Medieval Europe," in *Journal of Medieval History* 4 (1978), 189-215.

Bonmann, O., "Problemi critici riguardo ai cosidetti 'Statuta Bernardiniana' di Perugia (1425-1426)," in *Studi Francescani* 42 (1965), 278-302.

Brooke, R.B., *Early Franciscan Government. From Elias to Bonaventure* (Cambridge, Eng., 1959).

Cacciotti, A. and M. Melli (eds.), *I francescani e l'uso del denaro: atti dell'VIII Convegno storico di Greccio, Greccio, 7-8 maggio 2010* (Milan, 2011).

Campagnola, S. da, *Francesco e francescanesimo nella società dei secoli XIII-XIV* (Assisi, 1999).

Cenci C. and R.G. Mailleux (eds.), *Constitutiones Generales Ordinis Fratrum Minorum,* I (*Saeculum XIII*), Analecta Franciscana XIII, Nova Series Documenta et Studia, 1 (Grottaferrata, 2007).

Congar, Y.M.J., "Quod omnes tangit, ab omnibus tractari et approbari debet," in *Revue historique de froit français et étranger* 35 (1958), 210-259.

Cygler, F., *Das Generalkapitel im hohen Mittelalter. Cisterzienser, Prämonstratenser, Kartäuser und Cluniazenser* (Münster, 2001).

Cygler, F., "Le rayonnement des constitutions dominicaines au XIIIe siècle: quelques brèves observations," in M. Breitenstein, J. Burkhardt, S. Burkhardt, and J. Röhrkasten (eds.), *Rules and Observance: Devising Forms of Communal Life* (Münster, 2014), 239-250.

Cygler, F., "Les chanoines réguliers et le chapitre général (XIIe-début XIIIe siècle)," in M. Parisse (ed.), *Les chanoines réguliers: émergence et expansion (XIe–XIIIe siècles);*

actes du sixième colloque international du CERCOR, Le Puy en Velay, 29 juin – 1er juillet 2006 (Saint-Étienne, 2009), 265-296.

Cygler, F., "Pour une approche comparee des normes et de l'organisation de la vie regu-liere au moyen âge: Quelques pistes," in G. Melville and A. Müller (eds.), *Mittel-alterliche Orden und Klöster im Vergleich: Methodische Ansätze und Perspektiven* (Berlin, 2007), 163-186.

Dalarun, J., *François d'Assise ou le pouvoir en question. Principes et modalité du gouver-nement dans l'Ordre des frères mineurs* (Brussels, 1999).

Dalarun, J., *Gouverner c'est servir: essai de démocratie médiévale* (Paris, 2012).

Desbonnets, T., *Dalla intuizione alla istituzione. I francescani* (Milan, 1986).

Etzi, P., *Iuridica franciscana. Percorsi monografici di storia della legislazione dei tre Ordini francescani* (Padua, 2005).

Eubel, C. (ed.), *Provinciale Ordinis Fratrum Minorum vetustissimum Secundum Codicem Vaticanum Nr. 1960* (Florence, 1892).

Evangelisti, P., *I Francescani e la costruzione di uno stato. Linguaggi politici, valori iden-titari, progetti di governo in area catalano-aragonese* (Padua, 2006).

Evangelisti, P., "Per uno studio della testualità politica francescana tra XIII e XV secolo. Autori e tipologua delle fonti," in *Studi medievali* 3rd ser. 37 (1996), 549-623.

Evangelisti, P., "'Quis enim conservat civitatem, status et regimina?'. II linguaggio po-litico e la pedagogia civile di Giacomo della Marca," in F. Serpico (ed.), *Gemma Lucens: Giacomo della Marca tra devozione e santità: atti dei convegni, Napoli, 20 no-vembre 2009, Monteprandone, 27 novembre 2010* (Florence, 2013), 153-173.

Freeman, E., "What makes a monastic order? Issues of methodology in 'The Cistercian Evolution,'" in *Cistercian Studies Quarterly* 37 (2002), 429-442.

Galbraith, G., *The Constitution of the Dominican Order: 1216 to 1360* (Manchester, 1925).

Gaudemet, J. (ed.), *Les élections dans l'Église latine des origines au xvie siècle* (Paris, 1979).

Golubovich, G., "Le province dell'Ordine minoritico nei secoli XIII e XIV in Europa e nell'Oriente francescano," in *Bio-bibliografica della Terra Santa e dell'Oriente fran-cescano*, vol. 2 (Florence, 1913), 214-274.

Grélois, A., "Tradition and Transmission: What is the Significance of the Cistercian General Chapters' Statutes? (Twelfth to Fourteenth Centuries)," in K. Pansters and A.G. Plunkett-Latimer (eds.), *Shaping Stability: The Normation and Formation of Re ligious Life in the Middle Ages* (Turnhout, 2016), 205-216.

Hoffmann, C. *The Cistercian Evolution: The Invention of a Religious Order in Twelfth-Century Europe* (Philadelphia, 2000).

Lagarde, G. de, *La naissance de l'Esprit laïque au déclin du Moyen Age* (Louvain, 1934-1963).

Lagarde, G. de, "L'idée de la Représentation dans les Oeuvres de Guillaume d'Ockham," *Bulletin of the International Committee of Historical Sciences* 9 (1937), 425-451.

Leclerc, V., "Des Assemblées générales des ordres religieux au XIIIe siècle," in *L'Institut. Journal universel des sciences et des sociétés savantes en France et a l'étranger*. IIe section: *Sciences Historiques, Archéologiques et Philosophiques* 157 (1849), 3-7.

Lee, H-Y., *Political Representation in the Later Middle Ages: Marsilius in Context* (New York, 2008).

Mapelli, F.J., *L'amministrazione francescana di Inghilterra e Francia. Personale di governo e strutture dell'Ordine fina al Concilio di Vienne (1311)* (Rome, 2003).

Menestò E. and S. Brufani (eds.), *Fontes Franciscani*, Testi, 2 (Assisi, 1995).

Monahan, A., *Consent, Coercion, and Limit: The Medieval Origins of Parliamentary Democracy* (Leiden, 1987).

Moorman, J.R.H., *Medieval Franciscan Houses* (Saint Bonaventure, 1983).

Moulin, L., "La science politique et le gouvernement des communautés religieuses," in *Revue Internationale des Sciences Administratives* 1 (1951), 42-67.

Moulin, L., "Le gouvernement des communautés religieuses comme type de gouvernement mixte," in *Revue Française de Science Politique* 2, no. 2 (1952), 335-355.

Moulin, L., "Les origines religieuses des techniques électorales et délibératives modernes," in *Revue Internationale d'Histoire Politique et Institutionnelle* n.s. 3 (1953), 106-148; re-issued in *Politix* 11, no. 43 (1998), 117-162.

Moulin, L., "Une source méconnue de la philosophie politique marsilienne: L'organisation constitutionelle des ordres religieux," in *Revue Française de Science Politique* 33, no. 1 (1983), 5-13.

Musco, M. (ed.), *I Francescani e la politica. Atti del Convegno internazionale di studio Palermo 3-7 Dicembre 2002*, 2 vols. (Palermo, 2007).

Nederman, C.J., *Community and Consent: the Secular Political Theory of Marsiglio of Padua's Defensor Pacis* (Lanham, 1995).

Neukirchen, M. a, *De Capitulo generali in primo Ordine seraphico*, PhD Thesis (Rome, 1952).

Oakley, F., *The Watershed of Modern Politics: Law, Virtue, Kingship, and Consent (1300-1650)* (New Haven, 2015).

Pennington, K., "Representation in Medieval Canon Law," in *The Jurist* 64 (2004), 361-383.

Quillet, J., "Community, Counsel and Representation," in J.H. Burns (ed.), *The Cambridge History of Medieval Political Thought, c. 350–c. 1450* (Cambridge, Eng., 1988), 520-571.

Stasavage, D., "Representation and Consent: Why They Arose in Europe and Not Elsewhere," in *Annual Review of Political Science* 19 (2016), 145-162.

Stawski, J., *Le principe de la majorité (son histoire, son fondement et les limites de son applications. Études sur la formation de la volonté de Genève* (Geneva, 1920).

Sykes, K., "Cistercian influences on Gilbertine legislation," in *Citeaux* 59 (2008), 209-235.

Tierney, B., *Foundations of the Conciliar Theory: The Contribution of the Medieval Canonists from Gratian to the Great Schism* (Cambridge, Eng., 1956).

Tierney, B., "The Idea of Representation in the Medieval Councils of the West," in *Concilium* 187 (1983), 25-30.

Todeschini, G., "Le 'bien commun' de la *civitas christiana* dans la tradition textuelle franciscaine (xIIIe-xVe siècle)," in H. Bresc, G. Dagher and C. Veauvy (eds.), *Politique et religion en Méditerranée. Moyen Âge et époque contemporaine* (Paris, 2008), 265-304.

Tugwell, S., "The evolution of dominican structures of government," in *Archivum Fratrum Praedicatorum* 69 (1999), 5-60; 70 (2000), 111-242; 71 (2001), 5-182; 72 (2002), 26-159; 75 (2005), 29-79.

Vauchez, A., "Une campagne de pacification en Lombardie autour de 1233. L'action politique des Ordres mendiants d'après la réforme des statuts communaux et les accords de paix," in *Mélanges d'archéologie et d'histoire* 78 (1966), 503-549.

Waddell, C. (ed.), *Twelfth-Century Statutes from the Cistercian General Chapter: Latin Text With English Notes and Commentary* (Cîteaux, 2002).

CHAPTER 5

The Political Rhetoric of Capitals: Rome and Versailles in the Baroque Period, or the "Power of Place"

Peter Rietbergen

Introduction

Surely, amongst the world's capitals Rome is the one most captured in paintings, photographs, and films but, also, most subjected to scholarly scrutiny.[1] On the other hand, amongst the world's royal palaces Versailles undoubtedly is the one most pictured as well as researched.[2] Yet, people tend to forget that Versailles was more than a palace: it was also a city, and even, from the 1680s to the 1790s, the "de facto" capital of France, whereas the city of Rome, from the early sixteenth century onwards, became the greatly enlarged extension of that one, unique building complex, St Peter's basilica and the adjoining Vatican, or Apostolic Palace.

This contribution takes up the volume's theme of representation of power and public display by analysing and comparing both palace-cum-cities as rhetorical texts that aimed to proclaim a message of supreme power. I will concentrate on what historians customarily term "the early modern period" – which, when art-historians study it, coincides with both the Renaissance and the Baroque. My particular focus will only be on the Baroque. In doing so, my analysis of what one also might call the "semiotics" of these towns-cum-palaces will reveal both similarities and differences. This contribution will furthermore demonstrate how physical expressions of power can be seen as a prime instrument of legitimising power. I hope to contribute to the growing corpus of research that addresses the political rhetoric of the built environment in general and of the urban landscape in particular – "the power of place."

Obviously, the innate tendency of power to represent itself in as many ways as possible – including through the art of propaganda, which is the more

---

1　Cf. Rietbergen (2003).

2　For the complex role(s) of Versailles, see the historiographical, introductory chapter of: Sabatier (1999). However, amongst more recent studies Duindam (2003), is, easily, the most comprehensive and authoritative.

© PETER RIETBERGEN, 2019 | DOI:10.1163/9789004291966_006

This is an open access chapter distributed under the terms of the CC-BY-NC 4.0 License.

THE POLITICAL RHETORIC OF CAPITALS　　　　　　　　　　　　　　　　57

"active" form of representation –has always led rulers to try to structure the "loci" of their power in ways they felt to be "orderly," preferably referring to a hierarchical, authoritative and, indeed, often authoritarian order.

In many cultures, this desire has expressed itself in palaces and cities that mirrored the perceived order of the cosmos, an order, moreover, that often was seen as balanced and symmetrical.[3] This is not surprising for, as some psychologists such as Carl Jung (1875-1961) have argued, symmetry gives our mind a sense of primordial harmony and security as much as, or perhaps precisely because it also structures the physical universe.[4] Mircea Eliade (1907-1986), one of the founding fathers of comparative mythology, has stressed the importance of visual and, therefore, ceremonial and ritual "centrality" in many of the world's cultures as well.[5]

All over the world, this archetypal form of conceptualising space was also reflected in town-founding and town-planning, usually accompanied by geomantic rituals and, thus, resulting in a kind of cultural astronomy. In the Hinduist as well as in the Buddhist-Confucian "oikoumenai," this desire for order and hence control has resulted in the construction of imperial cities modelled on the "mandala," an "essence-container," a microcosmic "model" of the universe combining the square and the circle.[6] In Judaeo-Christian culture, the fundamental book of the Jews, the Old Testament, presents heaven as a place and, moreover, a temple, a tabernacle, a throne room. In the New Testament of the Christians, especially in the Book of Revelations, heaven is detailed as a world consisting of concentric circles, the innermost of which is a – or rather "the" – city, the "heavenly Jerusalem," the "City of God." Yet, the city itself is described as a square with, on each of its four sides, three gates. In it, God's throne-room is located.[7] Not surprisingly, medieval and Renaissance representations of Jerusalem and, consequently, Rome, often tended towards the circular[8] – as, for example, shown in the thirteenth-century so-called "Ebstorf-map," or the view of Rome in the fifteenth-century manuscript *Les tres riches Heures du Duc de Berry* and others[9] – though the actual topographies of these towns were anything but mandalaic.

3　For a very short survey: Patricios (1973); Bird (1977/2007). Concentrating mainly on recent developments, but offering a good general introduction: Minkenberg (2014).

4　Zabriskie (1995).

5　Eliade (1961) 20-40.

6　Cf., for example, Smith (1987); Narayan (2015), who also refers to classical Indian texts concerning city-building, and: Ten Grotenhuis, (1999), who deals with China as well. Last, but not least: Zhu (2004).

7　For a survey of various concepts of heaven: McDannell (2001).

8　A few examples are shown on: <http://mappingrome.com/medieval-rome/>.

9　Other examples are Taddeo di Bartolo's map in a fresco in the townhall of Sienna (ca. 1415), the maps adorning Ptolemy's *Cosmography* of the late 1460s, Alessandro Strozzi's

While many rulers did not hesitate to build palaces according to variants of these and other orderly visions, few actually succeeded in also creating an entire (capital) city "ex novo" – not only because financial and other practical considerations precluded such grandiose experiments, but also because existing capitals often were considered sacred, hallowed by the dynastic and imperial traditions that were part of the sovereign's heritage and, thus, of his (claims to) power. Abandoning them was, therefore, not advisable.

Still, in 1346 BC Pharaoh Amenophis IV, better known as Akhn-Aton, did decide to leave ancient Thebes with the unruly priest-caste he hated and created his new capital at Akhet-Aton (The Foundation of the Sun). In 836 AD, the Abbasid caliphs moved from Bagdad to Samarra. Likewise, in the early fifteenth century, the Yongle Emperor left Nanjing, and made Beijing the imperial city, constructed according to rigid geomantic-cosmological principles. And in India, in 1569, Emperor Akbar replaced Delhi with Fatehpur, the "city of victory." Last but not least, from 1598 onwards Shah Abbas, the ruler of Safavid Iran, created a new residence at Isfahan.

Yet, most monarchs had to satisfy themselves with imposing their visions of power on existing cities. In a sense, Rome and Versailles represent these two "types": the one an old capital constantly adapted to new visions of power, the other a new capital specifically devised to do so.

The "City Eternal"

To both secular and religious leaders the city of Rome, throughout its long history, offered unique possibilities for the representation of power. However, when the popes returned to Rome after their exile in Avignon, the city was not a sight that pleased them. While they were proud monarchs wanting to compete with and hold their own against the so-called new, absolute monarchies now slowly evolving in the European political landscape, the outlook of the city and the ordered and ordering view of the new, Humanist-Renaissance ideals of symmetry and classical balance did not quite fit their purposes.[10]

Nevertheless, their return had been ineluctable: the "mana" of the papacy originated in, and, indeed, remained insolubly tied to, the sacrality conferred

---

map of 1475, and Sebastian Münster's representation in his *Cosmographia*, of 1544. Even the far more accurate map in the famous Braun-Hohenberg-atlas of 1585 still suggests a circular city. Cf. however also: Müller (1961).

10 For this section, besides introducing new notions and ideas, I draw upon, and refer to my own, earlier work on papal Rome, specifically: Rietbergen (1983a) chapters II and VII; Rietbergen (2006) chapter IV; Rietbergen (2013); Rietbergen (2015) chapter I.

THE POLITICAL RHETORIC OF CAPITALS

on it by the tomb of St Peter's. The very foundation of papal power was, after all, their claim to primacy amongst the Church's many bishops, as the successors of the first among the apostles, who allegedly had been named his vicar by Christ himself, and whose very relics were embedded in the foundations of the basilica built atop his tomb. With its additional hundreds, or even thousands of graves of martyrs and saints, Rome was a sacred city, the capital of Christendom as well as Christianity.

In short, though during their years in Avignon (1309-1377) the Curia had succeeded in building both a formidable – as we now would say: proto-modern – bureaucracy and, as an important part of it, a fiscal system that gave the papacy enormous power, the popes could not afford to permanently leave the town of their origin. Without Rome, the pretences of the papacy were baseless. Consequently, precisely to preserve and even strengthen their position, they felt forced to return to it. But the Rome they found was not an "ideal," cosmically-oriented town. It was a "medieval" town, i.e., a town that had grown haphazardly, without any order, having evolved around the fortified residences of the warring urban aristocrats, who for centuries had competed with the popes. A town, also, strangely dominated by huge, half-ruinous monuments referring to an obviously great past that, however, only was dimly understood.

Still, before the popes could turn their attention to the town at large, a critical look at their ideological mainstay, the basilica of St Peter's, was necessary. It taught them that, after a millennium, the great church first built by the Emperor Constantine – to the terms of whose so-called donation the Curia still referred when defending the papacy's secular, princely power over Rome and central Italy – could no longer serve as the worthy reliquary of the Apostle's remains and hence as the church wherein they, his rightful and, indeed, only successors, would celebrate their power: not as bishops of Rome but as rulers of the entire, "universal" Church.

Therefore, already Nicholas V (1397-1447-1455) decided not to restore St Peter's to its ancient outlook but to replace it with a new, far greater church that would show the splendour of the imperial tradition in which it had been first conceived, a splendour that his advisers and architects now felt they could recapture because their Humanist learning allowed them to better understand those ancient times. While the plans of Nicholas did not mature, one of his successors, the great warrior-pope Julius II (1443-1503-1513), who managed to create what soon became the "state of the papacy," resumed his ideas.

Hence, in 1506, a start was made with the immense building that, more than a century later, became St Peter's as we now know it. Not surprisingly, the horoscope cast for laying the building's foundation stone – a typical Humanist practise – was constructed in such a way that the stellar constellation most propitious to it had been modelled on the one that reputedly held for Jesus of Nazareth himself. And, of course, the birthday of Christ traditionally had been linked to the day of the creation of the world.[11] Thus, the basilica became the nexus of Christian time and space, the navel of God's cosmos. Its Greek-cross ground-plan followed what were understood to be the basic elements of a representation of cosmic hierarchy and order: its perfect square was crowned by the perfect circle, Michelangelo's great cupola.

By the turn of the century, with the cupola complete, the then architect-in-chief, Carlo Maderno, proposed to surround the basilica with a series of lower chapels, each with its own cupola. If this design, which harkened back both to Michelangelo's and to the earliest plan for new St Peter's by Bramante, had been executed, the world would have seen the greatest mandalaic church ever, resembling both the third Hagia Sophia at Istanbul and, the epitome of such sanctuaries, the Borobudur on Java – both representations in stone of the "holy mountain" common to so many mythologies.

However, in 1607, it was decided that the old, Renaissance-Humanist plan of St Peter's was a "pagan" symbol. Yet, the new plan – based on a so-called Latin cross with, consequently, a proper nave – did not basically alter the basilica's function. Though both the Vatican and the Lateran palace had throne rooms, as did the papal summer palace on the Quirinal Hill, St Peter's is the real papal throne room – as well as, always, the most public one. Over the course of its long construction, the church went through a number of design stages. Still, all the architects involved – Michelangelo foremost amongst them – felt they were creating a truly imperial symbol, worthy of the man who combined the power of Christ's vicar with that of a secular prince ranking first amongst the monarchs of Christendom. There, the pope verily shows (the origin of) his unique power. For he celebrates under the huge, bronze canopy erected by Bernini in the 1630s, exactly above the tomb of the Prince of the Apostles. And behind him, all those present in the basilica – it can seat some 20,000 faithful, or, alternatively, accommodate some 60,000 people standing – see the "Chair of St Peter," encased in bronze in the apse. As an essential part of this symbolical-referential monument, a dove hovers over it in the stained-glass of the window whose light floods it all: the Holy Spirit is always with the papacy. In other words, this was the prime location for the pope to legitimise his power as well as the most appropriate place for the faithful to express their loyalty to God and to the pope.

Even if a Roman pontiff ever had considered creating a new capital for the Church he presented as universal, and, moreover, if he ever had had the means

---

11   Quinlan-McGrath (2001) 731 sqq.

THE POLITICAL RHETORIC OF CAPITALS61

to do so, he would always have been reminded of the basic fact already referred to above: without Rome, no papacy. If the popes wanted a capital that reflected their political, ideological, and religious beliefs – a town that, in short, resembled the ideal "Civitas Dei" – it had to be constructed within the materiality of contemporary Rome. To realise this vision, to make Rome into a "new Jerusalem" that would impress both the masses of pilgrims who annually arrived there – an important source of income, too – and the embassies of the Christian princes who sought out the popes both as temporal rulers of Central Italy and as arbiters of Christendom and, increasingly, as leaders of a truly global organisation, massive changes in the urban structure would have to be made.

Obviously, Rome once had been the capital of the greatest empire Western Eurasia had ever known. Indeed, from the fifteenth century onwards, precisely the representational significance as well as possibilities of the Caesarian ruins dawned upon the town's politico-cultural elite. Ideologically, this resulted in a vision of Rome that somehow gathered the remains of the "pagan," imperial city and the buildings created in more recent, Christian-papal times into one convincing synthesis.[12] In terms of city-planning, this vision was realised through a series of grandiose projects that were as practical as they were propagandistic.

Obviously, these schemes always involved St Peter's. However, the Vatican Hill, on which both the basilica and the adjacent palace had been built, lay outside the "original" Rome, the Rome of the imperial age and the "Middle Ages." The two needed to be linked, not only because the town proper held so many other significant Christian sites and monuments, not only because there the church-and-palace of the popes as bishops of Rome was situated in the Lateran quarter, but also because, since times immemorial, all roads which proverbially led to Rome literally converged upon the old centre.

Therefore, Pope Nicholas decided to integrate the Vatican quarter into Rome by no less than three new, rectilinear, porticoed thoroughfares which proudly would cut through the jumbled mass of medieval houses and other buildings covering the hill.[13] These constructions, he felt, would powerfully proclaim modern architecture, which, according to his advisers, now took on the reborn, classicist forms of the old empire. Although the original design was not executed, a few decades later a watered-down form was. Thus, today, streets in front of the basilica slope down to the banks of the Tiber, where an old bridge connects them to the city's main body and the roads that reach Rome from the North.

---

12   Rietbergen (2003) part I.
13   Westfall (1974).

Around the turn of the century, Julius II ordered the construction of the "Via della Lungara" and the "Via Giulia," two even longer streets which, running parallel to the banks of the river, linked the seat of papal power to Rome's venerable ancient centre: the Capitol. Given the propagandistic need of these projects, as had happened around the Vatican, people who owned property that stood in the way were either bought out or, sometimes, ruthlessly expropriated.

Three other pope-kings must be credited with the creation of papal Rome as we now know and see it. The first is Paul III (1468-1534-1549). Following ideas and constructions already started in the early decades of the sixteenth century, during his reign a piazza was laid out just inside the "Porta del Popolo," the ancient Roman gate which opened onto the Via Flaminia that led from Rome to Milan and on towards the Alps and Northern Europe from where most pilgrims came. From the piazza, like the prongs of a trident, three long, straight streets were "bored" into the corpus of the city: the left-hand one along the slope of the Pincio Hill to the bottom of the Trinità de' Monti, and the middle one, the Via del Corso – following the old "Via Lata" – going up to the Capitol. There, where the ancient Roman Republic had had its seat, Michelangelo now realised a new city centre, expressing the domination of papal authority over the once-independent communal leaders. The third and last of the three streets led from Piazza del Popolo to a point on the bank of the Tiber where one could see, on the other side, the majestic, though at that time still unfinished mass of new St. Peter's rising like a mountain on the city's horizon.[14] Together, these new thoroughfares should demonstrate the "Renovatio Urbis," the revival of Rome's imperial splendour.[15]

The second pope to address the ideological impact of Rome in its entirety was Sixtus V (1521-1585-1590, see Figure 5.1).[16] First, he finalised the building of the huge cupola of St. Peter's that dominates as well as characterises Rome's skyline even today, but whose construction, according to the design of Michelangelo, had lain dormant for decades. During the five short years of his pontificate, Sixtus also ordered the lay-out of a few more very long rectilinear streets that connected the city centre as defined in the previous pontificates to, specifically, the far-away but ceremonially-liturgically important basilicas of Santa Maria Maggiore, St John Lateran, and Santa Croce in Gerusalemme. Moreover, at all important intersections of these streets, as well as of the ones

---

14 Ciucci (1974). Also: Ackermann (1982); Frommel (1986) did not add much to either my own or other earlier contributions.

15 Cf. Delph (2006).

16 The literature about Sixtus's urban planning is extensive. See for a historiographical survey: Sinisi (2010) xxx, note 37.

THE POLITICAL RHETORIC OF CAPITALS 63

FIGURE 5.1 Portrait of Pope Sixtus V (r. 1575-1580). Published by Nicolaus van Aelst (Flemish, Brussels 1526-1613 Rome). Credits: The Elisha Whittelsey Collection, The Elisha Whittelsey Fund, 1949 (CC0 1.0) [accessed online 28.02.2019, <https://www.metmuseum.org/art/collection/search/369588>].

constructed during the preceding century, he had obelisks set up, the most magnificent one in front of the new St Peter's. Also, at strategic places monumental fountains were built. Thus, Sixtus completed the grid of streets created between the late fifteenth and the late sixteenth century. The result was an urban "net" in which the visitors of the Eternal City were captured – an effort at "spatial Christianisation," one might say, in which they were directed from one splendid sight to another, always ending up in front of one of the city's seven main churches. Visually, too, Rome had become a sacred city, *the* sacred city.

Indeed, even those who never were fortunate enough to visit Rome now could experience it, for from the sixteenth century onwards, both small and large printed maps – like the one produced by Antonio Tempesta in the 1590s, which shows some of Sixtus's streets – and engraved plates publicised Rome, enabling the wider world to see that the Eternal City was the most wondrous town of their world.[17] These publications were definitely intended to serve as printed propaganda for the urbanistic schemes of the papacy. Moreover, they formed a welcome for additional and pictorially attractive sources of information besides the traditional guidebooks usually presented under the caption "Mirabilia Urbis Romae," which included both short texts that gave pilgrims and other visitors a survey of the "Indulgentiae Ecclesiarum Urbis Romae," and the longer ones that (also) provided a "Historia et Descriptio Urbis Romae."[18] To address as large an audience as possible – i.e., both the actual pilgrims and other visitors, and the "armchair travellers" – these guides were published in a variety of languages. They were frequently updated to show the on-going changes in the townscape.

The third pope to leave his indelible imprint on Rome's cityscape and, indeed, to make it an enduring image of the papacy, was Alexander VII (1599-1655-1667). He tackled the problem of the very undignified sandy space stretching out in front of the grand basilica that had pained his predecessors for almost 150 years. From 1656 onwards, the design genius of his architect Gianlorenzo Bernini – and the manpower of several hundred artisans and other labourers – created a unique piazza: its form linked two circles into a grand oval.[19]

Meant as an open-air "theatre" – the very term was used at the time – for the church and, indeed, the Church, the piazza was defined and embraced by the

---

17   See, also, San Juan (2001).

18   Fundamental for our understanding of this complex "genre": Miedema (1996); Miedema (2003).

19   Cf. Kitao (1974).

THE POLITICAL RHETORIC OF CAPITALS 65

curves of two huge travertine colonnades. Their 284 columns carry an entablature crowned with the marble statues of 88 saints[20]; thus, heaven is represented on earth, with the "arms" of the colonnades, reaching out as if to receive the faithful in the fold of the "Ecclesia Romana": the only way to eternal salvation. At the piazza's heart stands the obelisk transferred there already in 1586 by Sixtus V. It serves as a gnomon, indicating the hours of the liturgy, while the open span between the arms of the colonnades themselves covers the moments of daily sunrise throughout the course of the year. Thus, the piazza seems to represent the cosmos as well. Looking up at the cross atop the obelisk and beyond it, towards the cupola of St Peter's, those who enter this space truly experience the totality of papal power that had succeeded in making Rome God's "city on earth".[21]

Of course, descriptions of this spectacular piece of architecture and urban planning immediately were incorporated in the guidebooks, as well as shown on the maps of Rome. Indeed, because the popes wanted propagandistically to use this, their last great architectural exploit, many artists – painters but also draughtsmen and engravers – now concentrated on views of Piazza San Pietro, depicting it in all its undeniable grandeur. It had become the apogee of the rhetoric of papal Rome.

The "City of the Sun"

While the popes in Rome searched for physical expressions of their power through St Peter's and through the city of Rome itself, in France we witness a different attempt of representation of power in the palace-cum-town that truly became the centre of a cult if not devoted to the Sun then, certainly, to the Sun King. Why Louis XIV, at the age of 23, started building and continued rebuilding his main residence in the old village of Versailles and, moreover, in 1682 transferred the entire business of government to it as well, thus for all practical and indeed also ceremonial purposes leaving Paris, is a question much discussed.[22] Admittedly, Louis's childhood memories of Paris had caused a trauma. As a young boy, he had felt the revolt, both of the French nobles and

---

20 The total is far higher if one also counts the statues crowning the buildings bordering the trapezoidal "square" in front of the basilica.

21 Rietbergen (1983b) 11-163, 237-41.

22 From the huge literature about Versailles, I cite: de Vinha (2009) and Torres (2015), not because they are the most scholarly but because they do present the history of the palace in some readable grand lines. For specifics: Bluche (1999); Berger (1985); Perouse de Montclos (1991).

of the Parisian population, against the rule of the queen-regent, his mother, and of her all-powerful adviser, Cardinal Mazarin, as a personal insult, an attack on the power and authority that by birth were rightly his, God-given to the kings of France. So, the choice to leave the Louvre, and even take up residence outside the ancient capital was, perhaps, not incomprehensible.

Moreover, certainly after the famous festivities staged in 1661 by the powerful director-general of France's finances, Nicolas Fouquet, at his newly-built palace of Vaux-le-Vicomte, not only Louis's jealousy was aroused – the "fête" speeded up Fouquet's downfall – he also very much became aware of the methods and means that would allow him to "fabricate" his own image and, hence, his kingship.[23] A new, modern palace adorned with everything the Arts could contribute would be the perfect vehicle for royal propaganda. Yet, the choice of Versailles remains enigmatic. Again admittedly, between 1632 and 1634, Louis's father, having bought the manor of Versailles which included a small village of that name, had built a hunting lodge there, of red brick and sandstone.[24] Still, piety can hardly have been his son's main motive to settle there, given that the site was insalubrious and certainly not spectacularly beautiful.

Last but not least, the suggestion that the little hill-and-vale where the village and the smallish chateau were situated, and that its very name referred to a site that was the ancient "centre" of France in a "val [vers] de Gallie" is, I think, nonsense, if only because such a history surely would have played a role in the subsequent mythological language of the palace.[25]

Though we cannot finally answer the question why Louis chose Versailles, there is no shortage of sources allowing us to interpret the symbolism and rhetoric of the constructions he built there. In doing so, we should realise that what remains of the 1660- and 1680-parts of the chateau and its park to a great extent really does reflect Louis's wishes. For he was passionate about architecture[26] – perhaps even more so than most Roman pontiffs – with, perhaps, the exception of his contemporary and, in a sense, rival, Pope Alexander VII, whose court architect, Bernini, Louis even tried to "steal."[27]

After having used his father's hunting-lodge during the years 1661-1668,[28] Louis decided to enlarge it – against the wishes of the new director-general of

---

23   Burke (1994). Cf. also Goldstein (2008).
24   J.-Cl. le Guillou (2011).
25   Nor do I go into the speculations of such men as, for example, Xavier Guichard and his ideas about the site of Alesia/Eleusis.
26   Berger (1994). Cf. also: Sarmand (2003).
27   Gould (1981).
28   Le Guillou (2011).

THE POLITICAL RHETORIC OF CAPITALS 67

the realm's finances, Jean-Baptiste Colbert.[29] During the following decades, thousands of farmers were requisitioned to work there; given the unhealthy site, many never left it – their dead corpses being carried away by the cartloads, as Madame de Sévigné tells us in a letter dated 12 October 1678. By 1685, some 36.000 men were "employed" in the building, while de-commissioned soldiers from the French army – at this time not, as usually, engaged in one of Louis's many bloody and costly wars – were toiling away there as well.

During the first building-phase, the original chateau was "encapsulated" in a far bigger, symmetrical structure, basically consisting of a wing for the king and one for the queen – both containing seven rooms – separated by a court-yard, but linked by an elevated terrace. The interior, especially on the king's side, was heavily symbolic. As André Félibien, the historiographer royal, wrote in his *Description sommaire du Chasteau de Versailles* (Paris 1674, and later):

> As the Sun is the devise of the King, the seven planets have been taken as the inspiration for the decoration of the seven rooms, in such a way that in each, one sees the actions of the heroes of Antiquity who are related to these planets and to the deeds of His Majesty.

Thus, the main reception room of the king's suite – placed right at the centre – was dedicated to Apollo, the Sun God himself, the ruler of the universe. Indeed, all over the palace, to start with the great wrought-iron entrance Gates, Apollo's emblem, the lyre, was in abundant evidence. In short, Versailles was a palace under the sign of the Sun.

Nor is it difficult to find some of the ideological-political roots of this choice. In September 1638, the French queen – at last pregnant with her first child, the much-longed for heir to the throne – had asked the Italian philosopher Tommaso Campanella (1568-1639) to cast her son's horoscope. Campanella had written extensively on the idea of a "Monarchia delle Nazioni," as well as about its "ideal" capital, the "Civitas Solis," the "City of the Sun" – the title of his 1623-book of which a new version was published in Paris in, incidentally, 1638. He foretold the queen that one day her boy would be the man in whom this "universal monarchy" would be personified.[30]

Campanella's tract was essentially a theological-political vindication of the various policies pursued by France's leading politicians – cardinals Richelieu and Mazarin foremost amongst them – to make France the leading state of Europe, and its king "by Divine Right" the arbiter of all the nations, foremost

---

29   Berger (1994) 33, 64, 72; Sarmand (2003) 326.
30   Grimm (1986).

amongst them the obnoxious Dutch and, of course, the two Habsburg dynasties, those of Austria and, even more so, of nearby-Spain, though both his mother and his wife were Spanish princesses.

No wonder Louis, who, after Mazarin's death in 1661 felt he finally became his own master, wanted to create a palace worthy of this prophesy – though, I would argue, Campanella's detailed description of the Sun City's central temple certainly was not repeated in the architecture of the palace (see Figure 5.2 and 5.3). No wonder, either, that the King himself used to explain the symbols of the various rooms his visitors were allowed or, rather, gently forced to see and admire. He would refer to Ovid's "Metamorphoses" – a source for many of the mythological stories depicted in Versailles – or, if need be, to the Bible. If his visitor was a military or naval man, the King would draw his attention to the decoration of the rooms dedicated to Mars and Neptune, or, for that matter, point out that the last of the rooms, connecting the king's wing with that of the queen, bore the sign of Venus, the Goddess of Love.[31] Thus, the progress through the palace's rooms took on something of a journey through cosmological time and space, in order to reach the universe's creative source. Not surprisingly, Louis's personal devise was *Foecundis ignibus ardet* – 'it [he] burns with fruitful fire'. To put it otherwise: Louis settled himself and, thereby, the monarchy. No longer did the French king, like his forebears, tour the realm, to show himself to, and, in a sense, to negotiate with his subjects. Like the Sun, he became the fixed centre of his kingdom, the source of all power[32] – or so he wanted people to believe.

In comparison to real models, Louis wanted his new seat both to emulate and to supersede what his brother-in-law, Philip IV of Spain, had created in and around Madrid.[33] In this palace, Louis told his courtiers in 1686: "Nous nous devons tout entier au public,"[34] indicating that the king of France was always on show – like an idol. Indeed, he also wanted to show himself and his power to all those who never would actually meet him in person, though they might visit Versailles, since the palace was in many ways an open place where tourists – "avant la lettre" – were welcome, if properly accoutred. Moreover, he wanted to impress the world at large. Therefore, printed descriptions of the palace and its decorations were widely distributed, for example in extensive articles – sometimes amounting to veritable booklets – in such journals as the

---

31 See the various instances given of Louis's own role as a "guide" in Hautecoeur (1953), and Guillou (1963), both summarised by Sabatier (1999) 32 sqq.

32 Sabatier (1985) 307-08.

33 Sabatier (2014).

34 Bernier (1836) 220.

THE POLITICAL RHETORIC OF CAPITALS 69

FIGURE 5.2 Versailles, during the first building campaign, ca 1670. Pierre Patel, ca. 1670. Credits: Wikimedia Commons, the free media repository [accessed online 28.02.2019, <https://nl.wikipedia.org/wiki/Bestand:Chateau_de_Versailles_1668_Pierre_Patel.jpg>]

FIGURE 5.3 Versailles, after the last building campaign, ca 1720. Pierre-Denis Martin, ca. 1720. Musée national des châteaux de Versailles et de Trianon. Credits: Wikimedia Commons, the free media repository [accessed online 28.02.2019, <https://en.wikipedia.org/wiki/History_of_the_Palace_of_Versailles#/media/File:Versailles_Pierre-Denis_Martin.jpg>]

Mercure galant and, of course, the government-sponsored *Gazette de France*.[35] Also, over the decades, the "royal printing office," as well as other commercial publishers, brought out a number of often illustrated guide-books. Large, engraved representations of the chateau and its surroundings were printed, too, accompanied by a short description. All in all, from the years between ca. 1670 and 1715, I count some 25 texts, including reprints that, of course, often were updated to document the many alterations the palace underwent.

For during the 1680s, the palace's disposition was greatly changed. On the first floor, the terrace linking the king's and the queen's wing was replaced with a magnificent gallery, lined with mirrors – think: light and Sun! – which, significantly, on the king's side one entered through the "Salon de la Guerre," and left again through the "Salon de la Paix" to gain the queen's side – an ideologically gendered sequence, one might say. However, in the "Gallerie des Glaces," the huge frescoes that adorned the walls and the ceilings no longer extolled a planet and its mythology, but Louis himself and his real, historical exploits on the (inter-)national scene, albeit in visual tales that, sometimes, distorted the actual state of affairs in the world. At the very centre, in a ceiling fresco glorifying the King, the various nations of Europe made subservient to him bow their knee – not to France, but to its apotheosed monarch, who is represented with the explication: "The King Governs by Himself." Indeed, by that time Louis had adopted a new motto: he now also felt *Nec pluribus impar*, which might be translated as '[he reigns] above all'. Maybe he remembered one of the sermons of his court preacher, J.-B. Bossuet, who had told his audience: "Vous voyez l'image de Dieu dans les rois," and, addressing the King himself while citing Scripture, had even said: "Vous êtes des dieux [...]," though yet warning his royal parishioner that he, too, would die like any mere mortal.[36]

Nevertheless, the king was, indeed, "idolised," with even the tiniest moments of his daily routine being used for the public display of his unique position. It was, also, part of Louis's much-discussed policy of binding France's nobles to his court and, indeed, his person.[37] Much of the ritual and ceremony took place in the "Chambre du Roi," the King's bedroom and, therefore, in a sense the most exclusive room of the chateau. After the major alterations of the 1680s, it now was situated right at the heart of the entire palace – but, more significantly, also on the central axis of the gardens and the town that slowly came to surround the "Dwelling of the Sun" like a planet's two halves. For

---

35   E.g. *Le Mercure galant*, December 1682, 6-13; December 1684, 1-84; April 1687, 14-56.

36   *Oeuvres Complètes de Bossuet*, X (1836) 385.

37   How successful he – and, indeed, the set-up of Versailles – was, remains a matter of much debate. Cf., for example, W. Newton (2000).

THE POLITICAL RHETORIC OF CAPITALS 71

during the last decades of the century, Versailles reached its final form. By then, the complex had come to encompass not only the building itself, but the world around it. Palace, park, and city now were (re-)designed as an ensemble meant to resemble the world of which the King's state rooms were the centre. Admittedly, given the enormous extent of the ensemble, this is more visible on the many printed plans and the painted or engraved bird's-eye perspectives of the time than it was, or is, in actual reality.

One of the circle's halves, extending outward from the terrace in front of the Gallery of Mirrors, is taken up by the huge gardens – covering some 1,000 hectares – designed by André le Nôtre. Though they have been considerably altered – even during Louis's reign – originally, they meant to achieve a number of goals at the same time. The lay-out presented the park as a cosmic space[38] of interlocking circles and squares, linked by radiating pathways, each half symmetrically flanking the central axis that, starting at the "Chambre du Roy," basically was formed by the 1.5 kilometre-long "grand canal." Everywhere such elements as, for example, four fountains representing the four seasons provided focal points. But the park also served as an open-air extension of the representational functions of the palace, with a dining-room, a ballroom, an audience chamber, et cetera, created by green walls – trained and clipped trees – and studded with statuary. No wonder, then, that the park was consistently used to impress foreign visitors: every diplomat who came to bow before the King not only was expected to inspect and dutifully admire the palace itself, but also to take the tour of the gardens – sometimes even accompanying Louis himself.[39] Indeed, in his later years, the King sat down and actually wrote a "Manière de montrer les jardins de Versailles," indicating the exact route that should be taken.[40]

Of course, Louis wanted those who could only read about his magnificence to be exhaustively informed as well. Therefore, a number of authors took care to set out and explain every detail of the park's decoration in descriptions and guide-books. I count at least fifteen specifically such between 1670 and 1715. Interestingly, they did not invite the audience to enjoy "nature" but, rather, to marvel at the way the King had managed to "embellir la nature, ou à la surpasser."[41] Actually, the texts almost exclusively stress man-made objects, showing Louis not only as the person who had built "le plus superbe Palais du Monde,"[42] but, as Félibien tellingly put it, who also "par une espèce de

---

38   Cf. Cosgrove (2001) 168-70.
39   Cf. Berger (2008).
40   Hoog (1982).
41   Pigianiol de la Force (1701) 2.
42   Morellet (1681) 3.

creation" had given the world this wonder.[43] Thus, the King became almost *Dieu* ruling over a world that no longer was chaotic, but ordered according to his will – as he pretended to order France and as he would have liked to order Europe.[44]

For let us not forget that both palace and gardens were constantly watched – by the King's guards and, indeed, by the new police force.[45] And of course they watched the "new" town of Versailles, too – for towns were, traditionally, hotbeds of the kind of unrest most feared by kings. Already in 1671, Louis, desiring to complete his vision of an ideal palace-cum-town, had decided to raze the old village and create a new city, by giving out building plots to people with the express obligation to actually construct their dwellings there. Until the end of the eighteenth century, all buildings had to be of the same height and colour, according to specifications expressly issued by the King himself,[46] to ensure the intended view-lines towards and, of course, from the palace.

Linking the new town with the capital was the "Avenue de Paris." Starting at the palace gates and bordered there by the enormous stable blocks needed to house the royal coaches and horses, it was an unheard-of 90 meters wide and ran straight for about one-and-a-half kilometre before, beyond the palace's horizon, joining up with the old road to the capital.

To complement this urban lay-out, two other avenues were created, thus forming a trident intersecting the half of the circle given to the town. Soon, distinct town-quarters developed, one around the newly-built church of Notre-Dame de Versailles, for which Louis personally laid the first stone in 1684, and another around the church of, significantly, Saint-Louis, which was finally built in the 1730s. These quarters slowly filled with houses and shops. Also, two monasteries, a hospital and, last but not least, a tennis-court for the King and the court nobles were constructed to accommodate the various needs of the ever-increasing number of people somehow serving the "economy" of the royal court and the central administration of the state.[47] For as indicated above, in 1682 the King did transfer his government from Paris to Versailles. Consequently, the number of inhabitants swelled from a few hundred in the 1660s to some 20,000 by the end of Louis's reign.[48]

---

43   Félibien (1674) 340.
44   E.g. Mukerji (1997).
45   Le Nabour (1991).
46   See: Dauphin (2004) for a very short introduction. For a detailed survey of the town during the "Ancien Régime": Bottineau (1988), as well as: Breillat (1986), which also gives a number of plans to show the town's development.
47   Da Vinha (2009) passim.
48   Cf. Lepetit (1977).

THE POLITICAL RHETORIC OF CAPITALS 73

When in 1715 the realm's regent, Philippe of Orleans, decided to return both the court and the business of government to Paris, the population of Versailles dwindled to half its size, again. Yet, from 1722 onwards, it rapidly became populous and prosperous once more. During the reigns of Louis XV and Louis XVI, some grand office-buildings were erected to house the ministry of foreign affairs and of war, respectively. Meanwhile, the number of inhabitants rose to some 50,000, making Versailles one of the larger towns of "Ancien Régime"-France. Nevertheless, it was not in any sense a "normal" town, with its own civic institutions, rituals and ceremonies. Rather, it was the inflated appendage of the palace and its inmates, under the strict control of a royal official.

Conclusion

After Louis's death, further changes were made both in the palace and the gardens of Versailles – in the 1740s and 1750s, and again in the nineteenth century. Still, the "Dwelling of the Sun" as he had envisaged it has remained not only as the exemplar of a royal palace but, also, as the embodiment in stone of royal absolutism, a piece of petrified rhetoric if ever there was.

Rome, too, underwent changes. Yet, though from the 1870s onwards the kingdom of Italy introduced its grand royal-bureaucratic buildings and, in the 1930s, the Fascist government tried to imprint it with its own specific brand of power architecture, the actual city-centre remains very much as the "Baroque popes" have left it in the late seventeenth century, with St Peter's Square and the basilica as its enduring symbol.

Comparing "Versailles" with "Rome," we now see the latter as the prime embodiment of a religious monarchy, or, even, autocracy, while the former stands for a secular one. However, the distinction between these two "realms" was far less clear-cut during the "Ancien Régime" than scholars sometimes assume. The popes, though ecclesiastical princes first and foremost – which meant they could and did use all references to religious and, indeed, transcendental power available – very much represented themselves with all the trappings of a temporal monarch. On the other hand, despite the largely secular base of their power, the kings of France never ceased to present themselves in a religious, transcendental context as well, employing both pagan mythology and Christian iconology. Actually, perhaps no one did so more comprehensively than the fourteenth Louis. His last great project, putting the finishing touch to Versailles, was the monumental palace chapel: modelled, significantly, on the thirteenth-century Sainte-Chapelle in Paris, the "national" shrine of France, and filled with symbols of Divine Right-monarchy.[49]

Nor were the two towns "normal" as were most other cities in Europe, in the sense that the population somehow could voice its concerns vis-à-vis the monarch who also lived there. In Rome, the papacy had succeeded in abolishing the erstwhile independence of the city council and its three "conservatori" on the Capitol. In Versailles, the power of the chosen syndic was, by and large, meaningless, too. In these towns, the ruler reigned supreme.

Last but not least, one might argue that "Baroque" Rome was an answer to at least two challenges presented to the papacy of the late sixteenth and the seventeenth century: the one by a Humanism seen as a return to paganism, and the other by the Reformation against Christianity and the universal role of Rome in it as understood by the popes.[50] Versailles also posed an answer to a challenge – the challenge of a polity in which both the urban elites and the aristocracy had tried to reduce royal power.[51] Both the popes and the French kings sought to uphold and even strengthen their position against the forces that, they felt, were undermining it. To make their pretences abundantly clear, as monarchs "by Divine Right" – the one through divinely-sanctioned birth, the other through divinely-inspired election – the men who ruled in Versailles and Rome fully exploited all aspects of visual propaganda. In doing so, they also elevated the political rhetoric of capitals to a new height.

Bibliography

Ackermann, J., "Rome in the Renaissance," in P. Ramsey (ed.), *Rome in the Renaissance, Medieval and Early Renaissance Studies 8* (Binghamton, 1982).

Bauval. R., *The Vatican Heresy. Bernini and the Building of the Hermetic Temple of the Sun* (Rochester, 2014).

Berger, R., and T. Hedin, *Diplomatic Tours in the Gardens of Versailles under Louis XIV* (Philadelphia, 2008).

Berger, R., *A Royal Passion. Louis XIV as Patron of Architecture* (Cambridge, Mass., 1994).

Berger, R., *Versailles: the Chateau of Louis XIV* (University Park, 1985).

Bernier, A., (ed.), [Marquis de Sourches] *Mémoires secrets et inédits de la cour de France*, II (Paris, 1836).

Bird, J., *Centrality and Cities* (London, 1977, repr. 2007).

---

49   Edmunds (2002). Cf. also Rietbergen (2016).
50   Labrot (1987).
51   Sabatier (1990) 307 sqq.

THE POLITICAL RHETORIC OF CAPITALS

Bluche, F., *Louis XIV* (Paris, 1999).

Bottineau, Y., "Essais sur le Versailles de Louis XIV. 1: La distribution du château et le plan du domaine et de la ville," in *Gazette des Beaux-Arts* 112 (1988), 77-98.

Breillat, P., *Ville nouvelle, capitale modèle: Versailles* (Versailles, 1986).

Burke, P., *The Fabrication of Louis XIV* (New Haven, 1994).

Ciucci, G., *La Piazza del Popolo* (Rome, 1974).

Cosgrove, D., *Apollo's Eye. A Cartographic Genealogy of the Earth in the Western Imagination* (Baltimore, 2001).

Dauphin, N., "Versailles, le château et la ville. Deux patrimoines distincts, duex mémoires antagonistes à l'époque contemporaine," in *Histoire urbaine* 9 (2004), 79-96.

Delph, R., "Renovatio, Reformatio, and Humanist Ambition in Rome," in R. Delph, M. Fontaine, and J.J. Martin (eds.), *Heresy, Culture and Religion in Early Modern Italy: Contexts and Contestations* (Kirksville, 2006), 73-92.

Duindam, J., *Vienna and Versailles. The Courts of Europe's Dynastic Rivals, 1550-1780* (Cambridge, Eng., 2003).

Edmunds, M., *Piety and Politics. Imaging Divine Kingship in Louis XIV's Chapel at Versailles* (Newark, 2002).

Eliade, M., *The Sacred and the Profane* (New York, 1961).

Félibien, A., *Description sommaire du Chasteau de Versailles* (Paris, 1674).

Frommel, C., "Papal Policy; the Planning of Rome during the Renaissance," in *Journal of Interdisciplinary History* 17 (1986), 39-65.

Goldstein, C., *Vaux and Versailles. The Appropriations, Erasures and Accidents that Made Modern France* (Philadelphia, 2008).

Gould, C., *Bernini in France* (Princeton, 1981).

Grotenhuis, E. ten, *Japanese Mandalas: Representations of Sacred Geography* (Honolulu, 1999).

Grimm, J., "Campanella in France," in J. Serroy (ed.) *La France et l'Italie au temps de Mazarin* (Grenoble, 1986), 79-86.

Guillou, E., *Versailles: le palais du Soleil* (Paris, 1963).

Guillou, J-C. le, *Versailles avant Versailles Au temps de Louis XIII* (Paris, 2011).

Hautecoeur, L., *Louis XIV, Roi-Soleil* (Paris, 1953).

Hoog, S., (ed.), *Louis XIV: manière de montrer les jardins de Versailles* (Paris, 1982).

Kitao, T., *Circle and Oval in the Square of Saint Peter's: Bernini's Art of Planning* (New York, 1974).

Labrot, G., *L'image de Rome. Une arme pour la Contre-Réforme (1534-1667)* (Seyssel, 1987).

Le Nabour, E., *La Reynie: le policier de Louis XIV* (Paris, 1991).

Lepetit, B., "Demographie d'une ville en gestation: Versailles sous Louis XIV," in *Demographie paroissiale. Annales de Demographie Historique. Societé de Demographie Historique* 11 (1977), 49-83.

Mapier, D., "Bernini's Anthropology: A 'Key' to the Piazza San Pietro," in *Anthropology and Aesthetics* 16 (1988), 17-32.

McDannell, C., and B. Lang, *Heaven: A History* (New Haven, 2001).

Morellet, L., *Explication historique de ce qu'il y a de plus remarquable dans la masion royale de Versailles* (Paris, 1681).

Miedema, N., *Rompilgerführer im Spätmittelater und früher Neuzeit* (Tübingen, 2003).

Miedema, N., *Die "Mirabilia Romae." Untersuchungen zu ihrer Überlieferung* (Tübingen, 1996).

Minkenberg, M., (ed.), *Power and Architecture: the Construction of Capitals and the Politics of Space* (New York, 2014).

Mukerji, C., *Territorial Ambitions and the Gardens of Versailles* (Cambridge, Eng., 1997).

Müller, W., *Die heilige Stadt: Roma quadrata, himmlisches Jerusalem und die Mythe vom Weltnabel* (Stuttgart, 1961).

Narayanan, Y., *Religion, Heritage and the Sustainable city. Hindusm and Urbanization in Jaipur* (London, 2015).

Newton, W., *L'espace du roi: la cour de France au chateau de Versailles, 1682-1789* (Paris, 2000).

Patricios, N., "Concepts of Space in Urban Design, Architecture and Art," in *Leonardo* 6 (1973), 311-318.

Perouse de Montclos, J-M., *Versailles* (Paris, 1991, repr. 2001).

Pigianiol de la Force, J-A., *Nouvelle description des chasteaux et parcs de Versailles* (Paris, 1701).

Quinlan-McGrath, M., "The Foundation Horoscope(s) for St. Peter's Basilica, Rome, 1506: Choosing a Time, Changing the Storia," in *Isis* 92 (2001), 716-741.

Rietbergen, P., "Sacralizing the Palace, Sacralizing the King. Sanctuaries and/in Royal Residences in Medieval Europe," in M. Verhoeven, L. Bosman, and H. van Asperen (eds.), *Monuments and Memory. Christian Cult Buildings and Constructions of the Past* (Turnhout, 2016).

Rietbergen, P., *Clio's Stiefzusters. Verledenverbeeldingen voorbij de wetenschap* (Nijmegen, 2015).

Rietbergen, P., *Rome and the World, the World in Rome* (Dordrecht, 2013).

Rietbergen, P., *Power and Religion in Baroque Rome. Barberini Cultural Policies* (Leiden, 2006).

Rietbergen, P., *Rome Gelezen. De retoriek van de Eeuwige Stad* (Nijmegen, 2003).

Rietbergen, P., "Pausen, prelaten, bureaucraten. Apecten van de geschiedenis van het pausschap en de pauselijke staat in de 17e eeuw," PhD Diss., (Catholic University Nijmegen, 1983a).

Rietbergen, P., "A Vision Come True. Pope Alexander VII (1655-1667), Gianlorenzo Bernini and the Colonnades of St. Peter's," in *Mededelingen van het Nederlands Instituut te Rome*, XLVI, Nova Series 11 (1983b).

Sabatier, G., and M. Torrione (eds.), *Louis XIV espagnol? Madrid et Versailles, images et modèles* (Versailles, 2014).

Sabatier, G., *Versailles, ou la Figure du Roi* (Paris, 1999).

Sabatier, G., "Versailles, un imaginaire politique," in *Publications de l'Ecole francaise de Rome* 82 (1985), 295-324.

San Juan, R., *Rome: A City out of Print* (Minneapolis, 2001).

Sarmand, T., *Les Demeures du Soleil. Louis XIV, Louvois et la surintendance des batiments du roi* (Seyssel, 2003).

Sinisi, D., and C. Genovese (eds.), *Pro Ornatu et Publica Utilitate. L'attività della Congregazione cardinalizia "super viis, pontibus et fontibus" nella Roma di fine '500* (Rome, 2010).

Smith, B.L., and H. Baker Reynolds (eds.), *The City as a Sacred Center. Essays on Six Asian Contexts* (Leiden, 1987).

Torres, P., *Les Secrets de Versailles* (Paris, 2015).

Vinha, M., de, *Le Versailles de Louis XIV* (Paris, 2009).

Westfall, C., *In this Most Perfect Paradise: Alberti, Nicholas V and the Invention of Conscious Urban Planning in Rome, 1447-55* (Philadelphia, 1974).

Zabriskie, B., "Jung and Pauli," in *Journal of Analytical Psychology* 40 (1995), 531-553.

Zhu, J., *Chinese Spatial Strategies: Imperial Beijing, 1420-1911* (London, 2004).

CHAPTER 6

Repertoires of Access in Princely Courts, 1400-1750

Dries Raeymaekers and Sebastiaan Derks

Introduction[*]

In the past four decades, the accessibility of those in power has become an important topic in historiography, particularly at the pre-modern court. Whereas most specialists of late medieval and early modern politics tend to agree that the study of access is the key to understanding power relations in these periods, opinions seem to differ as to exactly how the concept should be approached. For want of a clear definition, access has remained a rather vague category, the importance of which is often assumed rather than thoroughly explained. Similarly, the association between access and power is usually taken for granted, whereas the mechanisms behind it remain obscure. Scholars still struggle to understand how access was used by subjects to represent their claims in premodern centres of power, and the ways in which it was articulated and performed. By taking the full complexity of proximity to the monarch into account, this chapter means to broaden the scope and to explore how the many varieties of access enabled medieval and early modern people to express their voices and concerns.

The Key to Power?

In the last quarter of the twentieth century, the study of princely courts and households – after having lain under the dust for years – has been introduced anew into historical research concerning premodern politics. It did not take long before social, cultural, and economic historians also began to acknowledge the enormous potential of this topic of research. During the past few decades, then, the field of court studies has become a fully-fledged branch of

---

[*] This contribution is a revised version of the introduction we wrote for Dries Raeymaekers and Sebastiaan Derks, eds., *The Key to Power? The Culture of Access in Princely Courts, c. 1400-1750* (Leiden: Brill, 2016). Many of the themes presented in this essay are elaborated at greater length in that volume.

© DRIES RAEYMAEKERS AND SEBASTIAAN DERKS, 2019 | DOI:10.1163/9789004291966_007
This is an open access chapter distributed under the terms of the CC-BY-NC 4.0 License.

REPERTOIRES OF ACCESS IN PRINCELY COURTS, 1400-1750

historiography.[1] One development running parallel to this evolution is the rise of the concept of "access to the ruler" and the growing conviction that the study of it is fundamental for being able to unravel the early modern decision-making process in all its dimensions. In the 1980s the work of David Starkey provided a turning point in the research. In his view, having access to the monarch was of crucial importance in the political framework of the Ancien Régime.[2] Subsequent to earlier explorations by Carl Schmitt and Geoffrey Elton, it was Starkey who strongly posited that the right to access – and the possibility for personal interaction that issued forth from it – constituted an essential component of both the acquisition and the exercise of power.[3] It was of inestimable importance in the struggle among courtiers for individual advancement and representation. On the other hand, a lack of access could influence the course of this struggle in a negative sense. Starkey argued that the way in which the rule of successive English monarchs manifested itself – whether it be more "accessible" or "distant," according to the author – was defining for the workings of the political order in its entirety. Choosing one of either extreme led to varied policy-making with regard to the distribution of power, and demanded varied strategy in terms of those who wanted to acquire power. Both ways of acting, Starkey says, can essentially be traced back to contrasting methods of dealing with the relationship between prince and subject and, consequently, to contrasting visions concerning the nature and the legitimacy of monarchical rule.[4]

By now many historians have subscribed to Starkey's argument, and they have also added important insights concerning the nature of what has often been called the "politics of access."[5] In this way access has grown into a dominant explanatory factor in research with regard to early modern decision-making. In many studies the influence or power of courtiers is described in terms of proximity to the ruler. Without a doubt, access has become one of the most employed concepts in the steadily expanding field of court studies. Is access, though, always an indication of power? In the past the requisite caveats were already being made for this automatic association. In the influential collection *The Princely Courts of Europe*, John Adamson observes that "access and intimacy did not always equate with political power" but were, on the contrary,

---

1   See, for example, the overviews in Fantoni (2012).
2   Starkey (1987). See also Starkey (1973; 1977).
3   Cf. Schmitt (1954a; 1954b); Elton (1976).
4   See Starkey (1987), especially p. 8.
5   See, for example, Loades (1986) 85-95; Gunn (1993); Kettering (1993); Asch (1995); Weiser (2003); Jiménez (1996); Le Roux (2000); Hengerer (2004); Raeymaekers (2013).

always dependent on the nature of princely authority.[6] Jeroen Duindam, too, argues that access and political influence were not necessarily directly proportional, let alone mutually interchangeable.[7] Although both authors are of the opinion that the acquisition of access was, without a doubt, one of the most efficient ways for acquiring power, Adamson as well as Duindam postulate that access is only one aspect in a broad array of factors that have to be taken into account in research on the matter. Such reservations indicate that, despite its ubiquity in studies on the early modern court, the importance of access is still subject to debate. One of the reasons for this may be that it appears impossible to arrive at a clear-cut or workable definition of the concept. Over the years it has acquired a wide variety of meanings, rendering it difficult for scholars to reach a compromise on its nature and impact. How, then, can we move the debate forward?

The primary goal of our contribution, then, is to widen the scope of access as an analytical category by focussing not so much on its connection with the explicit exercise of power, but rather on the interconnected and complex practices in which the idea of access itself was shaped, expressed, and represented, for example in the visual and material culture surrounding the monarch. Thus, by examining the broad spectrum of manifestations of access from a cultural perspective, this contribution is mainly concerned with what we have termed the "culture of access." As will be explained in the following paragraphs, we argue that access should be viewed as a dynamic *process* – a constant interplay of spaces, strategies, personalities, rituals, artefacts, and events – that was "enacted" through a diverse repertoire of performances. By studying the latter, we may achieve a much more nuanced and thorough understanding of the meaning of access and of the ways in which it impacted the relations between rulers and ruled. This approach is one that the authors of this contribution, aided by a group of like-minded scholars, have introduced in a recently edited collection of essays.[8] In the following paragraphs, we build upon the wide-ranging expertise brought together in that volume, and explain how the idea of repertoires of access might contribute to the study of power relations in the late medieval and early modern world.

---

6 Adamson (1999) 109.

7 Duindam (2003) 234. See also the discussion on pp. 161-80.

8 Raeymaekers and Derks (2016). The volume itself contains the proceedings of an international conference on the same topic, which took place at the University of Antwerp on 8-9 November 2012.

The Culture of Access

Although historical research has convincingly revealed that "access" was an important factor in constantly changing power relationships, it has still proven difficult to designate general characteristics and norms. The reason for this difficulty is simple: we still do not know enough about how access worked in everyday practice and how it evolved. These lacunae may seem strange, in view of the variety of case studies concerning the politics of access at certain courts, but as yet there are no available systematic analyses of access in its entirety. In current literature the use of access is still seen, above all, as an important thematic line for penetrating into the complex organisation of the premodern centre of power. In this time period the princely court was a nebulous composite of political arrangements and social structures, as a result of which analysing it in its entirety is difficult to achieve. The great advantage of the notion of "access to the ruler" for historians is that it puts them in the position to approach the manifold nature of arrangements characterising courtly life in context, and to lay those structures bare. That may well explain the success of the concept of access. By directing their gaze at the topic of access researchers are able to describe how rulers and the people around them lived with one another, how they gave shape to their immediate lived surroundings, which groups knew how to keep access under strict control, and how access functioned as an instrument for political and social distinction. In this success for scholarship, however, there also lurks a paradox: although access is by now used by an entire pleiade of historians for analysing the multiform political world of the court, and is put forward as an explanatory factor for the nature of power relationships, many questions still remain concerning the meaning and scope of the concept. In spite of the broad consensus among researchers concerning its importance, access still continually escapes their grasp as well as their definitions. How access works in a concrete way and how defining it was in the development of early modern courts has, as a result, remained underexposed.

In the scholarly literature concerning access the emphasis thus lies specifically on reconstructing political relationships and on their role in the decision-making process. Seldom is the question posed, though, regarding what is involved in regulating access. Most studies take as their point of departure a somewhat restrictive conception of early modern politics, which largely mistakes the ritual and cultural dimensions of access. To this day, as a consequence of this misunderstanding, religious rites, architectural layouts, behavioural codes, and ceremonial solemnities have been insufficiently included in the analysis of access. Recent work has suggested, however, that the political reality of the early modern court was more multiform and diffuse than has been previously assumed.[9] Political power in this society was inextricably connected with reputation and social status. It was therefore no coincidence, either, that the ruler and his élites used their immediate surroundings to communicate their positions and claims to power. This made the princely court into a performative space, constructed by successive generations so as to convey certain messages. In a forum of this kind, rituals, objects, buildings, and clothing all were ways in which the rank of an individual or a group could be made visible in the hierarchy.[10] In this way they confirmed or defined power and position, so that these also became realities for the public in attendance. The neglect of this cultural dimension in the study of access is especially notable, because pre-modern courtiers were in fact obsessed with just these very performative actions and artefacts.

Another important argument for widening the perspective on access concerns the question as to continuity and discontinuity in dealing with access. Which developments are we able to distinguish in the rules, rituals, and cultural representation of access? Because existing case studies concentrate more often than not on the organisation of access in a certain era, they generally create little clarity concerning the dynamics of its regulations. The question is not only which forms of access prevailed at a certain court but also which social and political processes were coupled to these forms. Changes to being open or closed were often instigated by means of conscious policy of the rulers – to keep a grasp on their private surroundings – yet were also influenced by the expectations of the élites. Without support from the most important groups of the realm, governing was an onerous business. Often these groups each had their own opinions and claims concerning the degree of access at court. Regulating access in the early modern period was in that respect no one-way street but arose precisely in the interaction between the prince and his subjects. In this way it was always a process of *negotiation*. An important line for charting the difficulties that occurred during this process is the analysis of how access became formalised. Varied cases show that more formality in access was always supplemented with informal structures. Sometimes both kinds of measures were even at odds with each other, but generally they were clearly complementary.[11] Each formal measure for screening off rulers was, after all, inevitably followed by new informal stipulations so as to maintain a certain

---

9   See, for example, Asch and Birke (1991); Adamson (1999); Duindam (2003); Pečar (2003); Hengerer (2004); Horowski (2012).

10 Cf. the seminal studies by Stollberg-Rilinger (2008; 2000).

11 Cf. Hengerer (2004); Butz and Hirschbiegel (2009). On formality and informality in early modern politics see also Stollberg-Rilinger (2013).

flexibility and freedom of action. This process of formalising access can be pursued by way of court ordinances, the building of architectural divisions such as cabinet rooms, privy chambers, and enfilades, the handing out of symbolic keys, and the giving out of certain court offices. In short, whoever intends to trace the fault lines in the history of access cannot get around approaching the many forms and functions of access from a comprehensive historical framework. In the next paragraph we discuss what such a framework might look like.

Repertoires of Access

We have already pointed out that the notion of "access" is often made one and the same with the notion of "power," though without much critical sense, as if the connection between both concepts speaks for itself and the one always implies the other. All this is, among other things, the result of the fact that historians who use the concept are inclined to concentrate exclusively on politically oriented sources. In this way the perceptions of contemporaneous political figures and diplomats weigh heavily on the importance of access. However, it is questionable to what extent these perceptions and reality connect to each other. For that reason, we argue that the debate on the importance of access should not focus solely on its relationship with power, but also on the ways in which the idea of access was visualised, ritualised, symbolised, negotiated and performed. A study of this kind, which consciously takes socio-cultural practices as its starting point, necessarily uses an integrative method that combines a wide and very diverse set of historical sources. This allows for a more comprehensive insight into the function of access in the practice of early modern politics. Central to this approach is the idea that access should be viewed as a performance that may be understood by studying the diverse cultural repertoires through which it was enacted, taking into account the spatial, visual, and material dimensions concerned. The following repertoires can be identified and developed:

1   *Articulating Access*

How was access organised in a spatial sense? Since the emergence of the spatial turn in the historical sciences, it is clear that we not only have to know *where* precisely things happened, but that we also have to acquire insight just as much into *how* and *why* these things took place *in these particular spaces*.[12]

---

12   Cf. Warf and Arias (2009), especially the introduction. See also the pioneering work of Lefebvre (1991).

This is also valid for the early modern court. If access is viewed as a yardstick for defining which persons could and could not approach the prince in person, then the term can be taken quite literally. In this sense it is interesting to examine in what way physical access to the prince and his everyday lived space was facilitated, or in fact hampered, in practice. Put another way: what impact did the organisation of space have on the accessibility of the monarch? To answer that question a study of the princely residence is likely the most logical (yet not the only) point of departure. At almost all early modern courts the access to the princely quarters was constrained with the help of barriers like thick walls and strictly monitored gates and doors. A series of entryways, interior courts, staircases, and antechambers marked the route that led from the outermost palace walls to the proverbial *sanctum sanctorum*: the private quarters of the prince. An enfilade of chambers and halls functioned as a sluice in which visitors were sorted out beforehand so as to separate the rank and fashion from the *hoi polloi*.[13]

A well-devised type of palace architecture, in other words, contributed to the management of access to an important degree and could simplify access to the prince or, in fact, tie it into knots. In designing the residence – and also, by extension, its surroundings – court architects always took this concern into account to a greater or lesser degree. Over the course of the ages old buildings were adapted to new ideas concerning access, seclusion, and openness. At the same time, the fact needs to be taken into account that princes did not always stay behind the closed doors of their palaces. They went hunting, visited the town, took part in processions, went on horse rides, and so forth. On top of that, many of them travelled regularly, taking their lodging in tent camps, or in the residences of nobles they befriended, or in public buildings, abbeys, or monasteries. In these circumstances access to the prince had to be organised in another way. For example, studies on princely residences and joyous entries in French cities have underscored that in urban surroundings there was a clear tension between, on the one hand, being rigidly screened off on behalf of the political process and, on the other hand, being relatively open for ceremonial interaction with the urban population.[14] The visibility and the perceived accessibility of the ruler in the urban context, as these authors argue, also constituted an important factor in the ruler's self-fashioning. In this case it becomes clear that the concept of access was in no way static but rather particularly dynamic in nature, and that it also must be researched in that sense. At the same time, it is clear that the contemporaneous perception of the importance

---

13   See, for example, Fantoni, Gorse, and Smuts (2009); Asch (2009).

14   See, for example, Murphy (2016a; 2016b); Berland (2016).

REPERTOIRES OF ACCESS IN PRINCELY COURTS, 1400-1750

of access did not always agree with reality. Audrey Truschke has demonstrated that European diplomats, for instance, reported triumphantly about getting free access to the court of the Mughal emperor in India, but that that access led to little diplomatic success in practice.[15]

2 Regulating Access

How was access regulated? At most premodern courts, in addition to a well-devised organisation of space, a number of regulations existed which elaborated to the last detail either how the prince was to be screened off or in fact made accessible. In these regulations the court ceremonial and the accompanying ritual performance of accessibility played an important role. In order to be able to grasp the impact of access, it is important to examine in what way access was regulated by way of rules, agreements, and conventions, and – even more important – how in the process norms were related to practices. At almost every court in the late medieval and early modern periods, court ordinances were provided that stipulated who got access to the monarch, and who did not. These ordinances defined as well which courtiers were allowed to enter the princely quarters, in which sequence that happened, and at which moments during the day.[16] On top of that, they established who was allowed to speak to the prince, and how one was supposed to do so. The same was valid for the flow of affairs during public meals and audiences. Michael Talbot has convincingly shown how the Ottomans regulated the access to the sultan by way of a fixed sequence of spaces and rituals.[17] Talbot argues that the Ottoman court sent out important political messages to visitors as well via this ceremonial trajectory. Diverse sources – as well as the fact that ordinances regularly had to be promulgated anew – show, however, that the rules were in practice often trespassed against or gone around. Contemporaneous paintings and drawings show that the princely residence in the premodern era was as a rule a microcosm of busyness, in which courtiers as well as visitors and coincidental passers-by took part.

The palace complex needs to be imagined as a place where a significant hustle and bustle ruled every day (see Figure 6.1). Nobles, councillors, and servants all crossed paths at the entry gate, while coaches rode up and off. In the interior courts shops and market stalls were frequently set up where various merchants brought their wares to the man on the street. In the maze of corridors, staircases, and antechambers, visitors met to schmooze with one another

---

15   Truschke (2016).
16   Cf. Kruse and Paravicini (1999); Pangerl, Scheutz, and Winkelbauer (2007).
17   Talbot (2017). See also Talbot (2016).

FIGURE 6.1 A view of the palace of Versailles (after Jacques Rigaud). *Source*: Optica print by John Tinney. Rijksmuseum, Amsterdam, CC0 1.0 [accessed online 28.02.2019: <http://hdl.handle.net/10934/RM0001.COLLECT.402033>].

or to exchange bits of political news with the courtiers present. The palace gardens were also opened up to the public at set times.[18] In these kinds of circumstances it was nearly impossible to keep all the entrances and passages of the princely residence under surveillance 24 hours a day. In addition, one can suppose that balls, parties, ceremonies, parades, tournaments, and other festivities presumably attracted great throngs of not only desired but also undesired spectators to the palace. Although there is scarcely any proof for it, it can be assumed that the gatekeepers and porters were not averse to bribery.[19] In that context even the most screened-off parts of the residence proved not to be entirely safe from unauthorised persons and witnessed the many contemporaneous reports concerning robberies or undesired visitors.

One cannot lose sight of the consideration that the palace walls were not as impenetrable as might be thought in the first instance. The question arises, though, to what extent the "infiltrations" described here – in which various persons, wanted or not, could enter or penetrate the princely residence – were

---

18   Duindam (2003).
19   Cf. Raeymaekers (2013) 198.

REPERTOIRES OF ACCESS IN PRINCELY COURTS, 1400-1750

significant. Undoubtedly many (un-)invited guests hoped to catch a glimpse of the prince, draw his attention, perhaps even be addressed by him during their visit. That chance existed yet was extremely small. Having access to the residence was not the same as acquiring access to the monarch, and even if one succeeded in approaching him, he could in no way just simply be addressed. In his study about Charles II of England, Brian Weiser puts forward that "historians [tend to view] access in a binary manner: rulers are seen under the simple rubric as being either strict or easy of access. (...) But (...) in the sense of the ability to come into contact with the king, [it] was a more nuanced phenomenon."[20] Weiser rightly argues that the importance of access was not so much in physical proximity *per se* as in the possibility for interacting with the prince. Mark Hengerer, too, has emphasised the complexity of the concept and makes the case for shifting the focus of academic research to the connection between access and communication.[21] In an era in which long-distance communication was limited to correspondence – an efficient yet vulnerable medium and, on top of that, subject to lags in time – physical proximity proved to be an enormous advantage, though naturally only useful if communicating with the prince was possible (and permitted). More than *finding the prince*, access was a question of *finding the prince's ear*.

3   Monopolising Access

Who was entitled to access, and – perhaps even more important – who was not? The many strategies that existed at the early modern court for controlling and regulating the accessibility of the prince indicate that access was viewed as a desirable commodity. Nevertheless, it is clear that some persons were more assured of the right to access than others. While the majority of his contemporaries could only hope for an occasional meeting with the prince, others were entirely unable to spend time in his proximity, let alone interact with him. And yet there were a small number of persons who enjoyed free and unhampered access. In many cases these individuals held a high position in the household, whereby they were not only able to supervise compliance with extant rules in the matter of access but were in a position as well to manipulate or go around them.[22] In this way some among them were assured of a right to, or even a monopoly on, access to the prince. Ronald G. Asch has pointed out that this special status not infrequently went hand in hand with a special emotional relationship between the prince and the individual in question.[23]

---

20   Weiser (2003) 13.
21   See Hengerer (2004; 2016).
22   See, for example, Spangler (2016) and Duindam (2003) 90-110.
23   Asch (2016).

Without a doubt, quite a lot of family members, confessors, advisors, teachers and lovers of European princes readily made use of this privileged bond in order to acquire an influential position. Asch argues, on top of that, that this right to access sometimes was transferred from generation to generation, whereby in some cases it became an exclusive privilege that was reserved for certain families. In these kinds of circumstances, the *politics of access* was strongly interwoven with the *politics of intimacy*. In that sense the striking presence of favourites at European courts in the sixteenth and seventeenth century is characteristic for the strong impact that access could have upon early modern political life.[24] Some princes could deal with this phenomenon better than others. For example, princes still in their minority could be quite susceptible to the influence of third parties. The fierce contemporaneous criticism of these individuals demonstrates that a visibly unequal distribution of the right to access could also bring with it major political unrest.[25]

4 Visualising Access

How was access visualised? Various studies show that quite a lot of traditional acts and customs that were in vogue at the early modern court can in fact be seen as expressions of the interaction between looking for rapprochement, on the one hand, and maintaining distance, on the other hand. The representation of the process of access by means of rituals seems to be a constant that was present at all princely courts to a greater or lesser degree. The well-devised court ceremonial that was in fashion at all European princely courts, and which generally integrated detailed rules of access, can be viewed in this light as the example *par excellence*. Yet in the visual and material culture of the early modern court, too, we often find an externalisation of the process of access. That which most leaps to the eye, naturally, is the architecture of the princely residence itself, where walls and gates held back undesired intruders, and where antechambers and *enfilades* provided for the regulation of the flow of desired visitors. Even the decoration and the specific iconography of the residence contributed to the representation of access. Paintings, tapestries, and other forms of visual art frequently displayed scenes in which the interaction between the prince and the outside world take centre stage. The cycle of frescos in the so-called *Camera Picta* in the Castello San Giorgio in Mantua provides a nice example of this and can be interpreted as a symbolic expression of the accessibility of the duke of Mantua and of his willingness to communicate with his subjects.[26] Access was further made visual by means of other cultural

---

24   For general studies on favourites, see Elliott and Brockliss (1999); Kaiser and Pečar (2003); Hirschbiegel and Paravicini (2004).

25   See, for example, Williams (2006); Persson (2016).

26   Antenhofer (2016).

FIGURE 6.2
Charles-Alexandre of Croÿ (1581-1624), Marquis of Havré and Duke of Croÿ, was one of the *gentilhombres de la Cámara* [Gentlemen of the Bedchamber] of Archduke Albert of Austria (r. 1598-1621), sovereign ruler of the Habsburg Netherlands in the early seventeenth century. The key on the Marquis' tunic is the symbol of his office and represents his privileged access to the personal quarters of the Archduke. Source: Flemish School, 17th century (c.1610), oil on canvas: 78 × 43 5/8 inches, 195 × 109 cm. The Weiss Gallery, London [accessed online 28.02.2019: <https://commons.wikimedia.org/wiki/File:Charles-Alexandre_de_Cro%C3%BF_Marquis_d%27Havr%C3%A9_and_Duc_de_Cro%C3%BF..jpg>]

artefacts. During the festivities surrounding princely births luxury goods, relics, and decorative partitions were always employed to accent the elevated status of the prince and the elites.[27] At the same time these visual markers also made clear who belonged to the immediate circle of the prince. Another example is the famous golden or iron key, so prominently present in portraits of leading courtiers, which gradually evolved from an actually functioning instrument into a decorative object that possessed in the first instance a symbolic function (see Figure 6.2). Yet in the decorative treatment of uniforms, doorknobs, banquettes, and weapons as well as of other rather ordinary objects or

---

27   Thiry (2016).

those used every day, references to the process of access might, or might not, be hidden.

Conclusion

In summary, it can be stated that our approach may further the research into premodern power relations in two ways. First, it mitigates the need for a broad, systematic analysis of access by studying and – even more important – problematising the concept from diverse perspectives. Secondly, it demonstrates that access is in the first place a process of negotiation, which was presented and visualised in varied ways, and which in this light constituted an important component of the political culture of the early modern court. In this sense the study of the culture of access allows us to better comprehend early modern politics itself.

We are very much aware of the fact that a number of important topics, strongly related to the broader phenomenon of "access," could be added to the list of repertoires. One might, for example, consider correspondence or petitions as "alternative" forms of access that deserve to be studied in their own right. Yet, we do not intend to offer an exhaustive survey of all possible angles with regard to the role of access. Our contribution aims to juxtapose a number of extant and new lines of research that jointly expose the multiform nature of the phenomenon. Neither does this chapter intend to suggest an all-encompassing definition, nor to offer a comparative analysis. By bringing together a number of perspectives on the culture of access in diverse courts and time periods, it wants to lay bare differences and similarities and to spotlight recurrent patterns and topics. In this way it aims to generate debate about the importance of access for our knowledge of the world of the late medieval and early modern court. There is still much that we do not know. Yet this is also what makes our search for a key to better understanding this centre of power so captivating.

Bibliography

Adamson, J., "The Tudor and Stuart Courts, 1509-1714," in J. Adamson (ed.), *The Princely Courts of Europe: Ritual, Politics and Culture under the Ancien Régime, 1500-1750* (London, 1999), 95-117.

Antenhofer, C., "Meeting the Prince Between the City and the Family: The Resignification of Castello San Giorgio in Mantua (Fourteenth-Sixteenth Centuries)," in

D. Raeymaekers and S. Derks, *The Key to Power? The Culture of Access in Princely Courts, c. 1400-1750* (Leiden, 2016), 235-267.

Asch, R.G., "Patronage, Friendship and the Politics of Access: The Role of the Early Modern Favourite Revisited," in D. Raeymaekers and S. Derks, *The Key to Power? The Culture of Access in Princely Courts, c. 1400-1750* (Leiden, 2016), 178-201.

Asch, R.G., "The Politics of Access. Hofstruktur und Herrschaft in England unter den frühen Stuarts 1603-1642," in W. Paravicini (ed.), *Alltag bei Hofe. 3. Symposium der Residenzen-Kommission der Akademie der Wissenschaften in Göttingen* (Sigmaringen, 1995), 243-66.

Asch, R.G., "The Princely Court and Political Space in Early Modern Europe," in B. Kümin (ed.), *Political Space in Pre-industrial Europe* (Farnham, 2009), 43-60.

Asch, R.G. and A.M. Birke (eds.), *Princes, Patronage, and the Nobility: The Court at the Beginning of the Modern Age, c. 1450-1650* (Oxford, 1991).

Berland, F., "Access to the Prince's Court in Late Medieval Paris," in D. Raeymaekers and S. Derks (eds.), *The Key to Power? The Culture of Access in Princely Courts, c. 1400-1750* (Leiden, 2016), 19-39.

Butz, R. and J. Hirschbiegel (eds.), *Informelle Strukturen bei Hof: Dresdener Gespräche III zur Theorie des Hofes.* (Berlin, 2009).

Duindam, J., *Vienna and Versailles: The Courts of Europe's Dynastic Rivals, 1550-1780* (Cambridge, Eng., 2003).

Elliott, J.H., and L.W.B. Brockliss (eds.), *The World of the Favourite* (New Haven, 1999).

Elton, G., "Tudor Government: The Points of Contact: III. The Court," in *Transactions of the Royal Historical Society* (1976), 211-228.

Fantoni, M. (ed.), *The Court in Europe* (Rome, 2012).

Fantoni, M., G. Gorse, and R.M. Smuts (eds.), *The Politics of Space: European Courts ca. 1500-1750* (Rome, 2009).

Gunn, S.J., "The Courtiers of Henry VII," in *English Historical Review* 108 (1993), 23-49.

Hengerer, M. "Access at the Court of the Austrian Habsburg Dynasty (Mid-Sixteenth to Mid-Eighteenth Century): A Highway from Presence to Politics?," in D. Raeymaekers and S. Derks, *The Key to Power? The Culture of Access in Princely Courts, c. 1400-1750* (Leiden, 2016), 124-153.

Hengerer, M., *Kaiserhof und Adel in der Mitte des 17. Jahrhunderts: Eine Kommunikationsgeschichte der Macht in der Vormoderne* (Konstanz, 2004).

Hirschbiegel, J. and W. Paravicini (eds.), *Der Fall des Günstlings: Hofparteien in Europa vom 13. bis zum 17. Jahrhundert. 8. Symposium der Residenzen-Kommission der Akademie der Wissenschaften zu Göttingen* (Ostfildern, 2004).

Horowski, L., *Die Belagerung des Thrones. Machtstrukturen und Karrieremechanismen am Hof von Frankreich 1661-1789* (Sigmaringen, 2012).

Jiménez, C.G-C., "Etiqueta y ceremonial palatino durante el reinado de Felipe V: el reglamento de entradas de 1709 y el acceso a la persona del rey," in *Hispania* 56, no. 3 (1996), 965-1005.

Kaiser M. and A. Pečar (eds.), *Der zweite Mann im Staat: Oberste Amtsträger und Favoriten im Umkreis der Reichsfürsten in der Frühen Neuzeit* (Berlin, 2003).

Kettering, S., "Brokerage at the Court of Louis xiv," in *Historical Journal* 36 (1993), 69-87.

Kruse H. and W. Paravicini (eds.), *Höfe und Hofordnungen 1200-1600. 5. Symposium der Residenzen-Kommission der Akademie der Wissenschaften zu Göttingen* (Sigmaringen, 1999).

Lefebvre, H., *The Production of Space* (Chicago, 1991).

Loades, D., *The Tudor Court* (London, 1986).

Murphy, N., *Ceremonial Entries, Urban Liberties and the Negotiation of Power in Valois France, 1328-1589* (Leiden, 2016a).

Murphy, N., "The Court on the Move: Ceremonial Entries, Gift-Giving and Access to the Monarch in France, c.1440-c.1570," in D. Raeymaekers and S. Derks (eds.), *The Key to Power? The Culture of Access in Princely Courts, c. 1400-1750* (Leiden, 2016b), 40-63.

Pangerl, I., M. Scheutz, and T. Winkelbauer (eds.), *Der Wiener Hof im Spiegel der Zeremonialprotokolle (1652-1800): Eine Annäherung* (Innsbruck, 2007).

Pečar, A., *Die Ökonomie der Ehre. Höfischer Adel am Kaiserhof Karls vi. (1711-1740)* (Darmstadt, 2003).

Persson, F., "The Struggle for Access: Participation and Distance During a Royal Swedish Minority," in D. Raeymaekers and S. Derks, *The Key to Power? The Culture of Access in Princely Courts, c. 1400-1750* (Leiden, 2016), 202-233.

Raeymaekers, D., *One Foot in the Palace. The Habsburg Court of Brussels and the Politics of Access in the Reign of Albert and Isabella, 1598-1621* (Leuven, 2013).

Raeymaekers, D. and S. Derks (eds.), *The Key to Power? The Culture of Access in Princely Courts, c. 1400-1750* (Leiden, 2016).

Roux, N. le, *La faveur du roi. Mignons et courtisans au temps des derniers Valois (vers 1547-1564)* (Seyssel, 2000).

Schmitt, C., *Gespräche über die Macht und den Zugang zum Machthaber* (Stuttgart, 1954a).

Schmitt, C., "Im Vorraum der Macht," in *Die Zeit*, 29 July 1954b.

Spangler, J., "Holders of the Keys: The Grand Chamberlain, the Grand Equerry and Monopolies of Access at the Early Modern French Court, " in D. Raeymaekers and S. Derks, *The Key to Power? The Culture of Access in Princely Courts, c. 1400-1750* (Leiden, 2016), 155-177.

Starkey, D., *The Development of the Privy Chamber, 1485-1547.* Unpublished doctoral dissertation, Cambridge University, 1973.

Starkey, D. (ed.), *The English Court from the Wars of the Roses to the Civil War* (London, 1987).

Starkey, D., "Representation through Intimacy: A Study of the Symbolism of Monarchy and Court Office in Early Modern England," in I.M. Lewis (ed.), *Symbols and Sentiments: Cross-Cultural Studies in Symbolism* (London, 1977), 187-224.

Stollberg-Rilinger, B., *Des Kaisers alte Kleider. Verfassungsgeschichte und Symbolsprache des Alten Reiches* (Munich, 2008).

Stollberg-Rilinger, B., "Die Frühe Neuzeit – eine Epoche der Formalisierung?," in A. Höfele, J-D. Müller, and W. Österreicher (eds.), *Die Frühe Neuzeit. Revisionen einer Epoche* (Berlin, 2013), 3-27.

Stollberg-Rilinger, B., "Zeremoniell, Ritual, Symbol. Neue Forschungen zur symbolischen Kommunikation in Spätmittelalter und Früher Neuzeit," in *Zeitschrift für Historische Forschung* 27 (2000), 389-405.

Talbot, M., "Accessing the Shadow of God: Spatial and Performative Ceremonial at the Ottoman Court," in D. Raeymaekers and S. Derks (eds.), *The Key to Power? The Culture of Access in Princely Courts, c. 1400-1750* (Leiden, 2016), 103-123.

Talbot, M., *British-Ottoman Relations, 1661-1807: Commerce and Diplomatic Practice in Eighteenth-Century Istanbul* (Woodbridge, 2017).

Thiry, S., "Forging Dynasty: The Politics of Dynastic Affinity in Burgundian-Habsburg Birth and Baptism Ceremonial (1430-1505)," in D. Raeymaekers and S. Derks, *The Key to Power? The Culture of Access in Princely Courts, c. 1400-1750* (Leiden, 2016), 268-295.

Truschke, A., "Deceptive Familiarity: European Perceptions of Access at the Mughal Court," in D. Raeymaekers and S. Derks (eds.), *The Key to Power? The Culture of Access in Princely Courts, c. 1400-1750* (Leiden, 2016), 65-99.

Warf, B. and S. Arias (eds.), *The Spatial Turn: Interdisciplinary Perspectives* (New York, 2009).

Weiser, B., *Charles II and the Politics of Access* (Woodbridge, 2003).

Williams, P., *The Great Favourite. The Duke of Lerma and the Court and Government of Philip III of Spain, 1598-1621* (Manchester, 2006).

CHAPTER 7

The Image of Prime Minister Colijn: Public Visualisation of Political Leadership in the 1930s

Marij Leenders and Joris Gijsenbergh

Introduction*

In the 1930s, the parliamentary system in the Netherlands was under fire, as it was in most European democracies. Parliament, the political parties, and professional politicians were not held in very high regard. However, the critics of the parliamentary system did not actually distance themselves from the idea of political representation. On the contrary, they strove to achieve improvement of the system of representation. These critics were all searching for various, sometimes contradictory solutions to "the crisis of parliamentarism."[1] Some wished to restore the reputation of parliament in all its old glory. Others sought salvation in strong leaders, convinced that democracy could not continue without authority. They were convinced that these leaders should function as a symbol for the electorate. The debate about representation during the interwar period did not therefore only revolve around the position of parliamentary representation. The relationship between leaders and "the people" was also a recurring theme. The lamentation about parliamentarianism was based on various ideals of political representation and democratic leadership.[2]

This contribution will show the manifold ways in which parliamentary photographers and political artists portrayed Dutch political leaders in the 1930s. Prime Minister Hendrik Colijn, the most prominent statesman of the time, was especially frequently portrayed. The images of Colijn and his colleagues in the parliamentary arena are very relevant to a clear insight into the interwar history of representation. Photographers and caricaturists played an important role in the image-forming of these politicians. Their images drew a realistic view of the statesmen (mimetic representation) but also *framed* a particular type of politician (aesthetic representation).[3] The photographers and artists literally formed the image held by the greater public, of politicians and politics.

---

*   This chapter is mainly derived from Leenders (2014) and Gijsenbergh (2014).
1   "De crisis van het parlementarisme en de democratie," *Het Vaderland*, 7 Jan. 1926.
2   Gijsenbergh (2015) 117.
3   Ankersmit (1987) 363.

© MARIJ LEENDERS AND JORIS GIJSENBERGH, 2019 | DOI:10.1163/9789004291966_008
This is an open access chapter distributed under the terms of the CC-BY-NC 4.0 License.

PUBLIC VISUALISATION OF POLITICAL LEADERSHIP IN THE 1930S   95

Their photos and political caricatures gave a positive or negative impression of Dutch leaders. Analysis of this visual source material clearly shows the various ideals of political representation as it was presented to the public.

Some of the photographers and caricaturists of the 1930s longed back to the nineteenth century, a time when the political arena was populated by respectable and aloof gentlemen.[4] Compared to France and Germany, democratic participation in The Netherlands started relatively late. Holland resembled Great Britain in that respect. Although Thorbecke's constitutional revision of 1848 already sowed the seeds for a parliamentary form of government, the Dutch parliament remained a closed, aristocratic kind of institute, in which but a very small part of the population felt involved. The "representatives" were free and unfettered to practice their mandate, at a huge distance from the voters. The need to actually represent or express the will of the people was not high on the agenda in The House. After all, Members of Parliament (MPs) were notables, distanced from society, and considered their main task to be to promote general well-being to the best of their ability.[5]

At the end of the nineteenth century, this aloof method of politics made way for the kind that aimed at mobilisation and communication. Political artists such as Pieter de Josselin de Jong (1861-1906) portrayed late-nineteenth century politicians and parliament, but it was specifically several politicians themselves who managed to bridge the gap between politicians and citizens. The leaders of the new political parties in particular, such as the anti-revolutionary leader Abraham Kuyper, and the leader of the Social Democrats Pieter Jelles Troelstra, profiled themselves as spokesmen for their rank and file.[6] They achieved this not only in the House of Commons, but also in the partisan media and – as far as the Social Democrats were concerned – during mass demonstrations. To these demagogues, politics was not just a matter of business for the pompous gentlemen of The Hague to be concerned with, but something for everyone. They associated politics no longer with business-like, rational discussion, but – as historian Henk te Velde has convincingly demonstrated – with an emotional way of representing various groups of the population.[7]

After 1917, political representation once again changed character, following upon the introduction of the general right to vote (1917/1919) and the system of proportional representation (1917). On the one hand, this new step bridged the

---

4 Aerts (2009) 19.
5 Aerts (2014) 150-51.
6 Te Velde (2001) 23.
7 Te Velde (2000) 155-58; Te Velde (2002).

gap between politicians and citizens. More and more politicians now understood the necessity of seeking contact with their voters. Prior to 1917, parliament consisted of district members that often enough rather cherished their distance to local voters. The introduction of proportional representation ensured that MPs now reflected the political ideological divisions of the whole of the Dutch population as accurately as possible.[8] The introduction of the general right to vote also led to more voters being able to influence political decision-making. On the other hand, political leaders retained the need to keep their distance from "the general public." Now that the electorate was filled with the unskilled and the uneducated, the parties took it upon themselves to channel popular participation.[9]

In the 1930s, and against this background, public debate on representation burst loose. Some party leaders wanted to restore their aloof nineteenth-century type of relationships towards citizens. Other politicians considered such a return to be impossible, but did still want to lead their rank and file. To achieve this, they needed the confidence of the citizens. In the interwar period, the charisma of those in power was then of great importance, just as it had been for centuries already, from ancient times right up to the nineteenth century. Parliamentary photographers and caricaturists played a huge role in this because they helped to shape the image of various politicians. Their representation of Colijn and other leaders is central to this contribution. Editorial staff of magazines publishing the photographs and cartoons have also been considered in the analysis, because they were important intermediaries in the process of representation of leadership, too. Editors were responsible for selecting the images, helped make up the captions, and decided on how the images were printed.

This chapter distances itself from previous literature that emphasises how parliament was criticised *from all sides* during the 1930s.[10] Instead, this contribution will expand upon four recent tendencies within historiography. Following upon recent international historiography, we lay the emphasis here upon the diversity within the broad spectrum of interwar lament about parliamentary democracy.[11] Secondly, this article follows the literature on the Dutch shift in the formation of representative politics. Henk te Velde researched "the rise of political parties at the end of the nineteenth century" and how they served as catalyst in the process. Jasper Loots demonstrated how the debate on

---

8   Te Velde (2001) 23; Loots (2004) 21-23, 142, 207-210.

9   Gijsenbergh (2017) 140.

10   Berg-Schlosser (2000).

11   Gerard (2005) 504; Gijsenbergh (2015) 117.

PUBLIC VISUALISATION OF POLITICAL LEADERSHIP IN THE 1930S   97

representational reform only really took off around 1917, with the introduction of proportional representation.[12] This chapter shows how the various opinions on representation remained subject to change throughout the 1930s. The emphasis here lies on perceptions on the relationship between representation and authority because that was an important theme among publicists and politicians. This focus hooks up to a third historiographic tendency. Historians such as Moritz Föllmer and Joris Gijsenbergh have shown how the call to leadership in the 1930s was certainly not always directed at the abolishment of democracy. On the contrary, both in and outside The Netherlands, there were many advocates for firm authority who were in fact rooting for improvements of democracy.[13]

The analysis of visual source material forms the fourth way in which this contribution builds upon historiography. Lately, there are more and more historians analysing photographs and political cartoons, but they place these sources insufficiently in context. There appears to be only superficial interest exhibited in the historical connections, leaving photographs incorrectly dated and captions on the photos inaccurately reproduced. Especially where it involves photos by Erich Salomon, who is central to this article. Furthermore, previous authors have seldom made a distinction between the photographs that were published in the press of the time, and photos that remained in the archives. Only published photos can be utilised as a source of visual discourse during the interwar period because only these played any role in the public debate.[14]

One specific category of depiction is the caricature. These often only function in historical research as illustration. Even when they are central to the discussion, the attention often goes to one particular artist's work, the political subject of satire, or the history of a satirical periodical.[15] Caricatures, however, offer excellent insight as to how the functioning of politicians and the political system itself were sternly judged. Research into visual parliamentary culture is rare. Therefore, this contribution focuses on the visual representation of politicians and parliament in the interwar period. The images will be placed in historical context in order to discover how the photographer, the caricaturist, or the editor(s) wanted the image(s) to be "read."

The visual staging of Colijn's political leadership brings two different repertoires of representation to the fore – both of which garnered praise and

---

12   Te Velde (2001); Loots (2004).
13   Föllmer (2015) 178; Gijsenbergh (2017) 140.
14   Rose (2001) 69-99; Brandt (2013) 354; Burke (2001) 9-13; Beunders (2010) 121, 133-35.
15   Walter (2006); Mulder (1978); Mulder (1985); Van Weringh (1975); Van Weringh (1976); Van Weringh (1977).

derision in the 1930s. Advocates and opponents of these two ideal visions of representation collided regularly. The first section treats images portraying the PM as a "deliberative democrat," who, just as his predecessors in the nineteenth century, exchanged thoughts with other members of The House in a dignified, aloof manner. Photos by the famous Jewish photojournalist Erich Salomon, who fled to Holland after Hitler's rise to power, more than anything outlined a positive view of the deliberative House of Commons and Senate. Salomon praised his host country, where parliamentary manners and morals still existed. This positive vision of parliamentary democracy was not actually common in the Netherlands of the 1930s. The "Chat Club" was under fire from various quarters, such as the *Nationaal-Socialistische Beweging* 'National Socialist Movement' (NSB), which wanted to abolish democracy and various conservative groups which desired democratic reform. Caricatures in *Volk en Vaderland* and *De Haagsche Post* painted deliberative leaders as weak and inefficient.

The second section analyses specific images of Colijn as "disciplined democrat." These portray the PM as a strong, decisive leader, oozing authority. He serves the MPs imperturbably with adequate response and was literally shown to have "the ship's wheel" in his hands. There are several photos by Salomon – accompanied by captions, in the independent/liberal weekly journal *Het Leven, Geïllustreerd* – which suggested that Dutch democracy indeed benefited from just such a leader. This message was also conveyed in drawings in *De Haagsche Post* and *De Telegraaf*. Caricaturists did not always ridicule politicians: in these images we certainly see a positive depiction of Colijn. But not everyone welcomed a strong leader. According to the caricaturists of the progressive *De Groene Amsterdammer* and the Social Democratic *De Notekraker*, strong leadership could turn into authoritarian or even undemocratic leadership.

This chapter therefore touches on the concept of representation in two ways. Firstly, photographs and caricatures created their own representation of reality, by effectively *framing* political figures. Secondly, analysis of these visual sources brings ideal conceptions of political leadership to the fore. Politicians were portrayed as deliberative leaders or as decisive representatives of the nation. This offers some insight into the kaleidoscope of interwar opinions on authority within parliamentary democracy.

Colijn Portrayed as a Deliberative Democrat

The Conservative, orthodox-Protestant PM Hendrikus Colijn was portrayed many times from 1936 in Salomon's photographs. This photojournalist was the

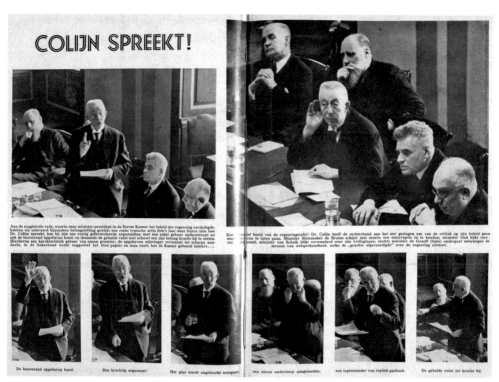

FIGURE 7.1 'Colijn speaks!' in *Het Leven*, February 22, 1936.
PHOTOS: ERICH SALOMON.

first to be given access to parliament (in 1936) in order to photograph MPs and the government in debate. He probably used his good relationship with Colijn to gain this position. He knew Colijn even before coming to Holland and Colijn was one of the first politicians in the Netherlands conscious of the influence of mass-media.[16] He was given an inordinate amount of press attention in the 1930s. Many a speech by Colijn was heard on the radio in Dutch households in the 1930s. Colijn also consciously employed (photo)journalists to build up his public persona. Erich Salomon was one of the first photographers to concern himself with Colijn. The selected photographs show Colijn as a deliberative leader, not afraid of and never avoiding debate in parliament.

The first example here was staged by the photographer to portray Colijn as an impassioned and superior statesman in a so-called "Parliamentary Film" with repetitive and explicit captions that emphasise the PM's stance when in debate with The House: "Colijn speaks, Colijn listens, Colijn directs" (see Figure 7.1). This picture shows us a rational and business-like statesman. On a

---

16   Langeveld (2002).

double-paged spread, the ministers are depicted behind the cabinet table; Colijn is the dominant figure in the middle during his speech. These photographs were taken from the public grandstand with light falling in from the window.[17] The deliberative aspect is shown in all its facets in the second example, showing how senator M.M. Mendels (*Sociaal-Democratische Arbeiderspartij*, SDAP) attacks Colijn's cabinet III. Cabinets III, IV, and V (1935-1939) did not possess a parliamentary majority. The opposition used this to express sharp critique of the government. During Colijn III (1935-1937), consisting of central/right parties, Mendels did not hold back in bringing the actual legitimacy of the cabinet into doubt. According to the Social Democratic senator, the PM had insufficiently researched whether the "States General of The Netherlands" had indeed approved this cabinet. In other words, did this cabinet in fact even have the support of parliament?[18] Salomon made a series of photographs of this debate on 6 or 7 February 1936 that firmly place Mendel's critical speech and Colijn's rejoinder, centre stage (see Figure 7.2). In the very same issue of *Het Leven* that portrays the debate in The House, we see senator Mendels (also a lawyer and journalist for the Social Democratic daily *Het Vrije Volk*) vehemently gesticulating on several occasions. *Het Leven* captions this as follows:

> One of the best speakers in parliament is indubitably Mr. Mendels, who frequently peppers his sharp criticisms with humour, and is always given great attention by The House. See the series of 'film' above to follow how he attacks the government [Colijn cabinet III] – surrounded by Dr. Polak, Count de Marchant et d'Ansembourg, Mr. van Vessem and Suze Groeneweg – with fierce gestures and with his hand on his heart to show his conviction.[19]

The fiercest attack on the unparliamentarian character of the new Colijn cabinet V came from the Catholic opposition. L.N. Deckers, party chairman of the *Roomsch-Katholieke Staatspartij* (RKSP), criticised Colijn that during the formation of his fifth cabinet, inaugurated on 25 July 1939, he had in no way

---

17   These photos have also been published in the *British Telegraph* and in the *Daily Telegraph* on 29 July 1939.

18   Related to this issue was the distinction between parliamentary and extra-parliamentary cabinets. Colijn interpreted that in his own way: "Purely parliamentary cabinets in the traditional sense of the word are very rare in the Netherlands, because very seldom did a homogeneous political group in Parliament possess the majority, which means that very seldom a cabinet could be formed of people, who completely politically agreed with that group." *Handelingen van de Eerste Kamer der Staten-Generaal* (HEK) 1935-1936, 267-68.

19   *Het Leven*, 29 Feb. 1936.

PUBLIC VISUALISATION OF POLITICAL LEADERSHIP IN THE 1930S 101

FIGURE 7.2 Parliamentary duel in The House in *Het Leven*, February 29, 1936.
PHOTOS: ERICH SALOMON.

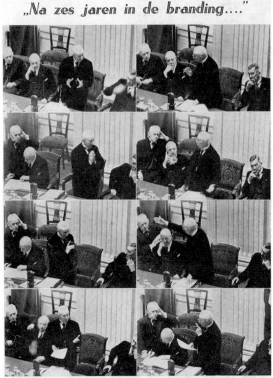

FIGURE 7.3
'After 6 years on the breakers...'
in *Het Leven*, August 8, 1939.
PHOTOS: ERICH SALOMON.

accounted for the wishes of parliament.[20] Deckers officially proposed for the inauguration of Colijn cabinet v to be denounced.

Colijn defended himself most audaciously, as can be seen in example 3, but it was to no avail. Decker's proposal was supported by a majority in The House and on 29 July 1939, the cabinet was under resignation.[21] Salomon recorded Colijn's speech in a series of eight "filmic" images. *Het Leven* published the photos under the title "After 6 years on the breakers...," a variation on the theme of Colijn's speech to The House where he referred to "standing in the storm for 6 years" (see Figure 7.3).[22] The accompanying editorial reads:

---

20 Moreover, Deckers argued that the resignation of the previous cabinet was unnecessary and undesirable, due to the economic and political crisis. *Handelingen van de Tweede Kamer der Staten-Generaal* (HTK) 1938-1939, 2228.
21 HTK 1938-1939, 2225.
22 Ibid.

PUBLIC VISUALISATION OF POLITICAL LEADERSHIP IN THE 1930S   103

> Colijn Cabinet no. 5 lasts only two days! Our colleague Dr. Erich Salomon took a series of charming photographs of the session wherein the formateur defends his decisions against critique from both left and right. Above: 'Dr. Colijn listening to Dr. Deckers's speech.'

Deckers is by the way not in the picture. The text continues about Colijn and "his big speech," about how "while the distinguished statesman speaks, he takes turns to face those on the right and then those on the left and does not hold back on the expressive gestures for which parliament knows him so well."

The photo reportage with a series of joined up fragments (snapshots) shows all aspects of a speech in progress, and the supporting body-language clearly aims at both convincing and moving the MPs. Due to the wording of the caption, not just the PM, but the ministers, too, were clearly being documented on their last day in function.

This method of photographing the same person in a series of photographs with short pauses between (see Figures 7.1, 7.2, and 7.3) gives an almost film-like effect. *Het Leven* comments on the results of Salomon's method, via captions. Gestures and expressions on Ministers, MPs, speakers, and listeners are actually give attention in his work, making it possible to accurately interpret their state of mind: "Colijn is obviously amused," "minister De Graeff (left) with his thumbs diplomatically pressed one against the other," and "Minister Oud who 'adds a smirk.'" The editorial staff described the PM as the conductor of the orchestra. *Het Leven* agreed with Salomon who had previously mentioned the importance of gestures during a speech.[23] Editors saw the photograph as an accurate depiction of reality (as was then usual to think so) and seemed unconscious of the influence a photograph could have on what was actually happening. Visual staging of Colijn as a rational, business-like, but above all charismatic PM seemed to connect neatly with existing portraiture. In any case, no critical commentary ensued.

Het Leven's intention of reproducing statesman Colijn's work as realistic could also be seen in the photos chosen of cabinet meetings. "Our readership can now form a clear picture of the cabinet wherein 'the country's most important decisions are taken!,'" as per their editorial.[24] Pictures of the tumultuous debate of 29 and 30 September 1936 showing Colijn's cabinet departing from "the gold standard" under pressure from parliament also make an attempt at clearly visualising political decision making. The captions emphasise Colijn's

---

23   Bottema (1936) preface, 108-11.
24   *Het Leven*, 7 March 1936.

huge difficulties in agreeing to this economic reform ("only if absolutely necessary").[25]

With the publication of Salomon's parliamentary photographs, *Het Leven* took a political stand – deliberately or otherwise. The editors "framed" the photos with their captions in such a way as to present parliamentary democracy positively, in a time that this form of government was being widely criticised. The captions of Salomon's photos suited the critics who actually believed in parliamentary democracy but who also proposed renewal and improvement to the system.[26] *Het Leven* worked together with Salomon to reveal how representation must take place via deliberation, with appeals for agreement among the majority of representatives. According to the editors and the photographer, parliamentary debate was not inefficient but indeed a noble component of the game of politics.

Salomon's style of parliamentary photography was closely followed by a few disciples in the interwar period. The work of photographic journalists like Wiel van der Randen and Henk Smits existed mostly of official, posed, political pictures at the start of the 1930s, and yet, photos taken after 1937 are barely distinguishable from Salomon's. There's an interesting depiction of Colijn as "deliberative leader" taken by Wiel van de Randen. In this, he portrays the PM while Colijn holds a relaxed "friendly chat" with the leader of the Communist Party among the parliamentary benches (see Figure 7.4). This portrait placed Colijn somewhere the PM probably could not have foreseen. After all, Colijn derived his authority and popularity, for a not unimportant part, from his image as a warrior *against* political extremism. This rather proves that Colijn quite clearly did not have his image forming entirely in hand. He was dependent on the photographer, or political caricaturist. Salomon's thematic of a positive image of deliberative leadership was continued here by other photographers. With the use of composition and the choice of just the right psychological instant, Salomon portrayed a determined, engaged leader.

However, this interpretation was not shared by all. Some political caricaturists considered deliberative leadership to be a sign of weakness because politics would become stuck in the quagmire of endless debate. Prime Ministers – Colijn leading the way – could always depend on criticism from the satirical press, specifically because they spent too much time in debate. Deliberative leadership was staged to look from mildly ridiculous to condescending, to reprehensible, in political cartoons. The artists working for the conservative/liberal oriented weekly publication *De Haagsche Post* (with a circulation of

---

25   *HTK* 1936-1937, 31- 60; *Het Leven*, 3 Oct. 1936.

26   Kennedy (2004) 13; Gijsenbergh (2015) 133-35.

Antipoden. Minister Colijn tegen de balustrade van het „stenograficum" in vriendelijk gesprek met den chef der communistische partij, den heer de Visser, achter wien een andere „extremist", de N.S.B.-er de heer Woudenberg, staat.

FIGURE 7.4
'Antipodes, Colijn having a friendly chat with the leader of the Communist Party Mr. de Visser with that other 'extremist', NSB's Mr. Woudenberg standing behind'. in *De Katholieke Illustratie*, December 9, 1937.
PHOTO: WIEL VAN DER RANDEN.

53-70,000 papers in the interwar period) provided mild critique on Colijn's political leadership. The caricature below appeared after "Prinsjesdag" 1935, the day that government expounds upon the policies for the coming year. Here we see how destructive the opposition can be when they really aim at an unsuspecting political leader. Colijn is portrayed as a weak leader, hiding from the hunters of the parliamentary opposition in his hare's lair. However, the artist aims his arrows more at the irresponsible leaders of the opposition. He deeply regrets that they are not at all constructive, but appear ready to shoot down government policies (see Figure 7.5).

The National Socialist newspaper *Volk en Vaderland* (circulation of 80,000) gave even more critique to Colijn's personal demeanour. The PM was portrayed as a weak leader. *Volk en Vaderland* did not just blame political parties but laid it squarely at Colijn's feet. For instance, the PM would be depicted as an easily influenced schoolmaster, and we see Mr. Colijn being addressed by his pupils while Anton Mussert, leader of the NSB, watches from the doorway. The pupils ask Colijn to stop Mussert entering the classroom because they are "scared" of him. The second cartoon has him doing just that, apparently being forced into

FIGURE 7.5
'Third Tuesday in September. Hunting season is opened...' in *Haagsche Post*, September 21, 1935.
ARTIST UNKNOWN.

it by the pupils hanging on to his belt and pushing him towards Mussert (see Figure 7.6a). These cartoons refer to the new regulatory measure Colijn had enforced to combat political extremism. The NSB was not initially affected by the ban that had been decreed under civil servants in the summer, but parliamentary pressure made Colijn decide to extend the ban to the NSB in 1933, and members of this party were given the choice: revoke your membership or leave the civil service. A third cartoon show the same schoolmaster and his pupils doing a little jig in the classroom: "Right boys, the danger has passed! He's gone!" (see Figure 7.6b). In the background, we can see the large figure of Mussert at the classroom window, with a resolute expression: they're not done with him yet! This is to symbolise Mussert's position both above and outside this parliamentarian spectacle. In the eyes of the NSB, Mussert was the only leader capable of tough leadership, not Colijn; no way would Mussert succumb to pressure from others, as Colijn had certainly done.

National Socialists used cartoons to corroborate that the parliamentary system made it impossible to govern decisively. In 1936, in *Volk en Vaderland*, Maarten Meuldijk portrayed the ministers in Colijn's third cabinet as horned

PUBLIC VISUALISATION OF POLITICAL LEADERSHIP IN THE 1930S

FIGURE 7.6a 'Primary 2 at politics school' November 1933. Boys: 'Sir, please ban Mussert. We are all scared of him!' December 1933. Schoolmaster: Get lost you spoilsport! Or they will all leave me! in *Volk en Vaderland*, January 6, 1934.
ARTIST UNKNOWN.

FIGURE 7.6b 'January 1934. Schoolmaster and teachers (together): 'Right boys, the danger has passed! He's gone!' in *Volk en Vaderland*, January 6, 1934.
ARTIST UNKNOWN.

FIGURE 7.7
'Nog méér voelhorens?' in *Volk en Vaderland*, November 20, 1936.
ARTIST: MAARTEN MEULDIJK.

slugs that left a trail of slime on their chairs in the Senate. A powerful image, suggesting that ministers are slow, indecisive individuals, too much attached to parliament and its plush velvety chairs to ever be decisive on anything. The sketch was accompanied by words attributed to the Catholic party chairman Carel Goseling who had earlier advocated that "the Cabinet [...] should have more 'feelers' in the House" (see Figure 7.7).

PUBLIC VISUALISATION OF POLITICAL LEADERSHIP IN THE 1930S   109

This "proved" to the NSB, even more, that the parliamentary-democratic system could never produce a decisive government. Administrators listening too closely to parliament could not be expected to lead. This was most unsubtly portrayed in a series of cartoons in *Volk en Vaderland*. "Democracy" was represented as an abyss; or a dangerous disease; or a frozen, muddy canal full of holes in the ice; or a murky pond with a corpse floating in it; or a politician with a mill-stone tied around his neck.[27] The message was clear: no good could be expected from democracy and its weak political leaders, so the democratic system should immediately be dispensed with.

Colijn Portrayed as Disciplined Democrat

The National Socialists were not the only Dutch with cravings for a "man of action."[28] The call to be authoritative resounded equally in Catholic, Protestant, and liberal circles. These conservative parties represented the majority of voters. Endless debate in parliament was discredited and more confidence was displayed towards decisive leaders in general. These politicians should not waste their time in parliamentary chitchat, but should solve national problems. They should put an end to "The Great Depression" that had held the Netherlands in its sway since 1931, as well as to the alleged undermining of authority by extremists and insurgents.[29]

However, Catholic, Protestant, and liberal groups differed from the NSB on two main points. In the first place, conservatives believed that democracy was indeed capable of enforcing authority, and parliamentary democracy was in no way a hindrance to any form of decisive government (as opposed to what the National Socialists insisted was the case). Moreover, authority was an indispensable part of the democratic system. This then meant that any call for a strong leader must not be looked upon as a rejection of democracy. It would be more accurate to speak of a desire for a "more disciplined democracy."[30] This term was launched by the lawyer Karl Loewenstein in the second half of the 1930s. He, too, had fled Nazi Germany, just as Salomon had done. In this conception of democracy, an inflexible leader was required – one that was not quickly disconcerted by any opposition. This leader must keep control of parliament and "the people." A true leader must be an "man of action" – resolute

---

27   "De twee honden en de doode ezel," Volk en Vaderland, 8 Jan. 1937; "Democratie is een gevaarlijke ziekte," Ibid., 15 Oct. 1937; "Goseling op glad ijs," Ibid., 23 Dec. 1938; "Monopolie-bus," Ibid., 6 Jan. 1939.
28   Houwink ten Cate (1995) 218-19.
29   Gijsenbergh (2015) 122.
30   Loewenstein (1938) 774.

and unshakable. The Catholics, Protestants, and liberals saw Colijn as the epitome of just such a leader. To them, that was actually the reason to support Colijn. It is characteristic of Colijn's stature as a statesman that many, even in the opposition, praised his leadership qualities in the 1930s. This was the second obvious difference to the NSB, who continually criticised Colijn's leadership.[31]

Colijn liked to present himself as a decisive leader. He postulated that government, by its very nature, had an "inherent right" to lay down the law to its subjects, whatever the will of the people. In his view, sovereign power did not rest in the will of the people, nor in a strong parliament, but in the inherent right of government ministers exercising their given authority. He was aiming here not only at a strong cabinet, but on an influential monarch. Colijn, along with many citizens at that time, envisioned a disciplined democracy with a strong leadership as requisite for the continuance of parliament in times of crisis. He warned, during an election speech in 1933: "A purposeful government, that does not completely ignore popular influence, should find a majority in parliament, upon which it can rely."[32] Colijn wished his cabinet to benefit from a powerful position, and therefore tapped into the widely felt need for authority.

Many magazines and their caricaturists reinforced Colijn's image as "man of action." He was portrayed as a strict, yet just, authoritative figure upon whom the Dutch people could rely. The compiler of *Colijn in Caricature* (1936) would for instance call this Prime Minister "Holland's Great Statesman."[33] Even Salomon, generally in pursuit of the concept of thoughtful leadership, presented Colijn at times as a figure of authority. He did so, for instance, in his report on a visit of guests from the Dutch East Indies to the Netherlands in 1937, which portrayed the PM in his official robes of office. These symbols of power provided Colijn with the authority pursuant to a long tradition of state. It also helped that the famous "Grote Kerk" in The Hague was the background of the picture, rather giving Colijn a divine blessing (see Figure 7.8).[34] Salomon hereby staged the PM's authority with this picture. He did so quite deliberately, as it turns out from an interview in the left/liberal periodical *De Groene Amsterdammer.* In 1937 he herein heaved a sigh, saying "conditions across the whole world would perhaps be improved if only leaders would actually lead."[35]

---

31   Gijsenbergh (2017) 140.
32   Colijn (1933) 314-15; see also Langeveld (2004) 40, 246-47.
33   Bottema (1936) 3.
34   "Bezoek van 'Indische gasten,'" *Het Leven,* 16 Jan. 1937. See also the photos published at the occasion of the engagement of Princess Juliana: De Vries (1963) 150, 154-55.
35   Salomon (1937).

FIGURE 7.8
Traditional staging of a statesman in *Het Leven*, January 16, 1937.
PHOTO: ERICH SALOMON.

Salomon's call for a leader who knew what he was talking about seems to defy his concept of thoughtful leadership. However, Colijn's purposeful leadership seemed legitimate to Salomon and indeed necessary in times of crisis, as long as it remained within the framework of the parliamentary system. Salomon's work in Germany illustrates this apparent contradiction more clearly. Salomon had attempted to portray the Weimar Republic's Reichstag using various photographic methods plus visually aesthetic means in order to make it appear as a type of parliament full of deliberating gentlemen who were both accountable and at the same time close to the people.[36] In his view, the Reichstag was not only the place of parliamentary debate, but also an arena for big performances by "statesmen." His intention was to portray the Reichstag as the representative centre of the Republic. His photographs of the bearing of various political chiefs, in their capacity as members of government, can all be

36   Biefang (2014) 33, 41, 88.

seen as a visual argument for the opinion – or better yet, the hope – that not only an authoritative regime but also a parliamentary democracy, was capable of producing authoritative political leaders. In Salomon's opinion, thoughtfulness and thoroughness were fine bedfellows. The rise of the *Nationalsozialistische Arbeiterpartei* (NSDAP) in Germany shattered that dream, and yet Salomon was not discouraged.

The call for strong leadership is also clear in the captions to Salomon's photographs in *Het Leven*. This was one of the many periodicals that welcomed Colijn's authority. Unfortunately, without seeing the actual correspondence, it is not possible to find out how much influence Salomon actually had on said captions. Some indications on the back of the original photos in the archives could indicate that his suggestions were adhered to.[37] And yet, it is likely that the editorial staff had the final say on any accompanying text, with which they were actually commenting on any pictures of Colijn. These captions were often concentrated on the parliamentary discussion as expounded upon in a previous paragraph, but often enough effectively emphasised Colijn's tight hold on the reins of leadership. A picture then emerges of how Colijn enjoyed his reputation and standing in parliament and how he really stood his ground against critical opponents within The House. The message implied that the PM deserved the respect of all Representatives as well as citizens, because he aimed to preserve national interests. *Het Leven* paid a great deal of attention to the parliamentary arena, but was a big advocate for strong leadership.

One good example is the text accompanying photos of the "parliamentary film" called "Colijn speaks, Colijn listens, Colijn directs" of February 1936 (see Figure 7.1). The title itself indicates that the PM is not only in debate with the Senate, but was entirely in charge. The tone of the caption tells us that *Het Leven* applauded this addition of the directorial element to democracy. The editorial staff glorified Colijn for his "huge intellect" that allowed him to defend government policy "majestically." They also emphasised that "[...] Colijn's raised index finger exhorts us to pay good attention." This "characteristic gesture made by our Prime Minister" does not go unnoticed because "The Parliament [listened] enthralled." When one MP deigned to criticise, "this opponent was summarily responded to." The caption for a *close-up* of the cabinet table (above, right) underlines here "just how far from being in agreement" the ministers listened to criticism. The editorial staff brings our attention to this, just in

---

37   Salomon himself glued the photos together, as a collage. That was meant as an instruction for the editorial staff. Furthermore, he wrote texts on the back of the photos, such as "Colijn thinks." Berlinische Gallerie, nr. 3 (1936) and nr. 18 (1939), Niederlande XII: Dr. Erich Salomon.

PUBLIC VISUALISATION OF POLITICAL LEADERSHIP IN THE 1930S   113

case readers themselves had missed the obvious irritation clearly legible on the faces of cabinet members.[38]

Colijn was indubitably satisfied with this representation by *Het Leven* because he had personally complained, during the debate in the Senate, that the fragmented parliament cooperated insufficiently with the cabinet.[39] Remarkably, the regional, Catholic newspaper *Nieuwe Venloosche Courant,* actually feared that the photo of the cabinet table in *Het Leven* could damage the State's reputation. This comment shows that this newspaper also felt that the PM should enforce respect. Unfortunately, there are no other comments in relation to this photo that could make it possible to work out how representative this Catholic newspaper's opinion was. What is clear, though, is that the *Nieuwe Venloosche Courant* felt that the evident staging of this photograph clashed with any dignity the government commanded:

> Mr. Oud's listless attitude gives us to assume that he is listening to a speech on fundamental, positive Christianity. Wizard Colijn holds his hands to his temples as shells, so imitating a bat; or perhaps a Maori. [...] We surely possess an imposing collection of respectable portraits of our ancestors. [...] But when history completes the chapter on the turbulent era of Colijn's Crisis Cabinet, just one such photo from the archives need be recovered and our descendants will only be able to assume that we all descend from a ridiculous bunch of idiots. What happened to honouring history?[40]

Het Leven's admiration and respect for the PM is further evident in the captions to Salomon's photographs of Colijn's situation at home. Public space was apparently no longer sufficient for a number of journalists to get on top of this politician's personality. They tried infiltrating the personal life of politicians.[41] Salomon hooked up to these new mores and photographed the Colijn family in a private capacity. Editorial staff at *Het Leven* used a photo of Colijn's dining room to indicate the importance of order and authority both at home and in the political arena: "Tranquillity and sobriety define this house, where Mrs. Colijn rules with an iron fist, just as her husband does in meeting rooms across the country." The captions on several photos of Colijn in his office spread the same message: "Under his leadership, the people of The Netherlands have

---

38   *Het Leven*, 22 Feb. 1936.
39   *HEK* 1935-1936, 272.
40   Cited in Bool (1979) 134.
41   Broersma, "Mediating Parliament," 180.

FIGURE 7.9   Private and public within politics in *Het Leven*, June 5, 1937.
PHOTOS: ERICH SALOMON.

rejected the extremists on both right and left, and are ranged closely around the House of Orange and the Dutch form of government [...]." *Het Leven* was indeed totally unsurprised that Colijn, during parliamentary elections for 1937, was once more awarded a huge "vote of confidence" from the electorate (see Figure 7.9).[42]

There were other papers besides *Het Leven* that showed appreciation for Colijn's strict style of leadership. *De Haagsche Post* and the popular newspaper *De Telegraph* led the way here. These papers praised his energy, not just in the articles in the paper but also in their political cartoons of Colijn. Their caricaturists also used multiple metaphors for "school" to depict his style of political leadership. This metaphor was however much more positively portrayed than it was in *Volk en Vaderland*. The politician – usually a minister – was now seen as a teacher with authority, leading the country and its parliament. For instance, Eppo Doeve of *De Haagsche Post* depicted Colijn as a stern looking schoolmaster, with all the MPs depicted as school children. Colijn towers above

---

42   "In intieme kring," *Het Leven*, 5 June 1937.

FIGURE 7.10
'The third Tuesday in September: 'Get to work!'. PM/School Master H. Colijn, calls the playing MPs/school children to attention, on the opening day of the parliamentary year in *Haagsche Post*, September 18, 1937.
ARTIST: EPPO DOEVE.

the playing children on "het Binnenhof" and calls them to attention. This cartoon appeared around the third Tuesday in September, the very day of the opening of parliament in "de Ridderzaal" in The Hague. This depicted Colijn's stature: he was the dominant figure in Dutch parliamentary politics and all members of parliament were subject to his authority (see Figure 7.10)

Most political caricaturists harked back to the ancient metaphor of the nation's flagship, captained most capably by the statesman. According to historian Te Velde, this had to do with the political climate of that decade which frequently put the government under a lot of pressure.[43] It was a powerful image that fitted very well to Dutch history with all its famous naval heroes. The power of the image was also evident in its versatility: the wild seas and dangerous rocks and cliffs representing threats the country had to endure. The

---

43   Te Velde (2002) 126-27.

FIGURE 7.11
Captain of the Ship of State in *De Telegraaf*, September 24, 1933.
ARTIST: LOUIS RAEMAEKERS.

rudder and sails of this great ship also played their role: symbolising "good" fundamental concepts that would help steer those ocean highways. It required an able man at the helm to ensure that the great ship was never sunk. Following "Prinsjesdag" on 19 September 1933, caricaturist Louis Raemakers made use of this image. He depicted PM Colijn as a composed captain on the "ship of state," well prepared for the storms to come. The image fitted the call for a powerful statesman capable of guiding The Netherlands through the most turbulent of storms (see Figure 7.11).

Leen Jordaan also depicted Colijn in *De Groene Amsterdammer* as helmsman of a great ship in the middle of a fierce storm. Holding tight to the ship's wheel ("parliamentary democracy") with, in the background, two ships of state, run aground beneath the cliffs: France and Austria had been "sunk" through "politics" and a "cabinet crisis." "Politics" had obvious negative connotations in this cartoon. Both countries had indications of huge instability:

PUBLIC VISUALISATION OF POLITICAL LEADERSHIP IN THE 1930S 117

FIGURE 7.12
'Hold that course!' Here we see PM Colijn depicted as Captain of HMS of State 'Holland', holding fast to the wheel of 'parliamentary democracy' and steering the ship well away from the cliffs of 'politics' and 'cabinet crisis', upon which France and Austria have already floundered in *De Groene Amsterdammer*, October 28, 1933.
ARTIST: LEO JORDAAN.

France was constantly changing from one government to the other, while violent attacks by members of the National Socialist party in Austria caused unrest. This shows that even a progressive paper had faith that Colijn could save the country from ruin (see Figure 7.12).

At the same time, the summons "Hold that course!" above the cartoon can be read as a warning to Colijn. The Dutch HMS of State could only defy all storms if Captain Colijn kept to the course determined by parliamentary democracy.[44] If the prime minister would systematically ignore the parliament, or even shut down his critics, parliamentary democracy was under threat of extinction from within. This cartoon evokes not only the classical image of Colijn as capable helmsman, but made evident the fear that the PM's continued insistence on action could be at the expense of the will of the people.[45]

44 L.J. Jordaan, "Hou koers," *De Groene Amsterdammer*, 28 Oct. 1933.
45 Gijsenbergh (2015) 254-56.

Jordaan's cartoon exposes just how far the "navigation" metaphor could be taken. Progressive supporters of parliamentary democracy were willing to accept strong pilots, on condition that they worked within the framework of democratic representation. Jordaan made this plain more than once, exposing his own less than complete support of the idea of a disciplined democracy.[46]

The Social Democrats were clearer in their aversion to a disciplined democracy and strong leadership. Their complaint was that Colijn – who demanded to be allowed to govern, unhindered – gagged any opposition. This concerned them greatly because the SDAP was invariably in opposition until 1939. Social Democratic cartoonists protested that strong leadership was contradictory to true democracy because a "man of action" refused to listen to critique.[47]

Albert Hahn Jr. criticised Colijn's lack of respect for anyone else's point of view, by portraying him as a man putting up his collar and dashing through a storm of papers full of criticism for his policies as they rain down upon him. The caption shows just how unimpressed this Social Democratic cartoonist was by Colijn's defence that "White Papers" were demagogic: "despicable demagogy [...] but where is it actually relevant?" This caption addressed the government's reaction to criticisms made by (among others) Social Democratic MPs on the government's financial-economic policy. The government had informed parliament that "it could only be a remarkable lack of perception, or indeed a despicable demagogy" that could incite anyone to voice this critique, because the government had after all no say in international financial-economic developments.[48] De Notekraker explained this differently: the use of the harsh term "demagogy" showed that there were apparently no relevant arguments to be made against the critique given by the SDAP. The cartoon literally depicted Colijn running away from his responsibilities, instead of subjecting himself to democratic control and answering the questions of the parliamentary opposition about his cabinet policies. With this sketch, Hahn showed a different view than Salomon's photos and their corresponding captions in *Het Leven*, which showed understanding towards cabinet ministers' frustrations at having to endure critique from the parliament.[49]

Social Democrat George Van Raemdonck went further than Hahn – he threw Colijn in the same pile as other aspirant "strong men" like the leader of the NSB, Mussert, and the foremen of fascist splinter movements. Van Raemdonck accused Colijn of actually awakening fascism. In his cartoon, he has

---

46   Jordaan, "Kamerontbinding" and "Begrootingsdebatten", *De Groene Amsterdammer*, 18 Feb. 1933 and 10 Nov. 1934.

47   Gijsenbergh (2013) 164.

48   *HTK*, 1934-1935, no. 362, sub no. 3.

49   *Het Leven*, 22 Feb. 1936; Bottema (1936) 108-11.

PUBLIC VISUALISATION OF POLITICAL LEADERSHIP IN THE 1930S   119

Colijn nursing an emaciated baby at the breast, wrapped in a swastika. In Van Raemdonck's view, Colijn was no better than the National Socialists and fascists, who also both rushed to provide milk. Van Raemdonck placed PM Colijn in line with persons and groups that the artist himself called extremist or reactionary. On this list he counted NSB leader Mussert, W.M. Westermann (chief of the *Verbond voor Nationaal Herstel* (VNH), B.Ch. de Savornin Lohman (prominent protestant member of the Senate and a great admirer of Colijn), A.R. Zimmerman (the authoritarian Mayor of Rotterdam), anti-Semites, Catholic fascists, and the Lutheran Church.

This caricature shows how political commentators in the 1930s could not avoid "the strong man." All sorts of politicians, from the National Socialist Mussert through to the disciplined democrat Colijn, presented themselves as the decisive leader. This self-representation was reinforced through photographs and political cartoons. The call for decisive leadership was generally repeated, but in progressive circles, protests could be heard against this form of political leadership.

Conclusion: Iconography on Leadership in Dutch Democracy

During the interwar period, the image of Dutch political leaders partly depended on cultural imagery. PM Colijn and other persons in charge could win the confidence of the voting public if they were portrayed in a positive way, but were at risk of losing that same vote of confidence if they were shown in an unfavourable light. Leadership representation mostly appeared in printed newspapers and magazines, given that this media had the largest coverage. Parliamentarian photographers, caricaturists, and editing staff of illustrated journals also influenced the reputation of politics. Although the number of illustrated journals was limited, they brought the political area literally "in the picture." Of course, this did not result in a realistic depiction (mimetic representation) of these "men of state." On the contrary, the illustrated journals tended to place the politicians in a particular light (aesthetic representation). Their compositions, use of metaphors, and their captions rather "framed" the political leaders' demeanours. They attempted to legitimise as well as delegitimise certain types of leadership. This indicates that visual sources support us in analysing the intangible process of representation. Analysis of photographs and political cartoons has shown which ideal images of leadership were presented to the citizens of the Netherlands.

The first idealised image of politics was deliberative leadership, in which cabinet members held courteous, constructive discussion with members of parliament. MPs played an important part in this repertoire of representation because they controlled the government. There were indeed proponents to be found for this type of independent parliament. It was especially the Social Democratic caricaturists who sketched parliament of the 1930s as the central arena of Dutch politics, where the masters, those in charge, should be thoroughly investigated. Previous scholars have too often emphasised that Social Democrats were reluctant to exchange their old revolutionary strategies for parliamentarian tactics. Most Social Democrats in the 1930s embraced a strong parliament, especially in the hope of being heard, despite their position in opposition.

Caricatures in National Socialist and conservative journals instead advocated authoritative leadership. In their view, the "man of action" should pay as little heed as possible to critical members of parliament. The NSB went far in this and postulated that strong leadership was only possible after the abolishment of parliamentary democracy. Conservative cartoonists working for *De Haagsche Post* and *De Telegraph* were somewhat milder. They deemed it possible to combine democracy with strong leadership. Colijn fitted the picture there, as far as they saw, by leading the country as a stern schoolmaster, or a capable skipper. They appreciated the fact that Colijn appeared to hold the reins in the Binnenhof.

These two ideal images of political leadership were often enough combined – for instance in the images in *De Groene Amsterdammer*, in the photos by Erich Salomon, and in the relevant captions in *Het Leven*. It is understandable that Salomon craved debate *and* spirit, given his personal experience of the rise of the NSDAP in his homeland. After seeing the demise of the Weimar Republic, Salomon put the spotlight on the auspicious side of the Dutch parliament that reminded him of the nineteenth century parliament filled with dignified and respectably deliberating gentlemen. At the same time, he realised that his ideal was unrealistic now that the economic crisis had led to complaints about a parliamentary "chat club." Salomon's solution was to have a strong leader who solved problems *within* the framework of the parliamentarian system. This particular feature of Colijn was just what Salomon appreciated, so he was happy to promote Colijn's image of "man of action." The image took off in Holland because it hooked up nicely with both the Dutch tradition of deliberation from the nineteenth century and the desire for momentum in the 1930s.

The various ways Colijn was represented demonstrate the huge diversity in Dutch interpretations of democratic leadership. The PM's style of leadership was both criticised and praised, based on manifold arguments. How the PM was to lead was subject to debate but despite all the differences of opinion on the matter, an important shift became visible in the shape of representative politics throughout the 1930s. A return to the nineteenth century, with parliament populated by eminent gentlemen, was ruled out. Deliberating parliamentarians did not exactly disappear from the stage, but they did now have to tolerate a strong Prime Minister among them. Most Dutch citizens welcomed such developments. It was not seen to be as a hollowing-out of the democratic system, but more as an improvement to it. Exactly how the leader should comport himself remained controversial, but it was undisputed that he now, himself, represented the nation. The photographs and caricatures here researched enhanced his charisma and the acceptance of his power.

Bibliography

Aerts, R., "Besloten openbaarheid. De representatie van het Nederlandse Parlement," in A. Biefang and M. Leenders (eds.), *Erich Salomon & het ideale parlement. Fotograaf in Berlijn en Den Haag, 1928-1940* (Amsterdam, 2014), 137-160.

Aerts, R., *Het aanzien van de politiek. Geschiedenis van een functionele fictie* (Amsterdam, 2009).

Ankersmit, F.R., "Politieke representatie. Betoog over de esthetische staat," in *BMGN – Low Countries Historical Review*, 102, no. 3 (1987), 358-379.

Berg-Schlosser, D., and J. Mitchell (eds.), *Conditions of democracy in Europe, 1919-1939* (Basingstoke, 2000).

Biefang, A., "Het einde van deliberatie. De foto's van Erich Salomon van de Rijksdag 1928-1931," in A. Biefang and M. Leenders (eds.), *Erich Salomon & het ideale parlement. Fotograaf in Berlijn en Den Haag, 1928-1940* (Amsterdam, 2014), 21-88.

Bool, F., "Foto '37," in F. Bool and K. Broos (eds.), *Fotografie in Nederland 1920-1940* (The Hague, 1979), 127-143.

Bottema, T., E. Doeve and A. Hahn (eds.), *Colijn in de caricatuur. Honderd uitgezochte caricaturen met een voorwoord van Dr. Colijn zelf* (Baarn, 1936).

Reunders, H, and M. Kleppe, "Een plaatje bij een praatje of bron van onderzoek? Fotografie verwerft geleidelijk een plek in de historische wetenschap," in *Groniek* 187 (2010), 121-139.

Brandt, B., "Writing Political History after the 'Iconic Turn,'" in W. Steinmetz, I. Gilcher-Holtey, and H-G. Haupt (eds.), *Writing Political History Today*, (Frankfurt am Main, 2013), 351-357.

Burke, P., *Eyewitnessing. The Uses of Images as Historical Evidence* (London, 2001).

Colijn, H., *Wankelen noch weifelen. Rede ter opening van de deputaten-vergadering, gehouden te Utrecht op donderdag 9 maart 1933* (Amsterdam, 1933).

Föllmer, M., "Führung und Demokratie in Europa," in T.B. Müller and A. Tooze (eds.), *Normalität und Fragilität. Demokratie nach dem Ersten Weltkrieg* (Hamburg, 2015), 177-197.

Gerard, E., "Een schadelijke instelling: kritiek op het parlement in België in het interbellum," in *BMGN – Low Countries Historical Review* 120, no. 3 (2005), 497-512.

Gijsenbergh, J., *Democratie en gezag. Extremismebestrijding in Nederland, 1917-1940* (Enschede, 2017).

Gijsenbergh, J., "Contrasting Complaints about Parliamentarism in Western Europe (1918-1939)," in K. Palonen and J.M. Rosales (eds.), *Parliamentarism and Democratic Theory. Historical and contemporary Perspectives* (Berlin, 2015), 117-139.

Gijsenbergh, J., and H. Kaal, "Kritiek op de parlementaire democratie in Nederlandse spotprenten," in A. Biefang and M. Leenders (eds.), *Erich Salomon & het ideale parlement. Fotograaf in Berlijn en Den Haag, 1928-1940* (Amsterdam, 2014), 201-220.

Gijsenbergh, J., "The semantics of 'democracy' in social democratic parties. Netherlands, Germany and Sweden, 1917-1939," in *Archiv für Sozialgeschichte* 53 (2013), 147-173.

Houwink ten Cate, J.H., *De mannen van de daad en Duitsland, 1919-1939. Het Hollandse zakenleven en de vooroorlogse buitenlandpolitiek* (The Hague, 1995).

Kennedy, J.C., "De democratie als bestuurskundig probleem: Vernieuwingsstreven in de Nederlandse politiek sinds 1918," in *Jaarboek Parlementaire Geschiedenis* (2004), 12-23.

Langeveld, H., *Schipper naast God. Hendrikus Colijn, 1869-1944* (Amersfoort, 2004).

Langeveld, H., "De verzuiling doorbroken. Hendrikus Colijn en de liberale en ongebonden pers," in J. Bardoel and H. Wijfjes (eds.), *Journalistieke cultuur in Nederland* (Amsterdam, 2002), 37-49.

Leenders, M., "Op zoek naar het ideale parlement – Erich Salomon in Den Haag 1936-1940," in A. Biefang and M. Leenders (eds.), *Erich Salomon & het ideale parlement. Fotograaf in Berlijn en Den Haag, 1928-1940* (Amsterdam, 2014), 89-122.

Loewenstein, K., "Legislative Control of Political Extremism in European Democracies. Part II," in *Columbia Law Review* 38, no. 5 (1938), 725-774.

Loots, J., *Voor het volk, van het volk. Van districtenstelsel naar evenredige vertegenwoordiging* (Amsterdam, 2004).

Mulder, H., *Een groote laars, een plompe voet. Nederland en de Nazis in spotprent en karikatuur, 1933-1945* (Amsterdam, 1985).

Mulder, H., "De politieke spotprent tussen de beide wereldoorlogen," in C. Blotkamp and M. Boor (eds.), *Kunst en Kunstbedrijf. Nederland 1914-1950* (Haarlem, 1978), 168-208.

Rose, G., *Visual Methodologies. An Introduction to the Interpretation of Visual Materials* (London, 2001).

Salomon, E., "Het onbescheiden oog," in *De Groene Amsterdammer*, 19 June 1937.

Velde, H. te, *Stijlen van leiderschap. Persoon en politiek van Thorbecke tot Den Uyl* (Amsterdam, 2002).

Velde, H. te, "De spiegel van de negentiende eeuw. Partij, representatie en geschiedenis," in *Jaarboek Documentatiecentrum Nederlandse Politieke Partijen* (2001), 19-40.

Velde, H. te, "Van Thorbecke tot Den Uyl. Distantie en nabijheid in de Nederlandse politieke traditie," in D. Pels and H. te Velde (eds.), *Politieke Stijl. Over presentatie en optreden in de politiek* (Amsterdam, 2000), 152-175.

Vries, H. de, and P. Hunter-Salomon (eds.), *Erich Salomon. Porträt einer Epoche* (Frankfurt am Main, 1963).

Walter, A.S., and J.J.M. van Holsteyn, "Pim in prenten. De weergave van Pim Fortuyn in politieke tekeningen," *Jaarboek Documentatiecentrum Nederlandse politieke partijen 2005* (2006), 176-205.

Weringh, K. van, *De Houten Pomp: AR Caricaturistisch weekblad, 1922-1930* (Amsterdam, 1977).

Weringh, K. van, *Getekende wereld, de kijk van F. Behrendt en Opland op het wereldgebeuren, 1961-1975* (Amsterdam, 1976).

Weringh, K. van, *Albert Hahn: tekenen om te ontmaskeren. Biografie van de bekendste Nederlandse tekenaar* (Amsterdam, 1975).

CHAPTER 8

Postwar Popular Politics: Integrating the Voice of the People in Postwar Political History

Harm Kaal and Vincent van de Griend

Introduction

Both inside and outside of academia, a declining trust in politicians and the rise of populism has catalysed a debate about a supposed "crisis of democracy."[1] Political decision-making has increasingly escaped public control, particularly at the level of the European Union. The public sphere spiralled into decline when citizens turned into passive consumers who focused on private instead of public concerns.[2] Moreover, with the laws and mechanisms of the mass media dictating political communication, parliamentary democracy has transformed into a mediacracy or drama democracy. Against this background, populist politicians have emerged on the scene, promising to restore the power of the people.

One should, however, be careful not to integrate populist notions of crisis and of confrontation between political elites and the people into the historical analysis of political representation. We argue that at the heart of the discourse of crisis is a lack of understanding of the multifaceted ways in which politicians and the people have interacted. In this chapter, which is based on a case study of the Netherlands, we first offer a reconceptualisation of the notion of popular politics by mapping the repertoire of communicative practices through which political representatives and the people they represented have interacted in the postwar years. Second, we zoom in on one of these practices: letters people sent to their representatives. The analysis will be aimed at identifying popular perceptions of political representation that were articulated in these letters. Third, we end by offering a way forward for historical research on the interaction between politicians and the people.

The vast scholarship on political representation in parliamentary democracies has been mostly oriented towards the "formal" aspects of political representation treating it as a status that results from particular political procedures and constitutional arrangements with research being dedicated to an investi-

---

1 Rosanvallon (2008); Saward (2010).
2 Habermas (1962).

© HARM KAAL AND VINCENT VAN DE GRIEND, 2019 | DOI:10.1163/9789004291966_009
This is an open access chapter distributed under the terms of the CC-BY-NC 4.0 License.

gation of how representatives take up their role.[3] Recently, however, several scholars have introduced alternative accounts of the notion and history of political representation that allow for a more dynamic approach of the relationship between politicians and the people. One of them is the French historian and political scientist Pierre Rosanvallon. In *La contre-démocratie. La politique à l'âge de la defiance,*[4] he attacks the "myth of the passive citizen" that is omnipresent in accounts of the recent historical trajectory of democracy and political representation. Rosanvallon brings in the notion of "counter-democracy" to show that built into the political system are practices through which citizens hold their representatives to account. He distinguishes between three mechanisms (apart from elections, which he claims are losing significance) through which the people act upon politics: surveillance (through the media, the omnipresence of public opinion, and other forms of oversight and calls for transparency), prevention (e.g. through actions of protest movements), and judgment (e.g. court cases with citizens as jurors, watchdogs, and other forms of investigation). Together they make up a "durable democracy of distrust."

Although Rosanvallon's conceptualisation of counter democracy tends towards a focus on technical and quasi-institutionalised forms of popular participation in the polity, particularly the mechanism of surveillance does offer a new perspective on the interaction between politicians and the people. In postwar democracies, politicians are continuously confronted with, and need to take into account, public opinion – "the essential manifestation of the people as an active and permanent presence"– which is presented to them through, among others, the media, opinion polls, and demonstrations.[5] Surveillance also amounts to holding politicians to account in terms of their behaviour by uncovering scandals and reports on improper conduct. These durable expressions of distrust have forced politicians to offer "transparency" and to show consistency in terms of their public and private behaviour.

Where Rosanvallon has focused on unpacking the notion of democracy, political scientist Michael Saward has presented an alternative approach to political representation that centres on the concept of representative claim-making: the claim to act and speak on behalf of others. He sees representation as a "process that involves the making of claims to be representative."[6] In his analysis of the nature of political representation, Saward contests the claim of Carl Schmitt that representation is to be understood as the "realization of the unity

---

3 The classical study is Pitkin (1967).
4 Rosanvallon (2006), translated as: *Counter-Democracy. Politics in an Age of Distrust*, Rosanvallon (2008).
5 Rosanvallon (2008) 31.
6 Saward (2005) 184.

of an authentic community." Referring to Anderson and Bourdieu, Saward contends that "[c]onstituencies, like communities, have to be 'imagined'" and that politicians are engaged in the "active constitution of constituencies."[7]

Saward makes clear that claim-making is not limited to politicians. His framework allows us to explore how representation "works," also beyond the sphere of parliament, at various levels in- and outside of what is traditionally regarded to be the "political sphere."[8] The British historian Jon Lawrence in turn has convincingly argued that the formation of political identities and constituencies – including the making of representative claims as Saward would call it – was not a top-down process. Politicians were faced with "pre-existing popular beliefs and aspirations" they needed to tap into. This brings Lawrence to a discussion of the reception of the language of politics and the need to study

> The interaction between the worlds of 'formal' and informal politics, conscious that the relationship between the two is never unmediated, and that our analysis must therefore always be sensitive to the tensions and ambiguities in the relationship between 'leaders' and 'led'.[9]

Historians, however, have found it hard to find ways to explore politics from below. In a recent overview of the state of the art in political history the authors argue that "governments, monarchs, parties, or parliaments [...] still get the bulk of the attention."[10] Lawrence himself acknowledges that a lack of sources leaves "much [...] to inference – to the critical and interpretative skills of the historian."[11] As a result, popular perceptions of the political often remain to be a black box.

Practices of Popular Politics

British historians often use the term "popular politics" to refer to political communication from below, by ordinary people. Although the concept often lacks a clear definition, it is mostly used as the opposite of formal, organised (party) politics. In historiography on nineteenth century British politics, popular politics refers to the rough and tumble of uncontrolled, spontaneous, and very

---

7   See: Kaal (2017).
8   Saward (2006) 302.
9   Lawrence (1998) 61; see also Black (2001).
10 Steinmetz (2013) 20.
11 Lawrence (1998) 67.

visible popular involvement in politics (and the degree to which this gradually made way for a more disciplined political culture).[12] Furthermore, the concept is used in studies that reflect on postwar popular political action in the form of demonstrations and manifestations initiated by social movements in the 1960s and 1970s.[13] The tendency to narrate postwar popular involvement in politics in terms of active citizenship and social movements has, however, obscured our view on other forms of popular politics that fall beyond this rather limited realm of civic engagement. Recent work by Rosanvallon, Saward, and others has shown that popular involvement in the political as a communicative space was much broader. Opening up the concept of popular politics to include the broad range of communicative practices through which the interaction between citizens and their representatives took shape might help us to overcome the tendency among political historians to still focus their studies on the history of "governments, monarchs, parties, or parliaments."[14] The identification of these practices enables us to subsequently explore popular perceptions of political representation and of "the political" more in general: what did citizens expect from their representatives, what did they conceive as "good politics" at any given time? This in turn helps us to identify shifts in the norms, conventions, expectations, attitudes, and emotions that guided their interaction with politicians in the postwar years.

"Popular politics" is also a characterisation of the political culture of a particular era. British historians, for instance, have long debated the question when in the nineteenth century popular politics made way for "party politics", that is, for a more controlled, organised, and disciplined culture of popular political engagement. "Popular politics" also captures much of the political culture that developed from the late 1950s onwards. In the 1950s, in Western democracies like Britain and the Netherlands, discussions arose about a growing gap between the political (party) elites and "the people." Blame was put on the development of parties into professional organisations that had become alienated from the public at large. The traditional election meeting – with politicians delivering a speech in front of a loyal crowd of electors – was in decline: fewer people showed up and fewer meetings were held.[15] The distance that had marked the political culture of the early postwar years was now identified as a problem. Restraint, trust in the political system, and, given the recent experiences of political extremism, distrust of forms of interaction and repre-

---

12   Vernon (1993); Lawrence (2006) as well as earlier work by Lawrence.
13   Davis (2008); Eley (2002).
14   Steinmetz (2013) 20.
15   Lawrence (2009) 154-55.

sentation that deviated from the formal institutions and procedures of parliamentary politics had been the norm and had made politics in the words of Martin Conway "neat, controlled and ever so slightly boring."[16]

The call to reinvigorate the relationship between politicians and the people was prompted by broader shifts in society. From the late 1950s onwards, the notion of "the people" was reconceptualised. A compartmentalisation of the people in terms of distinct social blocs gradually, but steadily, lost force. In what Bernard Manin has characterised as the era of party democracy – roughly between the late nineteenth century and the 1960s – representatives were exponents of the various social groups in society they represent: there was "sociological similarity" between them and the people they represented. In the Netherlands, sociologists used the term "pillarisation" as a metaphor for the coexistence of several socio-religious communities (pillars) that were united around a shared class or religious identity. When the ties between class, religion, and political identity formation loosened (de-pillarisation), the concept of the people became somewhat diffuse and intangible. This could potentially harm the stability of parliamentary democracy. After all, the stability and legitimacy of a representative system depends on the ability of politicians to translate the abstract notion of the people into a meaningful category to which both politicians and the people they aimed to represent could relate, a category with which voters could identify.

Rosanvallon has argued that with the demise of party democracy, representatives were no longer expected to "make present" the various groups in society, but to "be present." Being present means that representatives were expected to present themselves as in sync with the everyday experiences of citizens, with their "trials and tribulations."[17] And since people identified themselves no longer primarily along lines of class or religion, but along lines of shared experiences of social, economic, material, cultural, and historical conditions, representatives who showed empathy for one citizen, were simultaneously tapping into a constituency of citizens with shared conditions. The popular politics of the late 1950s and beyond put a bonus on those politicians who were approachable, who were willing to engage with citizens and to open themselves up from input of the people. In an attempt to *be present*, politicians across Western Europe started to look for new ways to interact with the people they aimed to represent. In this contribution, we first briefly map four of these practices of interaction and discuss how they can help us to explore popular perceptions of political representation. Subsequently, the remainder of this

---

16   Conway (2002) 59-60.

17   Rosanvallon (2011) 188.

POSTWAR POPULAR POLITICS

chapter will be dedicated to one of these practices: the letters people sent to politicians.

Four Practices of Interaction between Politicians and the People

First, personal letters, and more recently emails, addressed to politicians are the communicative practice that comes closest to giving direct access to popular views.[18] Politicians' personal archives bear witness to the fact that many people used it to address their representatives. Compared to demonstrations or manifestations, letter writing was a fairly easy and "safe" way to address politicians but also a significant one: politicians used letters to gauge public opinion and many made sure to send a reply.[19] Although letters do not give direct access to "the mind of the people," recent research within the field of life writing has shown their importance in constructing identities-through-dialogue;[20] they thus give us access to how "ordinary citizens" expressed their political identity in interaction with their representatives. Studying this form of popular politics therefore provides us crucial insights in the nature of popular conceptions of political selfhood, citizens' expectations of politicians, and in what people perceived as "political."[21]

Newspapers also offered a platform for the voice of the people. They published letters-to-the-editor and stimulated interaction between politicians and the people. In the run-up to general elections, Dutch newspapers, for instance, invited readers to send in questions for party leaders by mail or phone and published the politician's response a couple of days later.[22] This engagement of the printed press has been characterised as a transition from a partisan logic – in which the media acted as a rather uncritical platform for political communication – towards a public logic in the 1960s, when journalists adopted a far more critical approach.[23] Their increased orientation on the voice of the people might be explained by the fact that also the newspapers were looking for new ways to engage with their public. When the close ties between particular news media and socio-political communities were severed in the 1960s, journalists were less sure about what kind of public they were representing. One way to solve this issue was reader research, another way was to open up

---

18   Hauser (1999); Fenske (2013); Beyen (2014); Zimmermann (2008).
19   Sussmann (1963).
20   Eakin (1999).
21   Kaal (2018).
22   "Speciaal voor u," *Het Vrije Volk*, several editions in 1971.
23   Brants (2006).

newspaper columns to the voice of the people. That said, we still know very little about the role the printed press played in offering citizens a platform for the articulation of popular views on politics.

Second, television offered an important platform for the articulation of popular views on politics and for interaction between politicians and the people. Thanks to television, the popular politics of the late 1950s and beyond was marked by a similar sense of risk and suspense as the confrontations with the general public in the late 19th century platform meetings. In Britain in the 1959 general election campaign, politicians were confronted with a very hostile studio audience in *The Last Debate*.[24] In a similar setting, Dutch politicians answered questions from the audience in a televised debate in the 1967 campaign. In both cases, these confrontations were one-off events, at least for a long time to come.[25] In slightly adapted fashion, the confrontational format however did continue to pop up in the 1960s and 1970s. On the radio, politicians answered questions phoned-in by listeners, and in discussion programmes they discussed key issues with panels that included members of the general public. Moreover, from the 1950s onwards, politicians were also confronted with the opinion of the general public in news broadcasts. Voxpops – journalists interviewing people on radio or TV – brought "ordinary" citizens into the public limelight. From the mid-1950s onwards, voxpops were used to represent the diversity of popular opinion and thus offered opportunities for identification to the audience watching and listening at home. When they were first introduced, voxpops revealed a new appreciation of popular opinion: apparently, the opinion of members of the general public was now to be taken seriously, rather than ignored and dismissed as uninformed.

Third, opinion polls, introduced in much of Western Europe after the Second World War, resulted in a reconceptualisation of the notion of public opinion. Opinion polls *represent* popular opinion on political representation in that advanced scientific tools and techniques are used to construct something that could not be imagined before: "the" public opinion on particular issues.[26] Its constructed nature also speaks from the fact that polling agencies formulate questions, on their own or commissioned by customers like newspapers and news networks or political parties, and deliver a particular interpretation of the results. The deconstruction of poll surveys therefore reveals what polling agencies, or their customers deemed politically relevant, but also shows how people could imagine themselves as political subjects, i.e. as members of

---

24   Lawrence (2009) 168-69.
25   Kaal (2014).
26   Igo (2007).

POSTWAR POPULAR POLITICS

a group of people who held particular views on politics. In the words of Sarah Igo, opinion polls provided us as citizens with "knowledge about ourselves."[27] It enabled people to identify themselves as members of a majority or minority, as members of particular constituencies, marked by shared demands, beliefs, and social, economic, cultural, and material conditions. Simultaneously, opinion polls and other forms of sociological research based on polls and survey data brought with it a new conceptualisation of the people as, to quote Sarah Igo once more, "anonymous, atomized individuals holding discrete views." This taken into account, polls still also provide us with unique data on popular opinion on political representation: on the conduct, actions and personality of politicians. Governments and political parties indeed treated opinion polls as a very welcome instrument to get access to the hearts and minds of the people, and to grasp the undercurrents of popular political views and sentiments.[28] Their analysis is therefore a vital element of our aim to map the changing nature of popular perceptions of political representation.

Fourth and finally, popular culture, which pluralised and expanded massively throughout the post-war period, offered a new platform for interaction between politicians and the people. Media like popular magazines and TV shows of course do not merely reflect popular sentiments: they both tapped into them and informed popular views on political representation. They handed their readers and viewers a frame through which they could narrate and imagine political reality and their place within it.[29] By paying attention to popular culture we are, according to Lawrence Black, putting "politics in its wider social setting."[30] John Street in turn has argued that we should approach the interaction between politics and a massified and pluralised popular culture as "a legitimate part of the complex ways in which political representation functions in modern democracies".[31] Political representation in this case refers to the way in which claims to power and to act and speak on behalf of others are articulated (and contested) in the public sphere. In the period under investigation, the practices and discourses of popular culture became a significant part of the repertoire through which these representative claims were articulated. Popular culture thus emerges as a communicative space in which politicians are making representative claims and in which political identities are constructed and articulated. Elements of communication that are typically associated with popular culture – looks, emotions, dress, body language, a fo-

---

27   Ibid. 2.
28   Van Dixhoorn (2006) 23.
29   Strinati (1992); Van Zoonen (2005); Fielding (2014).
30   Black (2010) 3.
31   Street (2004) 436.

cus on the private self – therefore need to be taken seriously as crucial elements of *political* communication as well.[32]

Through these four practices – but not limited to these practices – both politicians and the people have tried to articulate what constituted political representation. Taken together, they offer an angle to explore popular ideas of political representation and to map their historical development in the postwar years.

Epistolary Interaction

Epistolary interaction formed an important element of the repertoire of interaction between politicians and the people. In the 1960s, Dutch research on popular feelings of political efficacy, i.e. the "feeling that individual political action does have, or can have, an impact upon the political process,"[33] showed that 52 per cent of the population perceived writing a letter to a politician as an effective means towards solving a particular issue. Respondents had been asked to judge the effectiveness of a number of individual and collective actions, like "take matters into your own hands" (88 per cent), "joining an association" (78 per cent), "signing a petition" (59 per cent), or "writing a letter-to-the-editor" (45 per cent).[34] Letters addressed to politicians are part of a broader family of written popular political communication that also includes petitions and other forms of popular appeals addressed to single politicians, office holders, or institutions such as Parliament. Letters, however, stand out because of their informal nature compared to petitions and appeals which are handled according to formal procedures.[35] One can even argue that personal letters addressed to politicians are a communicative practice that comes closest to giving direct access to popular views on politics. Letters provide us with sources *from* ordinary people, rather than the abundance of sources *about* them that are most often used in historical research.[36]

Letter writing is in itself a democratic act by citizens who are practicing their right and freedom to address politicians and to make themselves present beyond the ballot box.[37] In a sense, by writing a letter, by directly addressing a representative of the people, citizens are bridging the gap between politicians

---

32 Ibid. 444.
33 Hoogerwerf refers to Angus (1954) in Hoogerwerf (1967) 298.
34 Hoogerwerf (1967) 299.
35 Fenske (2013) 21.
36 Van Ginderachter (2007) 70.
37 Fenske (2013) 10.

and the people that is part of the system of political representation. By reading and processing these letters, politicians are not representing the will of the people, but confronted with it. This has, however, often been ignored in historical research that merely treats these letters as exponents of clientelism. Letters are indeed part of a long tradition of interaction between rulers and ruled, going back to clientelistic exchanges in the Middle Ages and Early Modern Era. Although clientelism was also part of epistolary interaction in the postwar years, citizens also used letters to comment and reflect on the political issues of the day and on the behaviour of politicians. Moreover, as Marnix Beyen has shown, by putting pen to paper, members of the general public contributed to the politicisation of particular issues: they triggered their representatives to discuss popular concerns in Parliament.[38] These letters therefore provide us with an angle to explore how the lifeworld of individual citizens became connected to the world of politics, how citizens perceived politics, how they made sense of political issues (their "political knowledge"), and the standards they used to evaluate the behaviour of their representatives.

It was not one-way traffic. Politicians, as research for Germany and the Netherlands has shown, received an increasing number of letters from members of the general public in the postwar years and took these letters very seriously.[39] They of course received mail from lunatics who ventilated conspiracy theories, but most of the letters made sense.[40] The Dutch social democrats developed an administrative procedure that enabled them to distribute letters to the appropriate expert within the party and made sure to send a reply. The need to treat letters seriously and to make sure that communication between citizens and government went smoothly also manifested itself in repeated discussions throughout the 1960s about the speed with which citizens should receive an answer to letters sent to municipal or national authorities and the use of polite forms of address in government correspondence with citizens.[41]

Although people at party offices were kept busy administering and answering incoming and outgoing mail (and phone calls), much of this correspondence has not survived history. To the dismay of the head of the Dutch Public Record Office, in the early 1990s the archive containing letters citizens had sent to their Prime Minister after 1945 was destroyed.[42] Luckily, some politicians

---

38   Beyen (2014) 30.
39   Fenske (2013) 20; Van de Griend (2016).
40   The liberal party for instance kept a separate register of incoming letters from lunatics ('gekken'). National Archives of the Netherlands (NA), Archive of the VVD (2.19.022), inv. nr. 35.
41   See for instance: "De Jong wil dat brieven sneller worden beantwoord," in *Trouw*, 7 March 1970.
42   NA, Archive of the Cabinet of the Prime Minister (2.03.01) 46.

and most political parties have left an archive behind that contains correspondence from and with citizens.

To illustrate how an analysis of letters addressed to politicians helps us to identify popular perceptions of political representation, we introduce a case study of letters citizens sent to the Dutch Labour Party, *Partij van de Arbeid* (PvdA), between 1966 and 1971. In the 1960s, against the background of a "party democracy" in decline, a sense of crisis captured the social democrats.[43] Party leaders questioned if the socio-economic agenda of social democracy sufficiently appealed to a younger generation. Moreover, after disappointing elections in 1966, young party members voiced their dissatisfaction with the course of events within the PvdA. In order to win back popular support, this group, presenting itself under the name of *Nieuw Links* 'New Left', tried to achieve a democratisation, radicalisation, and rejuvenation of the party.[44] This catalysed fierce debates within the party. Things settled down when New Left advocate André van der Louw was elected party chairman in 1971.

Historians have hitherto mainly approached these events from the perspective of the party elite, focusing on the clash between the "party establishment" and the newcomers of the New Left.[45] The clash, however, also triggered a response by "ordinary" party members. Here we present an analysis of the letters people sent to the chairman of the PvdA Sjeng Tans (1966-1969) and Anne Vondeling (1969-1971). Our research is based on an analysis of a corpus of some two hundred letters. The vast majority of these letters was written by men, only one out of ten by a female letter writer. Moreover, more than half of these letters came from party members. Our goal is three-fold. First of all, we aim to establish how "ordinary people" experienced and responded to the developments within the party. Historians have argued that the PvdA ignored signs that many people who sympathised with the PvdA felt alienated by the impact the New Left had on "their" party.[46] Second, we will use this corpus to establish more in general why people took up their pens, what they expected from the politicians they addressed, and how they conceived of themselves as political subjects. Finally, we will also address how the party responded to the input and questions they received by mail.

The majority of the letters sent to party chairmen Tans and Vondeling can be characterised as "comments." In their letters to the party, citizens commented on current events. Michaela Fenske has defined this as a form of

---

43   Kennedy (1995) 196.
44   Van Praag (1991) 41.
45   See Kennedy (1995).
46   Van Praag (1991) 75-79; Kennedy (1995) 197.

POSTWAR POPULAR POLITICS

'confrontation' or 'dispute' *Auseinandersetzung*, between citizens and their representatives.[47] This suggests that these citizens were informed, that they had access to channels of political information, and were therefore able to hold their representatives to account. In the 1960s, citizens were fed with information by an increasingly pluralistic mass media landscape that, as we have argued before, was characterised by a "public logic": the mass media acted as critical watchdogs of the political elite.[48] The letters provide an indication of the role the mass media played in shaping popular perceptions of politics.[49] "Nothing works as clarifying as this little 'window' called television," one woman wrote. "It is as if it delivers an X-ray of people, thereby providing a lot of insights in the human character, and boy, what little of importance is left."[50] Journalist and prominent social democrat Laurens ten Cate argued that the mass media contributed to turning citizens into an informed and critical audience that was no longer easily fooled.[51] The letters indeed show that citizens did not hesitate to confront politicians with inconsistencies. Although politicians publicly proclaimed openness, transparency, and a democratic spirit, to some citizens this came across as a hollow slogan. "I would like to bring something to your attention, that, despite all openness, is tenaciously concealed," one citizen for example wrote regarding the national immigration policy.[52] By pointing out such issues, people not merely responded to current events, but initiated the politicisation of particular themes.

Many comments concerned the impact of the New Left on the PvdA. The comments reflect the divide within the party between the older generation of social democrats and a younger generation that aimed to steer the party to the left. One group of letter writers expressed their "amazement," "agitation," and "confusion" with regard to the agenda of the New Left. Such criticism mainly concerned the New Left's sympathy for extra-parliamentary actions and the case it was making for the recognition of the communist German Democratic Republic. Many letter writers levelled their criticism against New Left frontman André van der Louw, characterising him as a "wolf in sheep's clothing"

---

47   Fenske (2013) 85.

48   Brants (2009) 90.

49   For example: International Institute of Social History (IISH), PvdA Archive, inv.nr. 376B, letter from J.P., 2 Feb. 1971; inv.nr. 487A, letter from J.B., 6 Feb. 1967; inv.nr. 487B, letter from Mrs. de G., 25 Jan. 1967.

50   IISH, PvdA Archive, inv.nr. 373A, letter from family N., 18 March 1969: "niets werkt zo verhelderend als het venstertje wat T.V. heet. De mensen die ervoor komen, staan als het ware in een röntgenfoto, je leert daardoor enorm veel mensenkennis opdoen en o wat blijft er weinig reëels van over" [*sic*].

51   Ten Cate (1967) 7.

52   IISH, PvdA Archive, inv.nr. 367A, letter from P. van S., 18 Nov. 1966.

and a carnivalesque figure who "killed" democracy and made politics "impossible."[53] Others were also critical of the role played by the left-wing broadcasting organization VARA. Thanks to the VARA, the clash between the New Left and the party establishment, which came to a climax at a party conference, was played out in front of a TV audience.[54] Such criticism mainly came from letter writers of an older generation, who had experienced national socialism and occupation. They championed a definition of politics as a serious business that was safe only in the hands of competent politicians, elected by the people, who discussed politics in parliament. Moreover, they perceived extra-parliamentary political action as a threat to the stability of the political system and often compared it with the political extremism of the interwar years. Finally, they expected politicians to have a sense of duty, to show restraint and be dedicated to reconstructing the country in the postwar years. Their hero was former party leader Willem Drees, prime minister between 1948 and 1958, who was also very critical of the role of the New Left within the party.[55] The New Left posed a threat to his legacy and should therefore be contained as soon as possible.[56]

The PvdA also received letters from citizens of a younger generation who supported the cause of the New Left. They, in turn, complained about an older generation of party members who were standing in the way of the necessary rejuvenation the New Left was bringing to the party.[57] One of these letter writers stated that the older generation "should accept, that their time has come, they have to make way for others. [...] Their old-fashioned ideas stand in the way of the progression of the party. That neither benefits us youngsters, nor the party."[58] Seen from this perspective, the provocative, extra-parliamentary activities of the New Left offered an alternative to the establishment clogged-up channels of politics that were controlled by the establishment.[59]

Although these comments reveal a sense of political engagement among ordinary citizens, many citizens also addressed politicians with personal requests. Most of these requests came from people who belonged to the more

---

53 IISH, PvdA Archive, inv.nr. 373A, letters from H.S., 30 March 1969; unknown, 9 March 1969; J.V., 27 March 1969.

54 IISH, PvdA Archive, inv.nr. 366D, letter from E. de J., 23 March 1966.

55 Gaemers (2007) 73; Aerts (2003) 20.

56 IISH, PvdA Archive, inv.nr. 373A, letter from A. van L., 12 March 1969.

57 IISH, PvdA Archive, inv.nr. 374A, letter from H.L. jr., 16 Feb. 1970.

58 IISH, PvdA Archive, inv.nr. 367B, letter from E.A., 23 Feb.1967: "[z]e moeten weten, dat voor hen de tijd gekomen is en dat ze plaats moeten maken voor anderen. [...] met hun ouderwetse ideeën remmen ze vooruitgang in de partij. Daar zijn wij niet bij gebaat en noch minder de partij"[sic].

59 De Jong (2014) 173-74.

POSTWAR POPULAR POLITICS

vulnerable groups in society such as the elderly, disabled persons, and unemployed people. The *Partij van de Arbeid* was known to defend their interests and the party had indeed delivered an important contribution to the construction of the postwar welfare state with social services that were provided by the General Pensions Act (AOW, 1956), the Social Security Act (ABW, 1965), and the Disability Insurance Act (WAO, 1966).[60] Against this background, citizens directed their letters at the PvdA to show the shortcomings of the existing package of social services.[61]

By turning to politicians, these letter writers bridged the distance between their peripheral social position and the centre of political decision making.[62] Doing so, they were engaging in a long-established practice of communication between the elite and the people that can be characterised as a clientelistic exchange. Citizens offered party membership and their support at the ballot box and now expected something in return. A schoolteacher who had recently lost her job and blamed this on the local branch of the *Partij van de Arbeid* threatened to "turn my back on the Partij van de Arbeid" and switch sides to the party that was willing to give back her job.[63] Citizens also tried to make their case stronger by claiming to defend the interests of a particular group of people, such as the elderly, the disabled, or the unemployed. They linked their case to the PvdA by reminding the party of the fact that it claimed to defend the interest of vulnerable groups in society.[64]

How did politicians respond to such interventions? As the American sociologist Leila Sussmann has pointed out in her study of the letters the American president Franklin D. Roosevelt received, understanding how politicians reacted to letters from ordinary citizens starts with an exploration of how the receiver valued the incoming mail.[65] Upon arrival in the mailbox of the headquarters of the *Partij van de Arbeid* in Amsterdam, the letters went through a thorough administrative procedure. A special staff opened the letters, read them and made sure to forward them to the appropriate person within the party. To this end, a note was attached to each letter that contained its administrative number, date of arrival, and the coded abbreviation of the office or official responsible for answering the letter.[66] In most cases, a copy of the answer was attached to the incoming letter and subsequently filed. The fact that

---

60   Schuyt (2013) 13.
61   IISH, PvdA Archive, inv.nr. 366D, letter from G.S., 8 Oct. 1965.
62   Fenske (2013) 71; Van Daalen (1987) 24.
63   IISH, PvdA Archive, inv.nr. 367E, letter from A.S., 30 Sept. 1969.
64   Den Uyl (1978) 126; IISH, PvdA Archive, inv.nr. 365E, letter from A.D., 9 Sept. 1965.
65   Sussmann (1956) 10.
66   IISH, PvdA Archive, inv.nr. 487C, letter to G.N., 21 March 1967.

the *Partij van de Arbeid* valued the mail they received also speaks from the nature of the answer people received to their letter. People hardly ever received a generic response, but a unique, personalised letter.

What effect did these letters have? Michaela Fenske has argued that these letters have an interruptive potential: the letters indeed prompted politicians to reflect on the impact of politics – in terms of policy making, laws, rules, and procedures – on the lives of ordinary citizens and on their role, as representatives of the people, in defending the interests of the people.[67] On several occasions, specific requests resulted in political action on part of the politician: party chairman and MP Tans for instance addressed questions to the Minister for Education after receiving a complaint by mail about the position of teachers working on a temporary contract.[68] Impressed by a letter he had received from a lonely, disabled woman, Vondeling asked fellow party member and tv-journalist Marcel van Dam to pay attention to the issue of social isolation in his television programme THE OMBUDSMAN '*De Ombudsman*'.[69] This, of course, did not mean that politicians were willing to satisfy all the requests they received. They took requests seriously, but they did not hesitate to explain to citizens that their inquiries had made clear that nothing could be done, or that a request was unfounded or unreasonable.[70] As far as the letters about the rise of the New Left were concerned, Tans and Vondeling in general tried to calm things down. People, mainly of an older generation, who were worried about the impact of the New Left, were told that the party needed to "stay in sync with the intellectual, younger generation." Extra-parliamentary activities did not threaten parliamentary democracy, they argued, but should be embraced as tools to counter political indifference and ignorance among the youth.[71] Finally, in general the letters addressed to the PvdA show that politicians and the people engaged in a meaningful form of interaction through and exchange of ideas and opinions, expectations, and justifications.

---

67   Fenske (2013) 21.

68   Aanhangsel Handelingen II 1965/1966, nr. 385; IISH, PvdA Archive, inv.nr. 366B, letter from A.P. Brandes, 15 March 1966; see also: IISH, PvdA Archive, inv.nr. 367B, letter to Ph.J. van der M., 23 Aug. 1967.

69   IISH, PvdA Archive, inv.nr. 375A, letter to M.P. van Dam, 15 Sept. 1970.

70   See for instance IISH, PvdA Archive, inv.nr. 365A.J. S.-S., 24 June 1965; Van de Griend (2017).

71   IISH, PvdA Archive, inv.nr. 374C, letter to M. van V., 2 July 1970; IISH, PvdA Archive, inv.nr. 374B, letter to A. K.-K., 27 March 1970.

Popular Politics: An Agenda for Future Research

The letters people sent to politicians are only one element in a far broader repertoire of popular political engagement that we have aimed to outline in this chapter. How might historians go about exploring this repertoire? How can we integrate the practices of popular politics in our understanding of post-war political history? The letters provide an excellent angle to respond to Jon Lawrence's call to study the interaction between the formal and informal world of politics. We, however, need to be aware of the fact that we are dealing with a rather unmediated practice of interaction. Letters are the odd one out in a broader repertoire of highly mediated practices of popular politics. Studying popular politics therefore requires historians to also study the nature of this mediatisation.

Among media and communication scientists, studying the articulation of popular views on politics through the mass media has developed into a very prominent area of research.[72] These scholars, however, do not offer a historical contextualisation of their research results, have mainly focused on the opportunities for popular agency in the Internet age, and tend to assume that "the public as a potentially empowered, active and participating force" is the hallmark of recent years.[73] The few studies that offer a historical perspective on the interaction between politics and the mass media in the postwar years often treat citizens as the passive consumers of information presented to them through the media, as the audience of a mass-mediatised performance of politics.[74] It is up to historians to integrate "the voice of the people" in research on the interaction between politics and the media.

One way to do so is by, first, deconstructing the communicative practices through which citizens voiced their political opinion in newspapers, on radio, and on television. This requires historians to pay attention to the different formats and modes of communication through which the voice of the people was mediated, such as letters-to-the-editor and street interviews. The feasibility of such research is enhanced by the availability of digital newspaper databases and repositories of radio and television broadcasts.[75] The second step involves an analysis of the content of the opinions voiced by ordinary citizens through these channels. Given the availability of digital data, historians should consider using tools and techniques of digital humanities in order to carry out

---

72   Liesbet van Zoonen (2005); Bakker (2013); Brants (2011) 126-45.
73   Brants (2017) 403.
74   Manin (1997); Habermas (1962).
75   For the Dutch case, historians can use the Delpher newspaper database <http://www.delpher.nl> and the Clariah Media Suite: <http://mediasuite.clariah.nl/>.

a longitudinal content analysis of the voice of the people. Third, such an approach should also include a discussion of how mass media actors (journalists and broadcasters) have reflected on their role in creating communicative practices through which the voice of the people was articulated: what were their motivations to do so? Fourth and finally, the analysis stretches out to the reception of "the voice of the people" by politicians. How did they process popular articulations of political representation? To what extent were politicians judged based on their ability to interact with ordinary citizens? What impact did the communicative practices of popular engagement have on styles of political leadership? Taken together, the answers to these questions might help us to truly incorporate "ordinary citizens" and their shifting perceptions and expectations of "politics" and the people who represented them politically in our understanding of postwar political history.

Bibliography

Aerts, R., "Emotie in de politiek: over politieke stijlen in Nederland sinds 1848," in *Jaarboek Parlementaire Geschiedenis* (Amsterdam, 2003), 12-25.

Bakker, T., *Citizens as political participants. The myth of the active online audience?* (Amsterdam, 2013).

Beyen, M., "Clientelism and politicization. Direct interactions between deputies and "ordinary citizens" in France, ca. 1890 – ca. 1940," in *Temp* 8 (2014), 17-32.

Black, L., *Redefining British Politics. Culture, Consumerism and Participation, 1954-70* (Basingstoke, 2010).

Black, L., "Popular politics in Modern British History," in *The Journal of British Studies* 40, no. 3 (2001), 431-445.

Brants, K., and P. van Praag, "Beyond Media Logic," in *Journalism Studies* 18, no. 4 (2017), 395-408.

Brants, K., and K. Voltmer, *Political Communication in Postmodern Democracy: Challenging the Primacy of Politics* (Basingstoke, 2011).

Brants, K., "Opgejaagd door Ceberus. De moeizame mediatisering van de politieke communicatie," in J. Bardoel, C. Vos, F. van Vree, and H. Wijfjes (eds.), *Journalistieke cultuur in Nederland* (Amsterdam, 2009), 85-100.

Brants, K., and P. van Praag, "Signs of Media Logic: Half a Century of Political Communications in the Netherlands," in *Javnost/The Public* 13, no. 1 (2006), 25-40.

Campbell, A., G. Gurin, and W.E. Miller, *The Voter Decides* (New York, 1954).

Cate, L. ten, "Tussen twee congressen: van de politiek naar de mensen," in *Opinie: veertiendaags orgaan van de Partij van de Arbeid* 22, no. 3 (1967), 6-7.

Conway, M., "Democracy in Postwar Western Europe: The Triumph of a Political Model," in *European History Quarterly* 32 no. 1 (2002), 59-84.

Daalen, R. van, *Klaagbrieven en gemeentelijk ingrijpen Amsterdam, 1865-1920* (Amsterdam, 1987).

Davis, B., "What's Left? Popular Political Participation in Postwar Europe," in *The American Historical Review* 113, no. 2 (2008), 363-390.

Dixhoorn, A. van, *De stem des volks. Publieke opinie, opinieonderzoek en democratie* (Den Haag, 2006).

Eakin, P.J., *How Our Lives Become Stories: Making Selves* (Ithaca, 1999).

Eley, G., *Forging Democracy. The History of the Left in Europe, 1850-2000* (Oxford, 2002).

Fenske, M., *Demokratie erschreiben. Bürgerbriefe und Petitionen als Medien politischer Kultur 1950-1974* (Frankfurt am Main, 2013).

Fielding, S., *A State of Play. British Politics on Screen, Stage and Page, from Anthony Trollope to* The Tick of It (London, 2014).

Ginderachter, M. van, "'If your Majesty would only send me a little money to help buy an elephant': Letters to the Belgian Royal Family (1880-1940)," in M. Lyons (ed.), *Ordinary Writings, Personal Narratives. Writing Practices in the 19th and early 20th-century Europe* (Bern, 2007), 69-83.

Gaemers, J., "Willem Drees privé verklaard," in H. Renders and G. Voerman (eds.), *Privé in de Politieke Biografie* (Amsterdam, 2007), 67-82.

Griend, V. van de, "Burgerpost met pantoffels voor PvdA-voorzitter Ko Suurhoff, maart 1961," in *Jaarboek Parlementaire Geschiedenis* (Amsterdam, 2017), 97-100.

Griend, V. van de, "De pen van het volk. Welke rol vervulde de burgerbrief in het contact tussen de PvdA en haar kiezers tussen 1966 en 1971?," (Master's thesis, Radboud University Nijmegen, 2016).

Habermas, J., *Strukturwandel der Öffentlichkeit. Untersuchungen zu einer Kategorie der bürgerlichen Gesellschaft* (Neuwied, 1962).

Hauser, G.A., *Vernacular Voices: The Rhetoric of Publics and Public Spheres* (Columbia, 1999)

Hoogerwerf, A., "De Nederlandse staatsburger: toeschouwer of medespeler? Partijactiviteit en opvattingen over politieke participatie," in *Sociologische Gids* 14, no. 5 (1967), 293-314.

Hunt, L., *Politics, Culture and Class in the French Revolution* (Berkeley, 1984).

Igo, S.E., *The Averaged American. Surveys, Citizens, and the Making of a Mass Public* (Cambridge, Eng., 2007).

Jong, W. de, *Van wie is de burger? Omstreden democratie in Nederland 1945-1989* (Nijmegen, 2014).

Kaal, H., "De cultuur van het televisiedebat. Veranderende percepties van de relatie tussen media en politiek, 1960-heden," in *Tijdschrift voor Geschiedenis* 127, no. 1 (2014), 293-316.

Kaal, H., "Reconstructing Post-War Political Communities. Class, Religion and Political Identity Formation in the Netherlands, 1945-68," in H. Kaal and S. Couperus (eds.), *(Re)Constructing Communities in Europe, 1918-1968. Senses of Belonging Below, Beyond and Within the Nation-State* (London and New York, 2017), 217-237.

Kaal, H., "The voice of the people. Communicative practices of popular political engagement in the Netherlands, 1950s-1960s," in *Archiv für Sozialgeschichte* 58 (2018), 183-200.

Kennedy, J.C., *Nieuw Babylon in aanbouw. Nederland in de jaren zestig* (Amsterdam, 1995).

Lawrence, J., *Electing our Masters: The Hustings in British Politics from Hogarth to Blair* (Oxford, 2009).

Lawrence, J., "The Transformation of British Public Politics after the First World War," in *Past&Present* 190 (2006), 185-216.

Lawrence, J., *Speaking for the People: Party, Language and Popular Politics in England, 1867-1914.* (Cambridge, Eng., 1998).

Manin, B., *The principles of representative government* (Cambridge, Eng., 1997).

Pitkin, H., *The Concept of Representation* (Berkeley, 1967).

Praag, P., van, *Strategie en illusie. Elf jaar intern debat in de PvdA (1966-1977)* (Amsterdam, 1991).

Rosanvallon, P., *Democratic Legitimacy. Impartiality, Reflexivity, Proximity*, translated by A. Goldhammer (Oxford, 2011).

Rosanvallon, P., *Counter-Democracy. Politics in an Age of Distrust*, trans. A. Goldhammer (Cambridge, Eng., 2008).

Rosanvallon, P., *La contre-démocratie. La politique à l'âge de la défiance* (Paris, 2006).

Saward, M., "Governance and the transformation of political representation," in J. Newman (eds.), *Remaking Governance: Peoples, Politics and the Public Sphere* (Bristol, 2005), 179-196.

Saward, M., "The Representative Claim," in *Contemporary Political Theory* 5 (2006), 297-318.

Saward, M., *The representative Claim* (Oxford, 2010).

Schuyt, K., *Noden en wensen. De verzorgingsstaat gezien als een historisch fenomeen* (Rotterdam, 2013).

Steinmetz, W., and H-G. Haupt, "The Political as Communicative Space in History: The Bielefeld Approach," in W. Steinmetz, I. Gilcher-Holtey, and H-G. Haupt (eds.), *Writing Political History* (Frankfurt am Main, 2013), 11-33.

Steinmetz, W., (ed.), *Political Languages in the Age of Extremes* (Oxford, 2011).

Street, J., "Celebrity Politicians: Popular Culture and Political Representation," in *The British Journal of Politics and International Relations* 6, no. 4 (2004), 435-452.

Strinati, D., and S. Wagg (eds.), *Come on Down? Popular Media Culture in Post-war Britain* (London, 1992).

POSTWAR POPULAR POLITICS

Sussmann, L.A., *Dear FDR: A Study of Political Letter Writing* (Totawa, 1963).

Sussmann, L.A., "FDR and the White House Mail," in *The Public Opinion Quarterly* 20, no. 1 (1956), 5-16.

Uyl, J. den, "De kwaliteit van het bestaan," in J. den Uyl (ed.) *Inzicht en uitzicht. Opstellen over politiek en economie* (Amsterdam, 1978), 116-127.

Vernon, J., *Politics and the People: A Study in English Political Culture, c. 1815-1867* (Cambridge, Eng., 1993).

Zimmermann, H-P., "Lebenswelt und Politik. Bürgerbriefe an Helmut Schmidt 1982," in P. Janich (ed.), *Humane Orientierungswissenschaft. Was leisten verschiedene Wissenschaftskulturen für das Verständnis menschlicher Lebenswelt* (Würzburg, 2008), 203-226.

Zoonen, L. van, *Entertaining the Citizen: When Politics and Popular Culture Converge* (Lanham, 2005).

CHAPTER 9

Majdan: Presence and Political Representation in Post-Communist Ukraine

Wim van Meurs and Olga Morozova

Introduction: Representation and Presence

Max Weber distinguished three ideal typical forms of authority and legitimacy. In their crudest form these three – charismatic, traditional, and legal-rational leadership – are typically construed as a sequence of progress toward modern liberal democracy.[1] More realistically, all individual and institutional authority is grounded in a specific amalgamate of these three types, even in the present era of popular sovereignty, professionalised bureaucracies, and universal suffrage. Having said that, in the twentieth century, authority *without* a representative claim referring to the people has become next to unthinkable.[2] Representative claims may differ widely, from representatives who considered themselves the democratically elected political voice of the legitimate interests of a specific part of the electorate, to righteous advocates of a common good, or to populists as mystic spokesmen of "the people" in singular. Similarly, for some, "politics" as the contest of representative claims should take place exclusively in the confines of the democratic institutions of parliament and government. For others, street politics is an acceptable complementary form of representation or even a superior form of democracy. Recent debates on direct democracy set out to re-introduce the *polis* ideal of the citizen expressing his interests without recourse to representatives or middlemen.[3]

The extraordinary case study of this chapter introduces, among others, citizens who take to the streets, rejecting *any* form of political representation and leadership, be it populist or not. Their claim is not to *represent* (part of) the people, but to *be* the people – a matter of presence instead of representation. The case study exemplifies two key issues of democratic contestation. First, the observation that today the principle of democracy in the widest sense (*dimokratia* – 'the rule of the common people'), is an integral part of any claim to political authority. Second, the observation that deciding what forms of

---

1 Weber (2008) 155-208.
2 Saward (2010) 35-56.
3 Setälä (1999); Hollander (2019); Lucardie (2012) 47-60.

© WIM VAN MEURS AND OLGA MOROZOVA, 2019 | DOI:10.1163/9789004291966_010
This is an open access chapter distributed under the terms of the CC-BY-NC 4.0 License.

PRESENCE AND POLITICAL REPRESENTATION IN POST-COMMUNIST UKRAINE   145

democracy are acceptable as "legitimate" often defies the very decision-making mechanisms of democracy. The state in question held a long tradition of universal suffrage and democracy as the exclusive prerogative of formal representative institutions (at least *de jure*), even though political practice amounted to authoritarian one-party rule. Once the ban on alternative forms of democracy and competing types of representative claims had been broken after the fall of the Soviet Union, political debate and action escalated rapidly. Historical references and symbolic *loci* became instruments in the increasing polarisation, featuring in makeshift expressions of claims to national and political legitimacy and authority. The purpose of this case study is to demonstrate that the political contests of post-communism were not only about political power and more or less sympathetic (from a Western point of view) holders of political office, but also about (un)acceptable forms of democracy and defining the limits of democratic representation.

The present case study concerns Ukraine, a "young democracy" by the standards of Western liberal democracies, although universal suffrage existed under the Soviet Constitution, applicable to the Ukrainian Soviet Republic from 1922 until its independence in 1991. For most of the twentieth century, the Communist Party claimed the status of sole representative of all Ukrainian citizens. Apart from Weber's legal-rational authority, some observers have ascribed "charismatic leadership" to the Communist regime.[4] In the 1990s, by and large politics and representative claims miraculously remained within the confines of the democratic institutions, despite the upheavals of the triple transition to independent statehood, market economy, as well as pluralist democracy and rule of law.[5] Apparently, the realities of seventy years of one-party regime notwithstanding, the institutions of democratic representation of independent Ukraine were not but an ephemeral emulation of a Western role model. They derived significant authority from indigenous institutional tradition, Weber's third type.

In sum, in the framework of this volume on repertoires of representation, Ukraine constitutes an interesting (and possibly trendsetting) case of a people's increasing disenchantment, not only with the political establishment, but also with its populist contenders. Conversely, the Ukrainian story also points to the firmness of a well-established tradition of parliamentary representation, even though for most of its recent history, Ukraine had been part of a one-party system and not a democracy. Arguably, the Majdan protesters have un-

---

4   Jowitt (1983), especially footnote 4.
5   Kolstø (1995); Melvin (1995); Wittkowsky (1998).

derestimated the inherent value of this institutional tradition, risking it all by making street politics a legitimate venue for politics.

This study of the discourses and actions of political representation in post-communist Ukraine focuses on two connected key episodes. The mass protests by Ukrainian-speakers from the western provinces and the capital city triggered by the rigged elections of 2004 constitute the first episode. These protests, the so-called "Orange Revolution," converged on Kyjiv's main square, *Majdan Nezaležnosti* ('Independence Square'). The second episode began when the pro-Russian candidate Viktor Janukovyč, defeated by the Orange Revolution, eventually became president ten years later. In 2013, he refused to ratify Ukraine's Association Agreement with the European Union, allegedly at Moscow's behest. Oppositional political constituencies gathered on the same square once again that now became known as Euromajdan, a much more protracted and violent confrontation between state authorities and radicalised protest movements (see Figure 9.1).

In view of the extreme ethnic and socio-economic polarisation in the country and a decade of rigged elections and blatant state capture, the relative absence of political violence and street politics prior to 2004 seems more remarkable and more deserving of an explanation than the temporary breakdown of political order in 2004 and again in 2013-2014 during the Majdan protests. The analysis below of the two eruptions of political contestation, however, will also offer explanations for the long and relatively calm intermezzos of institutionalised politics. Both democratic crises concerned contestations of political authority, including representative claims, in parliament as well as on Kyjiv's main square. These crises also concerned controversial forms of political action and their condemnation by political adversaries. We use the term "repertoire" for a coherent set of a legitimising discourse of representation and corresponding forms of political action. More often than not, one party to the conflict argued that both the actions of its opponents *and* their representative claim were illegitimate. Each party tried to reserve a representative claim for itself and the legitimate forms of action to go with it. The case study will show that these claimants typically failed in upholding exclusive rights to a repertoire.[6]

In 2004, the *Pora!* movement (Ukrainian: 'time's up!') mobilised citizens not to accept the outcome of the presidential elections as the pro-European liberal candidate Viktor Juščenko publicly accused the candidate form Eastern Ukraine Viktor Janukovyč of election fraud. *Pora!* argued that since the elections had been manipulated, street protests to ensure that the true winner

---

6 Tilly (2005); Laclau (1983).

FIGURE 9.1 Euromajdan in Kyiv on 1 December 2013. CC BY 2.0 [accessed online 26.06.2018: <https://commons.wikimedia.org/wiki/File:Euromaidan_Kyiv_1-12-13_by_Gnatoush_004.jpg>].
PHOTO: NESSA GNATOUSH.

becomes president were a civic and urgent duty. Once democracy had been lost, it could not be easily restored:

> For the foreseeable future, the presidential elections represented their only chance for greater freedom and more rule of law. Russia clarified the alternative with its just-held managed 'elections.' The choice was between democracy or Putin-style authoritarianism.[7]

Evidently, not all protesters were driven by such a principled defence of democratic principles. Many simply blamed president Leonid Kučma and his protégé Janukovyč, for unemployment, crime, poverty, corruption, and despair, rather than supporting Juščenko as victim of electoral fraud.[8]

Russian media in Kyjiv and Moscow had taken a negative stance on the Majdan protests (against the pro-Russian political establishment) in 2004. In 2014, however, they observed a fascist conspiracy instead of a rally of misguided citizens. In January 2014, *Argumenty i Fakty*, one of the Russia's main weeklies, called the Euromajdan a "brown revolt":

---

7   Åslund (2006).
8   Tolkačov (2009).

If any liberal will try to persuade you, that peaceful protesters in Kyjiv are violently protecting the 'European choice,' you can be sure that this person is a liar without honour or conscience. Last week's events have left no illusions: the mob in Kyjiv is attempting a fascist coup.[9]

This study focuses on Majdan as the location of such political contestation. The use, time and again, of the same location for political action adds layer after layer to the symbolic meaning of what is at first sight merely a large open space and traffic junction in the national capital. Apart from the alleged (dis)similarities of the 2004 and 2014 events, older historic events were also selectively added to the bowl in an effort to maximise the symbolic value of the location. Hence, the Majdan has all the qualities associated with a veritable *lieu de mémoire*.[10] In addition to the historical diachronic dimension, both the 2014 and 2014 events also abide with synchronous references. The Orange Revolution is often perceived as part of a series of so-called "colour revolutions" in former communist states and Soviet republics between 2000 and 2005. Similarly, 2014 concluded a series of "square revolutions" from Cairo in 2011 to Istanbul in 2013. Not unlike the diachronic dimension, here, too, the question arises what connotations and similarities the organisers of the protests (or their opponents) prefer to emphasise to substantiate their choice of "democratic" repertoire and legitimacy.

In this case, the truth is in the eye of the beholder. In the analysis, the emic perspective from within the social environment is more important than the outsider etic perspective. The revolutions in Belgrade, Kyjiv, and Tbilisi may have been engineered by the same American strategists,[11] but what really counts here are explicit references and acknowledged role models in the dynamics of political contestation – i.e., the ad-hoc perceptions of the insider rather than the ex-post analysis of the outsider. From a more pragmatic point of view, using the largest square available in the capital for a political mass demonstration seems an obvious choice. Conveniently, the largest square is often also home to some key institutions of political power (albeit not in the case of the Majdan in Kyjiv).[12] In terms of urban layout, a square in the centre of the capital is bound to have a long history of memorable political events and corresponding national monuments. It is, almost by default, a *lieu de mémoire* in and by itself.

---

9   Sidorčik (2014).
10   Nora (1989).
11   Beissinger (2007); Bredies (2004).
12   Except for the building of the City parliament until the Second World War.

Political scientists have authored most Western studies of either the Majdan events or the colour and square revolutions as generic phenomena. More often than not, they frame the events of 2004 and 2014 as an ethnic conflict between a nationalising state and a minority that happens to be co-nationals of a former imperial power.[13] And if they do, political scientists typically applaud these political revolutions as proof of the vitality and tenacity of democratic culture among the citizens under authoritarian regimes. Democratisation and national liberation are presented as two sides of the same coin. In the words of a Western sympathiser:

> The strength of popular empowerment that had overthrown the leadership of communist parties and their respective political systems was almost forgotten [...]. However, with the turn of the millennium, thousands of citizens returned to the streets and squares, waving banners and flags, protesting against their leadership, and demanding the minimum requirement of democracy: free and fair elections.[14]

Due to its normative justification, these accolades ignore the selective perceptions of the insiders as well as the unwelcome consequences for conventions of political culture and democracy as an institutionalised procedure. Who decides what is "democratic" and what is "undemocratic" behaviour? If pro-Western protesters have the right (or even obligation) to leave the bounds of institutionalised representation for the sake of the people or the nation, how about pro-Russian secessionists and regional constituencies? Therefore, unlike most studies of these revolutions, the analysis below focuses on the meta-level of repertoires of democracy and their proponents, likable or not. Hence, the study incorporates the views from pro-Russian politicians, too – public perceptions and redefined political conventions.[15]

Unsurprisingly, these perspectives often contradict each other. In his memoires *Posle Majdana* ('After Majdan') former Ukrainian president Leonid Kučma wrote that the Orange Revolution had been (merely) the product of social disappointment and guileless expectations:

> People wanted the promised 'Western paradise' to arrive as soon as possible. Many disliked capitalism out of Soviet inertia, but it did not prevent

---

13 The debate on the ethnic or socio-economic essence of the polarisation is beyond the scope of this contribution, see: Karklins (1994); Van Meurs (1999); Melvin (1995).
14 Gerlach (2014) 1.
15 Zunneberg and Van Meurs (2014).

them from living under the motto 'we want a European way of life!' However, under the 'European way of life' they understood only its material appearance, and not the thriftiness, skills to accumulate funds and resources, tireless work and constant learning.[16]

Ten years later, a journalist supportive of the new wave of protests, noticed a laconic banner asking for the understanding of drivers who found Majdan, a key traffic junction, blocked by citizens and barricades: "Please understand us, we are fed up!" Somewhat wilfully, he read this sign to imply that "the people were fed up with judges taking bribes, political repressions, endless corruption, absence of fair elections, 'Soviet'-type economy, and the lowest living standard in Europe."[17]

On the other side of these barricades, a quite different set of arguments prevailed. In justifying the resistance and separatism of the population of Crimea in 2014, democracy and representation were not the issue:

It so happened that the majority of the Crimean population consists of Russian speakers, Tatars and people of many other nationalities. These people have ancient traditions, history and cultural values of their own. They cannot throw everything at the feet of those, who chose Bandera as their leader and preach Nazism. Our grandfathers fought Nazis and shed their blood in order for us not to put their memory to shame.[18]

In sum, no lack of contentious historical and representative claims here to justify political mobilisation outside of the democratic institutions or a clampdown on street politics by the political establishment.

The Majdan in 2004 and 2014

The Constitution of Ukraine has been adopted in 1996 under the second president Leonid Kučma. This document cemented Ukraine's sovereignty and provided much-needed legitimacy. Ever since the fall of the Soviet Union and Ukrainian independence in 1991, the main challenge for Ukraine has been to preserve its statehood despite being heavily dependent upon Russia for energy resources and exports. Backed by oligarchic elites from southern and eastern

---

16   Kučma (2007) 24.
17   Stražnyj (2016) 69.
18   Anon. (2014).

Ukraine, Kučma was interested in free trade with Russia, but remained cautious about entering any agreements, which would require Ukraine to commit to the CIS integration.

During Kučma's second term in office (1999-2005), oligarchs and their political parties became even more influential in Ukraine and the democratic "orange" coalition, supported by the socialists, found itself in the opposition. The oligarchs' supporters were mainly found among the Russian-speaking population of the industrial cities of Eastern Ukraine – which were especially reliant on Russia for cheap energy and a market for their products. Every once in a while, Russia played the "Crimean card" to put pressure on Kyiv. The peninsula had been a "gift" to the Ukrainian Soviet Republic in 1954 at the occasion of the three hundredth anniversary of the first "alliance" between Russia and Ukraine. However, as Ukraine gained independence Russia could never make peace with having to part with a region of such strategic significance.

Once the richest Soviet republic and by area the largest state in Europe with more than 40 million inhabitants, Ukraine found itself stuck between the EU and Russia. It has always been half-hearted about the Russian-led regional integration projects like the Commonwealth of Independent States (CIS) or Eurasian Economic Union (EEU), while for Russia getting Ukraine on board with these projects has been a key strategic objective for over a decade. At the same time, Ukraine also struggled to make a commitment to the EU integration without a membership perspective and it was not until 2014 that the scales tipped in favour of westward integration and the unsolved Crimea issue finally backfired.

Along this road, the presidential elections of 2004 and the subsequent Orange Revolution have served as an important turning point. They were heralded as a major democratic breakthrough and definitely pointed in the European direction. The "orange" leaders Viktor Juščenko and Julia Tymošenko accused Viktor Janukovyč, the key contender from eastern Ukraine favoured by Kučma, of election fraud. The rigged elections' results gave Janukovyč a one per cent margin over Juščenko and immediately, thousands gathered on the Majdan in peaceful protest. These protests grew into organised rallies on Kyjiv's main square and a series of sit-ins, demonstrations, and strikes all over the country lasting for over a month. The largest demonstration with half a million participants took place on November 23, 2004 on the Majdan in Kyiv. Eventually, Ukraine's Supreme Court ordered a revote. Despite its eventual electoral victory, the revolution also demonstrated the extent to which Ukraine was sharply divided in a pro-Russian "East" and a pro-European "West." Juščenko gathered up to 93 per cent of the vote in some western provinces, whereas his opponent won in the easternmost provinces by similar margins.[19]

Upon becoming president, Juščenko started negotiations on a new EU-Ukraine agreement. On the EU's part, this decision was taken in the context of the European Neighbourhood Policy (ENP), inspired by the Orange Revolution. It was welcomed in Ukraine as a promise of future membership. The negotiations on what later came to be known as the Association Agreement (AA) started in 2007, followed by the negotiations on its economic part, the Deep and Comprehensive Free Trade Area (DCFTA), after Ukraine's accession to the WTO in 2008.

However, the Juščenko presidency resulted in a disillusion and Viktor Janukovyč came back with a vengeance, using the economic crisis of 2008 as a platform to become the next president. Upon becoming president, he sent Tymošenko to prison on propped-up charges and her confederates came to the fore as the new opposition leaders. During Janukovyč's presidency, the country had definitely started to lean more towards Russia, albeit inconsistently. Even though EU integration remained a strategic objective for Ukraine, the long-term perspective Brussels offered did not provide a solution for the most pressing issues of economic malaise and energy security. Nevertheless, the expectations for the Association Agreement were high among the people and had great symbolic value. Tymošenko's release was one of the EU's conditions for signing this agreement, but Janukovyč refused to comply. Instead, he chose a tough line, suppressing his domestic critics and ignoring international pressure. Eventually, Janukovyč was ready to sign the EU Association Agreement in November 2013. At that very moment, Putin offered him a favourable CIS Free Trade Agreement deal involving loans and cheap gas, and the Ukrainian president made a U-turn in Vilnius, refusing to ratify the EU document.

The Euromajdan, a peaceful demonstration in support of the agreement, had actually started before, but radicalised when news of the president's second thoughts spread. From this moment on, the word *majdan* no longer referred to Independence Square in Kyjiv, but stood for the whole revolutionary movement, its attributes, symbols, and traditions. In January 2014 three protesters were killed by snipers, the first casualties in a mass demonstration in post-Soviet Ukraine. The violence started spiralling out of hand quickly, marking the breakdown of the already weakened political system and a few days later, president Janukovyč fled the country. Hoping to regain power, he instigated separatist uprisings in his strongholds in the east of Ukraine. A month

---

19   Kuzio (2011); White (2009).

PRESENCE AND POLITICAL REPRESENTATION IN POST-COMMUNIST UKRAINE   153

later the Crimean Peninsula had been annexed by Russia and military conflict in the eastern provinces of Luhansk and Donetsk had started.

The victorious protesters from Euromajdan forced the *Rada* (Ukraine's national parliament) to install a transitional government and organise new presidential elections. In May 2014, Petro Porošenko, a prominent businessman who used to be close to Juščenko, was elected. He immediately renewed the Association Agreement negotiations and although the ratification process is almost complete by now, people's trust in the government has reached a new low. Moreover, it has become clear that the hybrid war in the Donbas region is not going to end any time soon and is de facto becoming another frozen conflict, providing the Kremlin with additional leverage over Kyjiv.[20]

Both in the Orange Revolution and in the Euromajdan a decade later, the protesters and the political establishment had ample choices of political repertoires to claim a voice in Ukrainian politics, with unforeseeable consequences. The fact that both these political clashes were associated with similar contemporaneous events elsewhere in the world further complicated the war of words and action on the Majdan. The next paragraph takes a closer look at these synchronous connections as an alternative to the more common diachronic references to preceding events and claims.

Synchronous Repertoires of Civil Mobilisation

In 2000, *Otpor!* ('Resistance'), a loose network of students all over Serbia ignited mass protests against fraudulent presidential elections and forced authoritarian leader Slobodan Milošević to acknowledge electoral defeat and resign. It succeeded, where oppositional political parties had failed time and again in the 1990s. The key to this success of *Otpor!* was non-violent demonstrations by youth and in particular students who were accepted by the population at large as genuine and a-political in their concerns. Their spokesmen, trained by Western strategists and spin-doctors, moreover, were the first to use world media as a political weapon systematically – to mobilise their fellow-countrymen, to spread their message and to unmask the repressive regime.[21] In retrospect, it became known that expertise and resources from US agencies and democracy-promoting NGOs had contributed substantially to *Otpor!*'s victory.[22]

---

20   Kuzio (2016); Samokhvalov (2015); Stepanenko (2015).
21   Richard Sakwa uses the term "informational warfare," Sakwa (2014) ix.
22   Beissinger (2007); Thumann (2004)

Otpor! quickly became a role model for urban youth in other authoritarian or "hybrid" (rather than outright dictatorial) states. Allegedly, US advisors and *Otpor!* activists played a part in the so-called Rose Revolution in Georgia two years later. Here, too, a civil youth movement, *Kmara*, fuelled protests against electoral fraud and toppled the regime of former Soviet foreign minister Eduard Ševardnadze without resorting to violence, but with the aid of Western public opinion and advisors. The so-called Tulip Revolution in Kyrgyzstan and the Cedar Revolution in Lebanon shared some of these characteristics and, like several other national protest movements, they tried to claim this pedigree (Belgrade and Kyjiv) and the promise of success it held, albeit without success.[23]

At the time, geographic proximity and strategic weight guaranteed the 2004 Orange Revolution in Ukraine the undivided attention of politicians and the media, both in the West and in Russia. The Majdan protests of 2004, too, have been led by a non-violent civil movement *Pora!* which consisted primarily of students who gathered in reaction to the repression, cronyism, and corruption during the run-off of the presidential elections. The similar names of the students' movements, the same clever media campaigns, and non-violent mobilisation strategies in reaction to fraudulent elections made the Orange Revolution part and parcel of a wider phenomenon of colour revolutions.

Although the common origins of the media campaigns and the advisors behind the scenes were proven only later, the Kučma/Janukovyč regime eagerly accused Western governments of instigating and financing unrest and discord in Ukraine. Juščenko, Tymošenko, and the *Pora!* movement took great care to present their protests as pro-Western and yet "spontaneous" and authentic.[24] The generic term "colour revolution" was coined in retrospect only, when protesters in Georgia and Kyrgyzstan explicitly stated their indebtedness to the Orange Revolution. By that time, the term became not only an analytical category, but also a political agenda, a wake-up call to civil opposition in other authoritarian states. Reportedly, the rulers in neighbouring Moldova replaced the (orange) uniforms of traffic wardens as a precaution.[25]

Correspondingly, newspapers and other media loyal to the regime claimed to have uncovered shady connections between the protesters and Western secret services (and with some justification). Drawing a parallel to Belgrade in 2000 and *Otpor!* might have backfired. Former Yugoslav president Milošević, now a detainee in The Hague, might be embraced as part of a Slavic brother-

---

23   Beissinger (2007); Levitsky (2010).

24   Kuzio (1997).

25   Negru (2010).

hood by the political establishment in Kyjiv, but his dictatorial regime and his fall in particular suggested unwelcome parallels more powerful than allegations of anti-national allegiances on the part of the revolutionaries.

It was hard not to notice a parallel between the Serbian *Otpor!* and Ukrainian *Pora!*, as *Pora!* activists, just like *Kmara* protesters in Georgia, were building on the Belgrade experience and had indeed been trained by the same people. During the Orange Revolution, this connection was not necessarily perceived as negative, as the 2004 Majdan itself has been meticulously organised. While the organisers took pride in the spontaneous and genuine support of the citizens, they also admitted that it took a well-planned strategy to outmanoeuvre the political nomenclature. According to one of the organisers, Vladimir Filenko, back then

> there were no spontaneous gatherings, but thoroughly planned actions. Maybe, precisely because everything has been consistently prepared beforehand, no-one died during the Orange Majdan. Yes, we are very proud of it. We have foreseen different options and courses of action, depending on the government's reaction. We have written A and B plans, sometimes even C for each operation.[26]

These connections to Belgrade resurfaced ten years later, albeit they were less obvious then:

> Currently, *Pora!*, after having been transformed into unsuccessful political parties, has become a brand, which is not being used anymore. However, on 1st of December in the Kyjiv streets one could see a bulldozer, which looked exactly like the one that 'attacked' the government building in Belgrade on the 5th of October 2000, when Milošević's regime was overthrown. So, in one way or another, *Otpor!* is present in Kyjiv once again, after it has already made Ukrainians 'happy' 10 years ago.[27]

References to *Otpor!* and its democratic victory in Belgrade four years before were quite rare in the partisan media as well as on the banners and pamphlets of the protesters. Implicitly, their task of reversing electoral fraud by a well-entrenched regime backed by Moscow in a strategically important major European state seemed much more daunting than toppling an isolated dictator in

---

26 Filenko (2014).
27 Džurkovič (2014).

Serbia, six times smaller than Ukraine. Pro-regime media indeed hinted at a Western conspiracy instigating "revolutions" in Russia's "near abroad":

> Revolutions toppled the regimes loyal to Russia one after another. Could it be a coincidence? Maybe someone has created an effective system of constant revolutions – 'rose,' 'orange,' 'singing' and others, and this someone completely disregards the laws of these countries?[28]

This quote labels the revolutions as alien and in violation of national law and order.

A decade after the Orange Revolution, the renewed protest on the Majdan had a distinctly different objective – the forced abdication of the democratically elected head of state rather than a re-run of presidential elections because of fraud. Arguably, the Ukrainian protests again fitted into a wider pattern of square revolutions. The Arab Spring of 2011-2013 set the stage with long-time dictators swept from office in Cairo, Tunis, Sana'a, and Tripoli. Even in Russia, Putin's re-election triggered civil protests on Bolotnaja Square, put down by the militia. The Majdan-like Tahrir Square in Cairo and Taksim Square with Gezi Park in Istanbul in 2013-2014 became symbolic hotbeds of civic activism and anti-politics to have popular accountability restored. During the Euromajdan, the Association Agreement with the EU was more of a catalyst than the sole bone of contention. Most of the protesters simply abhorred the rampant corruption and misgovernment of the political and economic establishment.[29]

This time, the other square revolutions predated Euromajdan. Strategically, role model acknowledgement was less problematic, as these revolutions had not been stage-managed by American or European agencies. The fact that these revolutions all occurred outside of the circle of former Soviet republics lessened the appeal of such references. Strong personal networks existed among democratic opposition in former Soviet republics and once in power they solidarized in their attempts to ward off Russian encroachments, using a combination of energy resources, economic sanctions, Russian minorities, military threats, and political pressure to maintain or regain a degree of control over these newly independent states. From a Ukrainian perspective, Cairo and Istanbul were quite alien contexts, despite the invigorating appeal of seeing a crowd of citizens succeed in standing up for its rights and interests.

---

28   Zuev (2009).
29   Onuch (2014).

PRESENCE AND POLITICAL REPRESENTATION IN POST-COMMUNIST UKRAINE   157

To some extent, the Western advisors and sponsors of the colour revolutions (more than the square revolutions) constituted a veritable and tangible transnational connection between these events and groups. Role model strategies and the encouragement of successful examples constitute more implicit connections. These connections are construed discursively. Framing by local and international media and political actors is decisive. Social media and twitter tags had multiplied the force and immediacy of international public opinion in a timespan of ten years. The very term "colour revolution" and the in- or exclusion of a specific country from the caucus of square revolutions constitutes framing and has a political impact.[30]

The next section deals with the much more common phenomenon of political entrepreneurs claiming historical pedigree to prove their legitimacy or, conversely, linking the opponent's actions to a negative predecessor in order to discredit the movement. From this diachronic perspective, too, the Majdan is again littered with positive and negative references to (recent) history and discursive weapons.

Diachronic Repertoires of National Resilience

When the demonstrators occupied the Majdan in 2004 and again in 2014, their astute media campaigners made the most of the location – not only the wide camera shots of hundreds of thousands of citizens and thousands of Ukrainian flags and orange banners taken from high-rise buildings lining the square, but also the symbolic ammunition the location provided. Conversely, the adversaries facing each other on Majdan also used negative imagery and historical associations to discredit and disqualify one another in the eyes of omnipresent world public opinion and local constituencies. No scriptwriter could have come up with a better setting for iconic images and dramatic shots heavy with meaning: top-down shots of the crowd and its blue-yellow and orange markers, menacing riot police in black combat gear, protesters clinging to the Independence Monument, the Majdan at night set ablaze by bonfires.

Sometimes, the high drama of images produces incidental but meaningful associations, noticed by history-savvy Western observers and astute local propagandists. The image of citizens scaling the monument and waving flags and banners against a backdrop of buildings hidden by smoke became almost as iconic as the tag *#euromaidan*. Whether it had been stage-managed or not, but the reference to Eugène Delacroix' famous Louvre painting "Liberty Leading

---

30   Beissinger (2007); Tucker (2011).

the People," an homage to the July Revolution of 1830 in France that toppled the restauration regime of Charles X is there. No written plea on the nexus between the nation, liberty, and the power of the people could have been more powerful.

In 2004, Juščenko and Tymošenko contrasted their own liberal-democratic and Ukrainian-national views to the political establishment's pseudo-democracy and subservience to Russian interests. Inevitably, they claimed to be the sole representatives of Ukrainian national interests. Hence, the very name of the location *Majdan Nezaležnosti* or 'Independence Square' was a first asset. The square, dating back to the nineteenth century, had been renamed (previously: Square of the October Revolution) in 1991 to commemorate the regaining of national statehood with the dissolution of the Soviet Federation. The protesters hoped to complete independence with the election of a truly democratic and independent president. The word *majdan* for 'square' in Ukrainian is of Arab rather than Slavic origin (compare: Taksim Square in Turkish: *Taksim Meydanı*) and primarily emphasises cultural distance to the Russian synonym *ploščad'* (or *plošča* in Ukrainian). The alternative name suggested in 1991, *Plošča Svobody* ('Liberty Square') would have chosen the Slavic synonym for "square" and liberty would have referred to both independent statehood of 1991 and the Russian Revolutions of 1917.

More importantly, the square features several important monuments, one to the legendary founders of Kyjiv, one to the folklore hero Cossack Mamaj, and one to the city's guardian saint, Archangel Michael.[31] All three constitute symbolic, rather than factual-historical references, to a glorious national past. Conveniently, the monument to the October Revolution had been removed. The domineering monument, however, is the victory column erected in 2001 to commemorate a decade of independence, a 200-foot-high column. The column is a quite eclectic brass statue of a young woman in national costume with a viburnum branch in her raised hands, allegorically representing Ukraine.

After the monument of the October Revolution had been removed from the Majdan in 1991, the Lenin monument on nearby Ševčenko Boulevard was considered the main communist symbol left in Ukraine. Since the early 2010s, the government began gradually removing Lenin monuments from the city squares all over Ukraine.[32] However, the unauthorised removal of the Ukraine's most revered statue of Lenin during the early stage of Majdan at the end of 2013 by the protesters has been highly controversial.

---

31   Anon. (2012); Anon. (2007).
32   Anon. (2013b).

The prime minister's office accused the protesters of destroying a monument from the UNESCO World Heritage list, an act of barbarism comparable only to the demolition of an ancient Buddha statue in Afghanistan by the Taliban. According to the Kyjiv City Administration this act of vandalism had "nothing to do with democracy." Nevertheless, the demolition of the Lenin monument has been criticised not only by the opponents of the Euromajdan. Ruslana, a famous Ukrainian Eurovision winner and an ardent supporter of both Majdans, wrote:

> While our peaceful initiative requires mutual solidarity and unity around Majdan and peaceful protests for the dismissal of the criminal government, destroying monuments and calling for aggression is absolutely counterproductive. It sets us further back from Euro-integration and humane society.[33]

At the same time, liberal Russian politician and human-rights activist Valerija Novodvorskaja welcomed the demolition and said that monuments of this kind have no place in a civilised city: "The demolition of the Lenin monument cannot be considered a provocation, just like a Hitler monument's removal cannot. The very fact of its existence is a crime. Such monuments can only be present where criminals and villains rule."[34]

For the campaign managers of 2004, recent memory offered useful associations of the ongoing anti-Kučma and anti-Janukovyč demonstrations to the large-scale protests of the 1990 student Revolution on Granite and the 2000-2001 "Ukraine without Kučma" demonstrations. The "granite" student strike movement compelled Ukraine's Communist leadership to pursue first sovereignty and next independence. The 2000-2001 demonstrations on the Majdan were a prefiguration of the Orange Revolution, demanding the resignation of President Leonid Kučma, but this early rebellion had been easily suppressed by the security forces. In 1994, a contest had been initiated for the best independence monument. Fearing another round of protests and encampments during the upcoming elections, the government in 2001 hurriedly picked a winner. The square was immediately enclosed by building fences under the pretext of beginning construction work. The demonstrations that took place, nevertheless, became known as "Ukraine without Kučma." Moreover, the current government, brought to power by Euromajdan, announced a "Territory of Dignity" tender to turn the Independence Square from an open space into a

---

33   Anon. (2013a).
34   Anon. (2013a).

park zone planted with trees. Thus, as much as the materiality of the square has shaped the protest movement, both protesters and vested powers have also set about to redesign the square to suit their purposes and projections.[35]

Apart from obviously and easily steering clear of all Soviet and Russian references, in 2004 the symbolism of the Majdan was like wax in the hands of the pro-independence campaigners. A decade later, the same legendary and heroic references embodied by the monuments were still valuable. The Euromajdan pledged adherence to the same national historic and cultural traditions.

When asked whether the Ukrainian "Majdans" are connected with each other, one of the Orange Revolution organisers, Vladimir Filenko, resolutely answered that he sees them as a continuation of the struggle for independence:

> Speaking of the most recent Ukrainian history, they all were continuing the Revolution on Granite, but if we consider the more distant past, the Majdans are a prolongation of the Hetmanate [an early-modern Cossack state in central and north -eastern Ukraine, OM] and the Cossack legacy. During the twentieth century alone we have had five attempts to restore Ukrainian independence [Filenko refers to the short -lived state-entities of the Ukrainian People's Republic of 1917, the West Ukrainian People's Republic of 1919, the Carpatho-Ukraine of 1938-39 as well as the declarations of independence of 1941 and 1991, OM] Actually, the word *majdan* is of Turkic origin. As we all know, we share common history with Turks and Tatars, so we borrowed this one from them too. Generally speaking, Majdan is not just a modern Ukrainian phenomenon, but is relevant to the global history as a whole. This notion emerged long before the Orange Revolution and I am happy to have been one of those, who succeeded in bringing it back to Ukraine.[36]

Just like two other prominent Majdan organisers, Taras Steckiv and Roman Bezsmertnyj, Filenko is a historian by education and saw the Majdan [as a generic and timeless locus of national resilience, OM] as a "manifestation of direct democracy."[37]

In sum, the Majdan revolutions in Ukraine have been explicitly framed in terms of national history and tradition. Indeed, this tradition refers back to the Cossacks, who used to hold meetings, where everyone from the crowd would

---

35   Anon. (2015).
36   Filenko (2014).
37   Ibid.

PRESENCE AND POLITICAL REPRESENTATION IN POST-COMMUNIST UKRAINE 161

give his opinion and the decisions would be taken by voting or consensus. These meetings gave the Ukrainian parliament its name – *Rada*, and were held on the central squares – *majdan*s. Hence Filenko's association with direct democracy. Supposedly, this form of government was widespread on a local level during the Hetmanate of the second half of the seventeenth and the beginning of the eighteenth century. This is also a radical "ideal type" of democracy without representation the most vigorous Majdan protesters championed when things were moving their way in 2014.

Thus, for Euromajdan, historical antecedents were much more complicated than for the 2004 protesters. Oddly enough, the Orange Revolution itself was the elephant in the room here. The high hopes placed in President Juščenko and Prime Minister Tymošenko in 2004 had quickly ended in utter and bitter disappointment. Tymošenko's terms of office (2005, 2007-2010) became synonymous to corruption, stalled reforms and malpractice. The next presidential elections in 2010, deemed relatively free and fair, had witnessed restauration with Janukovyč defeating Tymošenko.

Tellingly, in Ukraine, Euromajdan of 2014 is often referred to as *Revoljucija Hidnosti* ('Revolution of Dignity'), in contrast to the politicking of 2004.[38] This time, the protest movement was characterised by general distrust of all politicians and politicking, including the former heroes of the Orange Revolution. (Juščenko had left politics after his one term of office as president.) When in 2014 Tymošenko was released from prison on Brussels' intercession (convicted to a sentence of seven years for embezzlement and abuse of power), the protesters at the Majdan refused to welcome her as martyr, nor did they recognise her as their leader. Immediately upon release she hurried to the Majdan and delivered a speech in an attempt to take the lead over the revolution that was on its peak. The crowd, however, had mixed feelings about her appearance: some were praising her, while others shouted that they had no trust, referring both to her and the political class as a whole.[39] Tymošenko also cautiously hinted that she could become a "guarantor of the Constitution," if the people wished so. A few ardent supporters shouted "Tymošenko for president!", but the crowd failed to pick up on this slogan. People were whispering to one another that they were not standing on the Majdan to make her president, but for real changes for the better in their lives.[40] In a quite unique move, having learned the lesson of 2004, the protesters this time refused to be "led" or

---

38   Sakwa (2014) 81.
39   Anon. (2014b).
40   Anon. (2014c).

"represented," returning to the romantic ideal of popular sovereignty imagined as a coherent sequence from the Cossack Hetmanate to the Ukrainian Revolution of 1917 and the final milestone in 1991.

Despite the apparent similarities, this Revolution of Dignity was presented as fundamentally different from the Orange Revolution precisely because of its spontaneous character and absence of distinct leadership. The utter disenchantment with any forms of political leadership since 2004 led to a reversal of values a decade later: spontaneity instead of strategic planning; aggrieved citizens asserting themselves instead of defending a disenfranchised political representative.

As one Ukrainian observer noted in retrospect:

> Janukovyč's boorish behaviour regarding the Association Agreement has offended people more than any events since 2004. Because of the mass character and enthusiasm around these actions, they are even being compared to the Majdan of 2004. Contrary to the popular opinion about the spontaneity of the Orange Revolution, the 2004 Majdan had been thoroughly prepared. On the opposite, the organised actions during the Euromajdan were quite fragmentary. It can also be explained by the difference in circumstances – there are no presidential elections right now. In the course of the past nine years, many Ukrainians have become disappointed about the possibility of any changes and do not trust the politicians.[41]

Another sympathetic commentator concluded that revolutions were typically led by charismatic leaders, but not so in the case of Euromajdan:

> There were only coordinators: opposition deputies were 'responsible' for the parliament, ex-ministers of Foreign Affairs Boris Tarasjuk and Petro Porošenko – for the relations with international organisations, the camp-site commandant Andrij Parubij – for forage and defence, *Samooborona* (Self Defence) captains – for security, stage managers – for speeches and performances.[42]

In sum, the initiators of the second Majdan went to great lengths to dissuade any associations with the first one. Arguably, they even built their very reputation on being fundamentally different, as one of its participants has noted:

---

41 Šmajda (2013).
42 Stražnyj (2016) 229.

All in all, from the very beginning only place and time united these seemingly similar events. Both Majdans started in the same place – the Independence Square, and the same time – the 21st of November. However, during the Orange Majdan of 2004 with its light-hearted festive spirit, the most important thing was that people were sure the government would not start killing them. Back then, we naively shouted 'Police is with the people!' and the policemen, shyly smiling, stayed neutral. We chanted 'East and West are together!' – and it seemed as if there was no disagreement among us, nor could there ever be any. We called for Juščenko and thought that replacing Kučma with him would be enough.[43]

The new leaders of the pro-European protests were clearly professional politicians with diverging agendas and beliefs, sharing only the rejection of a future for Ukraine as Russian dependence. Only the party UDAR and its leader, former boxing champion Vitalij Klyčko, could claim some charismatic authority and popularity (locally and in the West). Not so for Tymošenko's conservative All-Ukrainian Union "Fatherland" and certainly not for the extremist and violent Right Sector led by the ill-reputed Dmytro Jaroš. The Moscow-supported separatism in eastern Ukraine and the annexation of Crimea created a state of national emergency in Kyjiv. Oligarch and entrepreneur Petro Porošenko became president and a national figure of sorts, but by no means the unblemished charismatic hero entrusted with the nation's future president Juščenko had been in 2004.

Both for domestic audiences and international public opinion, pro-Russian media in Ukraine and Moscow-based outlets made every effort to reduce the image of the protest movement and its leaders to the violent, extreme-nationalist, and xenophobic groups in the heterogeneous coalition of the Euromajdan. The Right Sector and excesses during the protests offered ample targets for such counterattacks. Apart from images of masked protesters wielding heavy weapons, the ubiquitous framing was "fascism." The new "illegitimate" regime was effectively and consistently labelled as "fascist" (rather than "undemocratic"). Since Soviet times, "fascist" had become a strong generic derogative term separated from any historical reference or comparison. In the secessionist action in eastern Ukraine and Crimea, liberation of the local (Russian-speaking) population from the new "fascist" government in Kyjiv was a strong legitimising and mobilising discourse.

In the context of Euromajdan, both sides remembered and instrumentalised the Ukrainian militant nationalist struggle for independence. However,

---

43   Anon. (2016c).

FIGURE 9.2   The headquarters of Euromajdan in January 2014, a prominent portrait of Stepan Bandera at the front entrance. [CC BY-SA 2.0, accessed online 26.06.2018: <https://commons.wikimedia.org/wiki/File:Headquarters_of_the_Euromaidan_revolution.jpg>].

while Ukrainians emphasised the anti-Bolshevik Ukrainian Revolution of 1917, Russians focused almost exclusively on Ukrainian Insurgent Army (UPA) that had fought against the Soviet regime during the Second World War with utter ruthlessness and ended up as allies of Nazi-Germany. In the same vein, Stepan Bandera, a Ukrainian nationalist leader from western Ukraine in the interwar period, was associated with Euromajdan by its opponents. The association involved racist nationalism, atrocities, treason, and collaboration with fascism.[44] His Organisation of Ukrainian Nationalists (OUN) had collaborated with Nazi-Germany in the war to free Ukraine from Soviet hegemony.

When accused of holding elections at gunpoint in his self-proclaimed Luhansk People's Republic, the separatists' leader Igor Plotnickij retaliated: "Porošenko's theory [...] is a blatant lie. It is just low. Porošenko himself came to power as a result of the violent pro-Bandera February coup in Kyjiv, which

---

44   Riabchuk (2016); Plokhy (2010).

PRESENCE AND POLITICAL REPRESENTATION IN POST-COMMUNIST UKRAINE   165

was anti-constitutional and bloody."[45] This type of negative framing appealed to many Ukrainians' fear of civil war, disorder and economic devastation. It also casted doubt on the credentials of Euromajdan as a whole in the eyes of Western public opinion that preferred to associate Euromajdan to national liberation and democracy, the image of Delacroix. Undeniably, the UPA featured regularly on Majdan and so did images of Bandera and OUN (see Figure 9.2). For part of the protesters these references constituted the strongest possible appeal to national resilience and hard choices for the sake of national sovereignty. In 2010, President Juščenko had awarded Bandera the title of Hero of Ukraine, a controversial decision immediately revoked by his pro-Russian successor and condemned by the European Parliament, which would backfire four years later when the Euromajdan broke out. The flip side of Ukrainian nationalism has become the main theme in Russian propaganda against Ukraine.[46]

The Third Majdan of Confutation

At the third anniversary of the Euromajdan, political scientist Oleg Saakjan observed:

> Politicians will not come out onto Majdan, because Majdan continued its life as the Revolution of Dignity in the work of volunteers, civil activists, experts and other people who are working to transform the country. For the politicians, the Majdan ended, because it brought them to power and therefore fulfilled its function.[47]

At the same time in late 2016, the call for a "third Majdan" appeared in (social) media. Informed by the above analysis of the Majdan's synchronous and diachronic connotations of representation and legitimacy, the term itself gives pause. Firstly, "third Majdan" suggests a sequence and continuity that the protesters of the second Majdan vehemently denied. The first Majdan had defended one half of the political elite against the other within the confines of representative democracy or defended these very rules of the game of representative democracy against the infringement of rigged elections. The second had moved to a new level of "revolution," ousting a democratically elected

---

45   Anon. (2017); quoted from: Bedritskiy (2015) 187.
46   Sakwa (2014) 20.
47   Anon. (2016b).

president because of the political choices he made. They thereby left the confines of representative democracy themselves. Consequently, the slogan "third Majdan" points to a common denominator – the people intervening and "supervising" politicians or politics as such as soon as they went astray. Given the regional and worldwide distribution of power, only a minority will blame President Porošenko and his government for failing to reverse the loss of Crimea and the bringing the secessionist easternmost provinces back into Kyjiv's fold.

A much larger proportion of the voters all over Ukraine has expressed utter disenchantment and frustration over the domestic track record of the new regime. Rampant corruption, the deterioration in the living standards, and the humiliating territorial losses have belied the promises of new beginnings associated with the radical second Majdan within years. Hence the understanding that all political elites are inherently unreliable and bound to prioritise their own enrichment over the interests of the people they are expected to represent. Consequently, "the people" has to be vigilant and ready to step in every once in a while, without the naïve idealistic belief that its new leaders will be any better. Optimistically, this utter political disenchantment implies the empowerment of civil society as the ultimate judge of democratic legitimacy. This may be a step forward in terms of classic democratic criteria by strengthening civil society.[48] There are, however, obvious risks involved in "the people" or "civil society" eclipsing the representative institutions and elected representatives at will. Yet, no matter how hard they try, "civil society" as a moral force cannot do without leaders, instigators, spokesmen to uphold the illusion of "the people" as a real-existing entity.

Reportedly, Julija Tymošenko urged citizens to instigate a new protest on Kyjiv's central square, pointing at artificially increased utility tariffs and inflation. During a press conference, she accused the president and the head of the National Bank of corruption. In a comment, Kyjiv's main radio station identified the motive behind all Majdans, past and future:

> Let's be honest. If we are hypothetically talking about the preparation of the 'third Majdan' or other mass protest actions in one way or another, the Ukrainian people has never come out onto Majdan for economy. It stood up when its political rights and freedoms were trampled down, especially those which have to do with personal dignity, but not the economic ones. If we take a look at 2004, people gathered on Majdan to defend their choice. No matter what, but it was a choice and it was not reckoned with. During the Revolution of Dignity people also did not

---

48   Freedom House's "strong civil society" or Dahl's "associational freedom," see: Dahl (1956).

stand up for economic reasons, but because of the political choice concerning the direction of further development for our country. Therefore, Tymošenko and *Batkivščyna* ['Motherland', her party, OM] will not succeed in igniting mass protests if they only keep relying on economic factors.[49]

Yet, Ukrainian politics too has entered the twenty-first century of fake news, social-media hypes and information bubbles. In parallel to the Ukrainian and western reports on Tymošenko and others threatening to incite a third Majdan, sympathetic Russian reporting on this call caused suspicions.[50] According to *EuromaidanNews*, it was Russian media and agents inciting Ukrainians to topple their government once more. Indeed, Russian media and pro-Russian media in eastern Ukraine previously not only vilified the Porošenko administration as illegitimate and outright "fascist," but have also vociferously condemned the first and second Majdan as a violent and treacherous coups d'état orchestrated by Washington and Brussels. All of a sudden, these very same media and their masterminds are applauding and welcoming a third Majdan. They claim that the EU has lost faith in Porošenko and that the Kyjiv regime is isolated and panicky, ready to use violence against the very people that swept them to power a mere three years ago.[51] In sum, are the people the playmaker here or are they being played? The only certainty remaining in this enactment of disinformation and incitement is that the Majdan will be the theatre.

Bibliography

Åslund, A., *Ukraine. How Ukraine Became a Market Economy and Democracy* (Washington DC, 2006).

Anon., "Glava LNR oproverg slova Porošenko o vyborax 'pod dulom avtomatov," *NTV*, 1 March 2017, [accessed online 19.06.2018: <http://www.ntv.ru/novosti/1258276/.slova-poroshenko-o-tom-chto-vybory-proshli-pod-dul/>]

Anon., "Sobrat ljudej na Majdan-3 na teme èkonomiki u Timošenko ne vyjdet – èkspert," *RIA Novosti Ukraina*, 24 November 2016a, [accessed online 19.06.2018: <http://rian.com .ua/interview/20161124/1018995087.html>].

Anon., "Majdan pryviv politykiv do vlady I na tomu dlja nyx zakinčyvsja – politolog," *UAInfo*, 22 November 2016b, [accessed online 19.06.2018: <http://uainfo.org/blog

---

49   Anon. (2016a).
50   Anon. (2016d).
51   Kazanskyi (2015); Anon. (2016d).

news/1479828371-maydan-priviv-politikiv-do-vladi-i-na-tomu-dlya-nih-zakinchiv sya.html>].

Anon., "Čim buv i čim ne buv Majdan," *Novoe Vremja*, 21 November 2016c, [accessed online 19.06.2018: <http://nv.ua/ukr/project/story-of-maidan-by-bondar-russ. html>].

Anon., "Timošenko pozvala ukraincev na tretij Majdan," *Lenta.ru*, 14 November 2016d, [accessed online 19.06.2018: <https://lenta.ru/news/2016/11/14/timoshenko/>].

Anon., "Ghost of Third Maidan," *Sputnik News*, 11 May 2016e, [accessed online 19.06.2018: <http://sptnkne.ws/dEsX>].

Anon., "Rekonstrukcija Majdanu može prizvesti do zniščenija istoričnix pam'jatok," *Džerkalo tižnja*, 5 July 2015, [accessed online 19.06.2018: <http://dt.ua/CULTURE/ rekonstrukciya-maydanu-prizvede-do-znischennya-istorichnih-pam-yatok-177934 _.html>].

Anon., "Janukovič-mladšij: Krym xočet otdelit'sja ot Ukrainy iz-za banderovcev I pro-povednikov nacisma," *Gordon.ua*, 16 March 2014a, [accessed online 19.06.2018: <http://gordonua.com/news/politics/yanukovich-mladshiy-krym-hochet-otdelit sya-ot -ukrainy-iz-za-banderovcev-i-propovednikov-nacizma-14081.html>].

Anon., "Vo vremja vystuplenija Timosjenko Majdan kritsjal 'Ne verim!' I 'Molodets!,'" *Segodnja.ua*, 22 February 2014b. [accessed online 26.04.2019: <https://www.segod nya.ua/politics/vo-vremya-vystupleniya-timoshenko-maydan-krichal-ne-verim-i-molodec-497991.html>]

Anon., "Snos pamjatnika Leninu: reakcija v Ukraine i mire," *Fakty*, 9 December 2013a, [accessed online 19.06.2018: <http://fakty.ua/173445-snos-lenina-reakciya-v-ukraine -i-mire>].

Anon., "Majdan z ostrogoju sprijnjav zakliki 'Timosjenko – president,'" *Ukrainski nat-sionalni novini*, 22 February 2014c.

Anon., "Pamjatnik Lenina snesli," *Ukrainskaja Pravda*, 8 December 2013b, [accessed on-line 19.06.2018: <https://www.pravda.com.ua/rus/news/2013/12/8/7005453/>].

Anon., "ŠČo uvičnjujut' pam'janiki Kieva?," *Tyžden.ua*, 4 April 2012, [accessed online 19.06.2018: <http://tyzhden.ua/History/49437>].

Anon., "Pokrovitelja Kieva trebujut 'otbelit' I 'pereodet,'" *UNIAN*, 31 July 2007, [accessed online 19.06.2018: <https://www.unian.net/society/56514-pokrovitelya-kieva-trebu yut-otbelit-i-pereodet.html>].

Bedritskiy, A., A. Kochetkov, and S. Byshok, *Ukraine after Euromaidan. Democracy under Fire* (2015).

Beissinger, M.R., "Structure and Example in Modular Political Phenomena. The Diffusion of Bulldozer/Rose/Orange/Tulip Revolutions," in *Perspectives on Politics*, 5, no. 2 (2007), 259-276.

Bredies, I., A. Umland, and V. Yakushik, *Aspects of the Orange Revolution. IV, Foreign assistance and civic action in the 2004 Ukrainian Presidential Elections* (Stuttgart, 2014)

Dahl, R.A., *A Preface to Democratic Theory* (Chicago, 1956).

Džurkovič, M., "Otpor vnov na Ukraine: Kto oni, psy (nenasilstvennoj) vojny?," *Russkaja Obščina*, 2 January 2014, [accessed online 19.06.2018: <http://www. russian.kiev.ua/ material.php?id=11608005>].

Filenko, V., "Vojnu vyigraem, kogda vypolnim trebovanija Majdana," *Korrespondent.net*, 26 November 2014, [accessed online 19.06.2018: <http://korrespondent.net/ ukraine/ politics/3448237-vladymyr-fylenko-voinu-vyyhraem-kohda-vypolnym-trebovanyia-maidana.

Gerlach, J., *Color Revolutions in Eurasia* (Heidelberg, 2014).

Hollander, S., *The Politics of Referendum Use in European Democracies* (New York, 2019).

Jowitt, K., "Soviet Neotraditionalism. The Political Corruption of a Leninist Regime," in *Soviet Studies* 35, no. 3 (1983), 275-297.

Karklins, R., *Ethnopolitics and Transition to Democracy: The Collapse of the USSR and Latvia* (Baltimore, 1994).

Kazanskyi, D., "The Third Coming? Is Maidan 3.0 possible, and what would it look like?," *The Ukrainian Week*, 17 December 2015, [accessed online 19.06.2018: <http:// ukrainianweek.com/Politics/154194>].

Kolstø, P., *Russians in the Former Soviet Republics* (London, 1995).

Kučma, L., *Posle Majdana 2005-2006. Zapiski prezidenta* (Moscow, 2007).

Kuzio, T., "Ukraine between a Constrained EU and Assertive Russia," in *Journal of Common Market Studies* 55 (2016), 103-120.

Kuzio, T., "Political Culture and Democracy" in *East European Politics and Societies* 25 (2011), 88-113.

Kuzio, T., "Ukraine and the Yugoslav Conflict," in *Nationalities Papers* 25 (1997), 587-600.

Laclau, E., "'Socialism,' the 'People,' 'Democracy'. The Transformation of Hegemonic Logic," in *Social Text* 7 (1983), 115-119.

Levitsky, S., and L.A. Way, *Competitive Authoritarianism: Hybrid Regimes After the Cold War* (Cambridge, Mass., 2010).

Lucardie, P., "From Crisis to Democracy. An Exercise in Political Imagination," in J. Gijsenbergh, S.K. Hollander, T. Houwen, and W. de Jong (eds.), *Creative Crises of Democracy* (Brussels, 2012), 47-60.

Melvin, N., *Russians Beyond Russia. The Politics of National Identity* (London, 1995).

Meurs, W. van, "Die Transformation in den baltischen Staaten. Baltische Wirtschaft und russische Diaspora," in *Berichte des Bundesinstitut für ostwissenschaftliche und internationale Studien* 6 (1999), 1-44.

Negru, N., *Twitter Revolution: Episode One Moldova* (Chişinău, 2010).

Nora, P. "Between Memory and History: Les Lieux de Mémoire," in *Representations* 26 (1989), 7-24.

Onuch, O., "Who Were the Protesters?," in *Journal of Democracy* 25 (2014), 44-51.

Plokhy, S., "The Ghosts of Pereyaslav: Russo-Ukrainian Historical Debates in the Post-Soviet Era," in *Europe-Asia Studies* 53 (2010), 489-505.

Riabchuk, M., "Ukrainians as Russia's Negative 'Other': History Comes Full Circle," in *Communist and Post-Communist Studies* 49 (2016), 75-85.

Sakwa, R., *Frontline Ukraine: Crisis in the Borderlands* (London, 2014).

Samokhvalov, V., "Ukraine Between Russia and the European Union: Triangle Revisited," *Europe-Asia Studies* 67 (2015), 1371-1393.

Saward, M., *The Representative Claim* (Oxford, 2010).

Setälä, M-L, *Referendums and Democratic Government: Normative Theory and the Analysis of Institutions* (Houndmills, 1999).

Sidorčik, A., "'Koričnevyj' mjatež na Ukraine," *Argumenty i Fakty*, January 20, 2014, [accessed online 19.06.2018: <http://www.aif.ru/euromaidan/opinion/korichnevyy_myatezh_na_ukraine>].

Šmajda, T., "Pomarančeva revoljucija I Evromajdan: vidminnosti, ščo možut' koštuvati peremogi," *Textu Analitičnij centr*, 25 November 2013, [accessed online 19.06.2018: <http://texty.org.ua/pg/article/editorial/read/49929/Pomarancheva_revolucija_i_Jevr omajdan_vidminnosti_shho_mozhut>].

Stepanenko V., and Y. Pylynskyi, *Ukraine After the Euromaidan. Challenges and Hopes* (Bern, 2015).

Stražnyj O., *Mentalitet Majdanu. Xronika podij – svidčennja* očevydciv (Kyjiv, 2016).

Thumann, M., "Putins Albtraum: Orange," in *Die Zeit* 50 (2004), 4-5.

Tilly, C., "Invention, Diffusion, and Transformation of the Social Movement Repertoire," in *European Review of History* 12, no. 7 (2005), 307-320.

Tolkačov, O., "Pora pomarančevogo Majdanu," *Radio Svoboda*, 22 November 2009, [accessed online 19.06.2018: <http://www.radiosvoboda.org/a/1884961.html>].

Tucker, J., "Enough! Electoral Fraud, Collective Action Problems, and Post-Communist Colored Revolutions," in *Perspectives on Politics* 5, no. 3 (2011), 535-551.

Weber, M, "Politics as a Vocation," in J. Dreijmanis (ed.), *Max Weber's Complete Writings on Academic and Political Vocations*, (New York, 2008), 155-208.

White, S., and I. McAllister, "Rethinking the "Orange Revolution," in *Journal of Communist Studies and Transition Politics* 25 (2009), 227-254.

Wittkowsky, A., *Fünf Jahre ohne Plan: die Ukraine 1991-96; Nationalstaatsbildung, Wirtschaft und Eliten* (Hamburg, 1998).

Zuev, V., "Ukraina i 'Cvetnye revoljucii,'" *Left.ru*, 5 January 2009, [accessed online 19.06.2018: <http://left.ru/2009/1/zuev183-2.phtml>].

Zunneberg, C., and W. van Meurs, "EuroMaidan. Democratie ten top of ten val?," in *Donau* 1 (2014), 64-69.

CHAPTER 10

Regulation without Representation? Independent Regulatory Authorities and Representative Claim-Making in the Netherlands, 1997-Now

Adriejan van Veen

Introduction

Independent regulatory authorities (IRAS) such as the US Federal Trade Commission (FTC), the British Office of Communications (Ofcom), and the Dutch *Autoriteit Financiële Markten* 'Financial Markets Authority' (AFM) wield considerable public power in today's capitalist democracies. They regulate the behaviour of businesses and professions in liberalised marketplaces such as telecommunications, energy, public transport, financial markets, and healthcare. IRAS set prices and standards, regulate market and infrastructure access, and provide consumer information. They enforce compliance through banning, fining, or "naming and shaming" transgressors. IRAS also advise lawmakers on new regulatory frameworks, participate in transnational regulatory networks, and speak out on sensitive political matters.[1] And yet, the decisions of these powerful public bodies are not fully controlled *ex ante* by either affected stakeholders or by democratic institutions such as government and parliaments. Even though their competences are demarcated by law, IRAS have the discretionary authority to independently make decisions on regulation and supervision.[2] The question might therefore be asked: who, or what, do IRAS represent?

This question, however, is rarely posed in the literature on independent market regulation. Three scholarly approaches regarding the position of IRAS in today's capitalist democracies can be distinguished. First, in the "technocratic" approach, the legitimacy of IRAS is based on the quality of their policy outputs. Because of their independence and expertise, IRAS are supposedly capable of delivering results that are qualitatively better than those of traditional political or bureaucratic institutions.[3] Secondly, in the "delegation"

---

1   Baldwin (2012); Levi-Faur (2011); Duijkersloot (2007); Coen (2005); Majone (1996).
2   Gilardi (2008); Verhey (2005); Zijlstra (2005); Thatcher (2002).
3   Maggetti (2010); Vibert (2007); Sosay (2006); Majone (1999).

© ADRIEJAN VAN VEEN, 2019 | DOI:10.1163/9789004291966_011
This is an open access chapter distributed under the terms of the CC-BY-NC 4.0 License.

approach, IRAs are democratically legitimate because government and parliaments have delegated public powers to them, and keep them in check through mechanisms of accountability and control. IRAs act as "agents" for their political "principals."[4] Thirdly, in the "relational" approach, IRAs are thought to derive legitimacy from their position in a field of public and private actors – including courts, businesses, and consumers – to whom they are responsive and whose opinions they balance when making decisions. This is variously described as "interactive" policy-making, "participatory" or "deliberative" governance, or "horizontal" accountability.[5]

Of course, each approach can be normatively criticised, while the approaches at some point are incompatible. IRAs that are too much kept in check by elected politicians might not be independent enough to achieve higher-quality results, while too much cosiness with private actors might likewise harm their independent stature.[6] Yet, despite these disagreements, adherents of all approaches in the literature seem to agree on one central tenet: that IRAs, because of their independence from political institutions and affected stakeholders, are "unrepresentative." According to the Swiss regulations scholar Fabrizio Gilardi, IRAs "do not conform to the representative model"[7] and according to Martino Maggetti they do "not rely on any claim of representativeness."[8] They are "non-majoritarian institutions" (NMIs), public bodies "that are neither directly elected by the people nor directly managed by elected officials."[9] Since delegation to these independent bodies constitutes a transfer of powers "away from elected bodies to unelected ones,"[10] they supposedly have a "non-elective and non-representative nature."[11] Power in capitalist democracies has therefore shifted from democratic institutions to "unrepresentative" bodies such as IRAs.[12]

In this contribution, I take issue with these statements about the unrepresentative nature of IRAs. While their establishment certainly constitutes a historic shift of decision-making power from elected to unelected bodies, this does not mean that IRAs have no representative claims. On the contrary: they do, and analysing the representative claims of IRAs is crucial to any evaluation

---

4   Vibert (2007); Thatcher (2005); Strom (2003); Epstein (1999).
5   Bovens (2010); Maggetti (2010); Black (2008); Sosay (2006); Sabel (2008); Yackee (2006); Majone (1999).
6   Maggetti (2010); Sosay (2006).
7   Gilardi (2008) 25.
8   Maggetti (2010) 2.
9   Thatcher (2002) 2.
10   Coen (2005) 300.
11   Maggetti (2010) 2.
12   Papadopoulos (2010) 1043.

REGULATION WITHOUT REPRESENTATION? 173

of their position in today's democracies. My analysis of the representative claims historically and presently made of, by, and around four IRAS in the Netherlands is based on recent advances in representation theory. In contrast to the literature on independent market regulation, in which "being representative" is equated with "being elected," representation theorists such as Michael Saward conceive of representation as a much more dynamic process. Representation is a discursive and performative process in which a claimant asserts that an entity stands or acts for a constituency – a claim that may or may not be accepted by an audience. Representation consists of the construction of a representative and "the represented" in an interactive relationship.[13] This happens in parliaments, where elected politicians claim to represent popular constituencies;[14] in civil society, where interest and protest groups do the same;[15] and, so I will argue, in the world of independent market regulation. Recognising this provides insight into a crucial historical change to representative democracies, and is, I will argue, a contribution to the existing approaches to the position of IRAS in these polities.

In the following, I will first discuss the theory of representation developed by Saward in *The Representative Claim* (2010). Then, I will show how the heuristic tool of the "representative claim framework" (RCF) can be applied to IRAS, and discuss my case selection. Subsequently, using the RCF tool, I will demonstrate how four Dutch IRAS were claimed by elected lawmakers in the 1990s and 2000s to represent – in a non-electoral, independent way – certain constructed constituencies on liberalised marketplaces. The four IRAS, I will then show, continued making representative claims after their establishment. Thirdly, I will show how the interaction between these IRAS and affected interests in consultation procedures constitutes a reciprocal process of representative claim-making and reception. Lastly, I will discuss the contribution of a representative claims analysis of IRAS to the three standard scholarly approaches to their legitimacy, and to our understanding of the historical change of representative democracies embodied by IRAS.

Representation as a Process of Claim-making and Reception

Representation is often equated with elections. A "representative democracy" according to many people is a political system in which a geographical and

---

13   Saward (2010; 2009; 2006; 2005).
14   De Wilde (2013); Severs (2010).
15   Marochi (2010).

cultural constituency – the people of a nation – elects a parliamentary body (and perhaps a president) on the basis of the "one person, one vote" principle. Historically, however, the term representation was more broadly applied,[16] and even today this remains so. Interest groups, social movements, independent ombudsmen, religious leaders, and celebrities all claim to represent constituencies, even though they are not elected. And often, their claims are accepted by democratic institutions and the public alike. Apparently, elections do not exhaust representation.

In *The Representative Claim* Saward offers a theorisation of representation as a discursive and performative process. It consists of a claimant asserting that an entity stands or acts for a constituency. An audience may or may not accept this representative claim. Representation is therefore dynamic, even ubiquitous: it happens across societies. But it is also unstable: audiences do not necessarily accept representative claims. This conceptualisation of representation sets it apart from earlier ones, in which representation was equated with institutional mechanisms like elections, or defined by normative values like political equality.[17] In Saward's view, representation is a communicative, reciprocal process playing out between claimants and audiences.

Saward's conceptualisation opens up the political world at large for investigations into representative claim-making and reception. Political and societal institutions, mechanisms, and communicative processes can be investigated for representative claims made about them or in them. To this end, he offers the heuristic tool of the "representative claim framework" (RCF). In representation, a *claim-maker* (an individual or collective, 'M') presents a *subject* (itself, or some other individual or collective, 'S') as standing for or acting in the interests of an *object* (a creative depiction of a constituency and its interests, 'O'). *Audiences* ('A') may receive, evaluate, and decide whether to accept or reject a representative claim – and thus consider 'S' a representative. To the extent that audiences recognise *themselves* and their perceived interests as implicated in a claim, moreover, they may consider themselves a *constituency* (see Figure 10.1).

Representation conceptualised as such happens in many physical and virtual spaces: in the parliamentary arena, in the news media, at election meetings, at protest marches, in governance networks, and so forth. Makers make claims about institutions, about persons, about themselves, acting or standing for constituencies, vis-à-vis audiences (including potential constituencies). Representation is flexible: a claim-maker can offer *him/her/itself* as the representing subject, but also *someone or something else*. Representative claims can

---

16   Pitkin (1967) 2-4.
17   See: Pitkin (1967); Eulau and Karps (1977).

REGULATION WITHOUT REPRESENTATION? 175

> A *maker* of representations ('M') puts forward a *subject* ('S') which stands or acts for an *object* ('O'), and is offered to an *audience* ('A').

FIGURE 10.1   The representative claim framework (RCF) (adapted from Saward 2010: 36).
    Note: In Saward's original model, a fifth element was included: the *referent* ('R'),
    or real-life entity of which the *object* is the representation. Since this entity is
    "unrepresentable" other than as a representation, however, I have dropped it
    from the framework. Saward (2010) 36-38.

be acts of self-representation and other-representation, while audiences can be multiple and diverse. They can consist of potential constituencies, as well as of outside observers.

Central to the dynamics between representative claim-makers and audiences are "cultural resources" and "constituency constructions." "Cultural resources," first, are employed by claimants to convince audiences (including potential constituencies) that they – or someone or something else – stand or act for someone or something else. Cultural resources can be conceptualised as the cultural meanings or normative principles that claimants and audiences must share in order for representative claims to be successful.[18] For example: the *transparency* and *regularity* of *elections* based on the principle of "one person, one vote" constitute powerful cultural resources for politicians in their claims to represent constituencies. Most audiences in contemporary democracies will accept these claims. Yet alternative and additional cultural resources exist and are regularly employed, including non-electoral ones:

- Ombudsmen may claim that their very *independence* from politics and the bureaucracy enables them to represent the interests of citizens vis-à-vis the administration;
- Interest groups or trade unions may claim that intra-organisational *authorisation and accountability mechanisms* connect them to their memberships, and that they therefore represent these constituencies;
- Climatologists or other specialists or professionals may claim that their *expertise* lends them authoritative insight into the "real" interests of a group or collective, and that they can therefore speak for or on behalf of them;
- Minority politicians, religious leaders or monarchs may claim that their *identity* connects them to their community, and that they therefore represent it;

---

18   Saward (2010) 75.

Constituency construction is a second crucial element of representative claim-making. Collective identities are never "natural" or "given," but always constructed in a socially discursive process.[19] Representative claim-makers make *assertions* about the identities and interests of the constituencies purportedly represented by them or others. They may paint constituency identities and interests precisely ("I represent the membership of the national association of dentists" or "the Turkish minority of Rotterdam") or vaguely ("I speak for the common people" or "the public"). Representative claim-making is a creative and aesthetic process.

Audiences, on their turn, employ cultural resources and evaluate constituency constructions to decide whether to *accept* or *reject* representative claims. The "success" of a representative claim largely depends, first, on the "match" between the cultural resources employed by claimants and those employed by audiences. A protest leader may, for example, not be considered a "true" representative by the news media, because he/she is not authorised by a constituency. Audiences, secondly, also have to recognise the constituency constructions of representative claim-makers as somehow accurate. Someone who does not consider himself a member of a downtrodden minority will likely not feel represented by this minority's purported spokesperson. Audiences may actively contest the claims of representative claim-makers, and offer an alternative picture of a constituency's identity and interests. In doing so, audience members become representative claim-makers themselves.[20]

Representative claim-making so can take many forms: electoral and non-electoral, formal and informal, explicit and implicit. Political rhetoric and debate often contain claims about institutions, organisations, or individuals being the best spokespeople or guardians *for* constituencies – because they are authorised by them, or, on the contrary, are independent from them. And these constituencies and their interests are necessarily discursively constructed – although they may be perceived as more or less accurate by audiences. Whether audiences and/or constituencies accept them, is another question.

According to Saward, neither cultural resources nor the accuracy of constituency constructions determine whether a representative claim should be considered democratically legitimate. Representative claims should be considered democratically legitimate when constituencies that a claimant *intends* to represent *actually feel represented*. In an open society, the demonstrable acceptance by this appropriate constituency of a representative claim about them – backed up by whatever cultural resources claimants employ, and

---

19   Saward (2010) 49, 74; cf. Ankersmit (1996); Anderson (1986).
20   Saward (2010) 48-56.

REGULATION WITHOUT REPRESENTATION? 177

constituencies accept, be they elections, authorisation and accountability mechanisms, notions of shared identity or of substantive expertise – should count for the democratic legitimacy of this particular claim.[21] Saward argues that it is up to researchers to investigate *who* makes representative claims, *what* their contents are, *how* they are received, and *why* they are accepted or rejected.

Studying Representative Claims in Regulatory Governance

IRAS are among the most powerful public authorities today. Their decisions in liberalised marketplaces affect millions of businesses, professionals, and consumers, and involve billions of euros and dollars. Yet they are anomalies in the "textbook model" of representative democracy: their decisions are not fully controlled *ex ante* by either affected stakeholders or by democratic institutions such as governments and parliaments. This has led many researchers to consider IRAS "unrepresentative." But are they? I argue they are not, and to support this argument I will perform a representative claims analysis on a selection of IRAS.

The four IRAS examined in this article are Dutch. The Netherlands is an interesting country setting for this project. Compared to other continental European countries, the Netherlands have since the 1980s been at the vanguard of liberalisation and privatisation policies in such domains as telecommunications, energy, railways, and healthcare.[22] The same goes for the delegation of public powers to independent agencies ("agencification"): Dutch IRAS by now are not as independent and powerful as their American or British counterparts, but more so than in most European countries.[23] IRAS have since the 1990s become a prominent feature of the Dutch governance system and have in recent years been the subject of controversy.[24] Hence it is very interesting to investigate who, or what, these unelected bodies (claim to) represent.

To ensure external validity with the population of IRAS at large, four Dutch cases were selected that were (a) formally independent from both the political sphere and affected interests (b) involved in market regulation (c) a public authority. To reflect variety in the wider population of IRAS, cases were selected

---

21   Saward (2010) 146-48.
22   Dan et al. (2012); Stellinga (2012).
23   Gilardi (2008) 59.
24   Van den Berg (2012); Van Gestel, Eijlander, and Peters (2007).

that operated in different economic domains, and had different goals and competences. This resulted in the following selection:

- the *Onafhankelijke Post en Telecommunicatie Autoriteit* 'Independent Mail and Telecommunications Authority' (OPTA): the Dutch telecommunications regulator from 1997 to 2013;[25]
- the *Nederlandse Mededingsautoriteit Energiekamer* 'Netherlands Competition Authority Energy Chamber' (NMa Energy Chamber): the Dutch energy regulator from 1998 to 2013;[26]
- the *Autoriteit Financiële Markten* 'Financial Markets Authority' (AFM): the Dutch financial markets supervisor since 2002;
- the *Nederlandse Zorgautoriteit* 'Netherlands Healthcare Authority' (NZa): the Dutch healthcare market regulator since 2006

Representative claims about and by these four IRAS were studied in the following way:

To study representative claims *about* these four IRAS, acts of establishment and related parliamentary debates were studied. These were expected to contain constructions of the IRAS as *subject* ('S'): bodies with a certain nature or properties, which enable it to act or stand for certain constituencies as *object* ('O'). These constituencies, likewise, are creative depictions of people as having a certain nature or interests. The *makers* ('M') of these representative claims are governmental and parliamentary lawmakers. In laws and debates, lawmakers publicly elaborate on the nature of IRAS and the constituencies they act or stand for. The Dutch citizenry may be considered the general *audience* ('A') of these claims.[27] Legislative representative claims about IRAS can be considered the "constitutive" representative claims of the independent bodies: henceforth they embody these.

To study representative claims *by* the four selected IRAS, their websites, annual reports, and policy documents were studied. These, too, were expected to contain constructions of the IRAS as *subject* ('S'): bodies that act or stand for certain constructed constituencies as *objects* ('O'). Now, however, the *makers*

---

25   In 2013, OPTA was merged with the competition authority *Nederlandse Mededingings-autoriteit* (NMa) and the *Consumentenautoriteit* 'Consumer Authority' to form the *Autoriteit Consument and Markt* 'Consumer and Market Authority' (ACM).

26   In 1998, this IRA was established as the *Dienst uitvoering en toezicht Elektriciteitswet* (DTe). In 1999, it became a chamber of NMa. From 2008 onwards, it was called *NMa Energiekamer* until the 2013 merger into ACM.

27   Potentially, audiences can be multiple and diverse. Since the intention of a claim-maker is not always clear, however, here the Dutch citizenry is considered the audience.

('M') of these representative claims are the IRAs themselves. In the public sphere, the independent bodies craft an image of themselves and the constituencies they claim to act or stand for. The Dutch citizenry, but also affected interests such as businesses and professionals, may be considered the *audience* ('A') of these representative claims.[28]

To study representative claims in the policy-making processes of the four IRAs, lastly, consultative procedures were studied. IRAs regularly consult affected interests before making decisions: corporations, professional groups, and consumer organisations who claim to have a stake in the outcome.[29] These consultative procedures were expected to involve a reciprocal process of representative claim-making and reception: assertions by IRAs and lobbyists alike about which constituencies and interests would be served by IRA decisions. Yet these consultations are not public, and therefore recourse was taken to 20 in-depth interviews with IRA staffers and 25 with lobbyists. This allowed insight into the representative claim-making strategies both IRAs and affected interests regularly employ when deliberating about regulatory decisions.

Except for the last section, the *reception* of the representative claims about and by IRAs was not studied. This would have involved survey research among the Dutch public. The following is therefore a qualitative account of representative claim-making in regulatory governance.

Representative Claims about IRAs: Representing Public Interests

The establishment of IRAs in the Netherlands followed the marketisation of economic and societal domains and the agencification of government organisations since the 1980s.[30] From the early 1990s onwards, Dutch lawmakers liberalised and marketised the telecommunications and energy sectors. State companies were gradually privatised, while new competitors were allowed. From the 2000s onwards, Dutch lawmakers enacted new regulations for the financial sector, while they liberalised and marketised the healthcare sector.[31] In all these sectors, lawmakers established IRAs: regulatory bodies whose decisions would not be fully controlled *ex ante* by affected stakeholders or democratic institutions. Which representative claims did lawmakers make about these new bodies?

---

28 Once more, however, intended audiences are difficult to pinpoint, and this will not be attempted.
29 Lavrijssen (2006); Yackee (2006).
30 Stellinga (2012); Verhey (2005); Van Thiel (2000).
31 Stellinga (2012).

The representative claims about the first generation of IRAS were rather general. Dutch lawmakers (*makers*) in 1997-1998 argued that the telecommunications regulator OPTA was to be temporarily independent from the political sphere because the state still had financial interests in the former state company KPN. OPTA was to be impartial, its decisions solely based on "expertise" (*subject*).

> The societal and economic interest (*object*) involved in the tasks is best served [...] with a division of tasks between a minister and an arms-length specialized administrative organ (*subject*).[32]

Lawmakers claimed that the economic interest served with OPTA's tasks was the "competitiveness of the Netherlands" (*object*), to which telecommunications liberalisation would contribute.[33] As an independent "guardian of general societal and consumer interests" (*object*),[34] moreover, OPTA (*subject*) would "protect" universal access to basic telecom services, freedom of choice for users, privacy, and state security.[35] Lawmakers thus claimed that OPTA, through its independent decisions – made beyond the purview of stakeholders and democratic institutions – would act in the interests of the Dutch economy and society. This was a representative claim, if a rather general one. The energy regulator DTe in 1998, meanwhile, was only made independent *de facto*, while Dutch lawmakers in the legislative package simply stated that energy liberalisation would give "customers and suppliers" more "freedom of choice."[36] Since lawmakers expected telecom and energy liberalisation to be accomplished quickly, they considered these IRAS temporary, exceptional bodies.[37] Their transitional nature apparently required no representative claims other than rather unspecific ones.

This changed around 2000, however, when criticism of the liberalisation and marketisation policies of the past decades erupted. Important Dutch advisory bodies such as the *Raad van State* 'Council of State' and the *Wetenschappelijke Raad voor het Regeringsbeleid* 'Scientific Council for Government Policy' (WRR) stated that after years of liberalisation policies, the balance with societal "interests" like the continuous availability, quality, and reasonable price of goods and services had to be rethought. The WRR wrote that Dutch lawmakers

---

32 Second Chamber (1996-1997a) 2-3.
33 Second Chamber (1996-1997b) 2.
34 Second Chamber (1996-1997a) 2.
35 Second Chamber (1996-1997b) 4.
36 Second Chamber (1997-1998) 7.
37 Second Chamber (1996-1997a) 9-10; Second Chamber (1997-1998) 6-7.

REGULATION WITHOUT REPRESENTATION?

"too often too unthinkingly and too unprepared had made a choice for marketisation, without having been sufficiently aware of the (necessity of guaranteeing) the public interests at stake."[38] Both advisory bodies called for an enhanced role of IRAS in this respect. And the Dutch government responded, making more specific and consistent representative claims about the unelected bodies.

The government, in a series of reports in 2001-2004, wrote that the elected political sphere – parliament and government – had to retain an important role in guaranteeing so-called "public interests" in liberalised domains. This rhetorical construct was new to Dutch political discourse at the time. Until then, the term "general interest" was often employed when referring to state intervention in economic domains, for instance to deliver goods and services to citizens via state companies.[39] Now, the term "public interests" became current, to signify concrete desiderata (interests) in economic and societal domains, and the exact beneficiaries (constituencies) of these desiderata. The Dutch government considered a well-functioning liberalised marketplace and transparent consumer information *economic* public interests, belonging to people constructed as *producers and consumers*. Universal service provision and the quality and safety of networks it also considered *non-economic* or *societal* interests, belonging to people constructed as *citizens*.[40] With this distinction, the government picked sides in a debate between competing schools of thought about regulatory rationales and constructed a constituency to be represented by IRAS.

Around 2000, one school of Dutch policy advisors held that ongoing marketisation policies necessarily were in the general interest, as they enlarged economic welfare. They depicted the beneficiaries of these policies strictly as *producers and consumers*. Only economic analysis could, in their view, determine whether any public interests *other* than free markets existed.[41] Another school, however, represented by the WRR, held that multiple rationales for determining public interests existed, one of them being *citizenship rights*: the right of every citizen, notwithstanding economic position, to certain goods and services. In their view, it was up to parliament to determine public interests – aided by economic analysis, but not exclusively so. And IRAS, according to the WRR, had an important role to play in independently guaranteeing and

---

38   Wetenschappelijke Raad voor het Regeringsbeleid (WRR) (2000) 162; cf. Raad van State (2000) 49-50.
39   De Pree (2008) 289-92.
40   Second Chamber (2003-2004a) 2-6.
41   Teulings (2003); De Pree (2008) 312-313.

furthering economic and societal public interests in liberalised domains.[42] The WRR called upon Dutch lawmakers to henceforth more explicitly formulate *within* regulatory legislation which interests of the public were at stake in liberalised domains, and how IRAS were to independently guarantee or further these.

Dutch lawmakers did exactly this in the early years of the twenty-first century. First of all, they gave a new interpretation to the capacities of IRAS that – so they claimed – allowed them to represent public interests. In 1997-1998, the early regulatory bodies OPTA and DTe had only hesitantly been hived off from *ex ante* political control because the state's ownership of telecom and energy companies required it. After 2000, Dutch lawmakers started to frame independence as an inherently desirable trait – a cultural resource that allowed the bodies to act or stand for public interests in a way the elected political sphere could not. IRAS in a 2001 report were called "indispensable" because they were "objective," "professional," and "fact-based."[43] When establishing the AFM in 2001 – an independent regulatory body in the financial sector, a domain in which the state did *not* have direct financial interests – lawmakers stated its independence was of "unabated value" to "expertise-based supervision."[44] And in 2004, the Dutch government proclaimed the independence of IRAS from politics an "uncontested" principle because it meant being removed from "today's thinking in politics."[45]

Secondly, Dutch lawmakers after 2000 more clearly delineated which publics and interests IRAS were to independently stand and act for. In 2004, they (*maker*) made the representative claim that a new and revamped OPTA (now independent for the near future and with expanded regulatory powers) would, on the basis of its expertise (*subject*), "further the interests of end users (*object*) in terms of choice, price and quality" of telecommunications.[46] In its decisions on market entry, universal provision, and privacy, it would place the "interests of citizens and businesses" (*object*) in the telecom sector at its heart.[47] That same year, Dutch lawmakers also made the representative claim that NMa Energy Chamber, now fully independent, would in its expertise-based decisions secure the "public interests" of energy consumers, businesses, and citizens in a competitive, non-discriminatory, and transparent marketplace,

---

42   WRR (2000).

43   Second Chamber (2000-2001) 12.

44   Second Chamber (2001-2002) 35.

45   Second Chamber (2003-2004a) 8.

46   Telecommunications Act Revision Act 2004 Art. I art. 1-3.

47   Second Chamber (2002-2003) 11.

REGULATION WITHOUT REPRESENTATION? 183

with quality networks and supply security.[48] In 2006, Dutch lawmakers made the representative claim that AFM in its expertise-based decisions, made independently from political and stakeholder control, would "guard" and "further" the "public interests" of financial businesses and consumers in an orderly, transparent financial marketplace marked by careful customer treatment.[49] And Dutch lawmakers in 2006 made the representative claim that the independent healthcare authority NZa in its expertise-based decisions would secure the public interests of the Dutch citizenry in the accessibility, affordability, and quality of marketised healthcare.[50]

After 2000, lawmakers specifically emphasised the public interests of one specific (constructed) constituency: consumers. They claimed that OPTA and Energy Chamber would further the interests of consumers in free choice and market transparency.[51] AFM's supervision was targeted at the "self-responsible consumer," who nevertheless required careful treatment.[52] The NZa was legally obligated to "put the general consumer interest first" in its duties.[53] And when OPTA, NMa and a third IRA – the Consumer Authority – were merged in 2013, this was claimed to be in the "interest of the consumer."[54] By then, Dutch lawmakers had established a host of institutions which were claimed on the basis of their expertise to represent the interests of various publics: businesses, consumers, and citizens. The IRAS would do so independently from democratic institutions and affected stakeholders.

Representative Claims by IRAS: Protecting and Emancipating Consumers

Since their establishment in the late 1990s and early 2000s, the four IRAS themselves have consistently reproduced these representative claims. On their websites, in annual reports, and in policy documents, they present(ed) themselves as independent and expert bodies. OPTA (*maker*) presented its ability to make independent decisions as a matter of "integrity" (*subject*);[55] NZa (*maker*) pres-

---

48   Second Chamber (2003-2004b) 1; cf. ibid. 1-5.
49   Second Chamber (2003-2004c) 28-30.
50   Second Chamber (2004-2005) 5-7.
51   Second Chamber (2002-2003) 11; idem (2003-2004b) 6.
52   Second Chamber (2001-2002) 14.
53   Healthcare Market Structuring Act 2006 art. 3-4.
54   Consumer and Market Authority Establishment Act 2013.
55   OPTA (2013a).

ents itself as independent "market master," "supervisor," and "advisor" (*subject*).[56] NMa (*maker*) on its website emphasised that it employed about 400 "highly educated people" (*subject*).[57] NZa (*maker*) claims that acting on the basis of "expertise" (*subject*) is one of its "core values."[58] But over the years, the IRAS have also begun to emphasise another quality: their communicativeness, especially vis-à-vis businesses and professional groups. OPTA publicly invited sectoral interests to "think along" and "exercise influence";[59] AFM emphasised its "dialogue" with financial interests, the political sphere, and the general public;[60] NZa stresses it performs its tasks "together with" the healthcare sector.[61] Being communicative now constitutes part of the representative claim of IRAS.

All four IRAS in their public presentation also have constructed constituencies in whose interests they claim to make their independent decisions. AFM (*maker*), in its annual reports, has depicted financial market participants, consumers, the general public, and the state (*objects*) as beneficiaries of its independent supervision of the financial sector.[62] NMa and AFM (*makers*), during the financial crisis of 2007-2008, (re)presented themselves (*subject*) as "restorers" of the Dutch public's (*object*) trust in free markets.[63] NZa claims with its independent decisions to represent "three public interests (*object*) in healthcare": accessibility, affordability, and transparency about quality.[64] Economic actors on free marketplaces and public interests figure prominently as constructed constituencies in the representative claims of the four IRAS about themselves, like they did in the original claims of lawmakers.

Over the years, moreover, the four IRAS have especially emphasised how their regulatory activities are "in the interest of the consumer."[65] In 2005, OPTA stated it would primarily pursue the consumer interest by stimulating market competition.[66] A year later, *both* market competition *and* consumer protection were stated to be the IRA's mission;[67] and in 2008, the consumer interest was claimed to be central to OPTA's activities, its annual report laced with pictures of consumers (see Figure 10.2).

---

56   NZa (2008) 8-9; idem (2010) 11; idem (2014a).
57   NMa (2013a).
58   NZa (2008) 9-10.
59   OPTA (2011) 69; idem (2013a).
60   AFM (2009) 36-38; idem (2013) 73.
61   NZa (2014a).
62   AFM (2004) 2; idem (2011) 2; idem (2013).
63   NMa (2009) 5; AFM (2011) 2; idem (2013).
64   NZa (2014a).
65   OPTA (2013b).
66   OPTA (2005) 45.
67   OPTA (2006) 5.

REGULATION WITHOUT REPRESENTATION? 185

FIGURE 10.2   OPTA depicts its constituency in its annual report. *Source*: OPTA, Jaarverslag 2008 [accessed online 6.2.2019: <https://www.acm.nl/sites/default/files/old_publication/publicaties/9795_jaarverslag-opta-2008.pdf>].

Likewise, NMa and its Energy Chamber in 2013 claimed: "All our efforts are aimed at benefits for the consumer." Its "ultimate goal" was to "create as many economic benefits to consumers as possible."[68] NZa, for its part, on its website explained its corporate logo (see Figure 10.3) – a "modern guardian angel" – in the following way:

> This angel symbolizes the protective role of the NZa regarding the interests of the healthcare consumer. At the same time the angel symbolizes the authority and expertise of the NZa, by which it gives insurers and

---

68   NMa (2013b).

FIGURE 10.3   NZa corporate logo. Source: NZa annual report 2010.

practitioners the right incentives to provide the consumer with efficient and good healthcare.[69]

In addition to making consumers a key element in their public self-presentation, the four IRAs have started to directly engage this constituency as well. From 2007 onwards, OPTA and NMa Energy Chamber on their website *ConsuWijzer* offered consumers "transparent" and "comparable" information on telecommunications and energy providers.[70] They also collected consumer complaints, claiming – if enough of them were received – to directly intervene in the sectors "to improve the position of the consumer."[71] The two IRAs have thus depicted themselves as responsive bodies, willing to intervene in marketplaces on behalf of consumer interests. Likewise, AFM's post-2010 supervisory project "Putting the customer's interest first" was to stimulate financial corporations to give consumers transparent information on the risks of financial products. This was to give the consumer "what he *needs*" rather than "what he *wants*" (original emphases).[72] AFM so portrayed itself as a representative of consumers with insight in their "true" needs.

Vis-à-vis the consumer constituency, the four IRAs have employed a discourse of tutelage and emancipation. OPTA and NMa Energy Chamber claimed *ConsuWijzer* "strengthens the consumer" and "strives to make the consumer assertive" by giving him tools to "get to work": model letters of complaint, scripts to practice conversations with shopkeepers, and an online coach to stimulate consumers to switch energy providers.[73] Likewise, AFM on its web-

---

69   NZa (2014b).
70   NMa (2013c) 46, 58.
71   OPTA (2013c).
72   AFM (2014).
73   NMa (2013c) 58.

REGULATION WITHOUT REPRESENTATION? 187

site offers games such as "More choice with money" and "One euro is not the same as another euro" to teach consumers how to make "rational" money choices.

The IRAs have thus depicted consumers as in need of information and critical skills, and portrayed themselves as their representatives who provide information but also teach them to help themselves. In this way, the IRAs have taken an active role in constituency construction: in transforming citizens into consumers on liberalised marketplaces.

Representative Claim-Making and Reception in IRA Policy-Making Processes

IRAs regularly consult affected interests before making decisions: corporations, professional groups, and consumer organisations who claim to have a stake in the outcome.[74] But what role do the representative claims about and by IRAs play in consultative procedures? As these consultations in the Netherlands are not public, interviews were held with regular participants in these procedures: 20 IRA staffers and 25 affected interest lobbyists in the four domains.[75] First, however, I will discuss which affected interests take part in IRA consultations, and why.

1   *Who Has Access to Consultations?*
The consultative procedures of Dutch IRAs are not universally accessible. The four IRAs, as prescribed by Dutch administrative or regulatory law, but also of their own volition, determine who has access to these procedures on the basis of criteria to judge the claims of external parties to represent affected interests. When prescribed by law, these criteria determine inclusion on the basis of the "personal," "distinctive," "objective," and "relevant" materiality of the interest at stake in a decision.[76] On this basis, OPTA and NMa Energy Chamber allowed telecommunications corporations such as KPN and Vodafone, energy network operators such as Liander and Stedin, energy production and supply companies such as Nuon and Eneco, interest groups such as EnergieNed and Netbe-

---

74   Lavrijssen (2006); Yackee (2006).

75   Interviews were conducted between 2010 and 2014. The questionnaire can be found in my dissertation, *Regulation without Representation?*, which is publicly available at <https://dspace.library.uu.nl/handle/1874/306252>. Interview transcripts are available at request.

76   Lavrijssen (2006) 30-31; De Poorter (2003) 131-32. This may include organisations that represent the "general and collective interests" of others, such as interest groups and consumer organisations.

heer Nederland, and organisations for large-scale industrial energy consumers into their consultative procedures.[77]

AFM and NZa have drawn up additional criteria to evaluate the claims of external parties to represent affected interests. Parties admitted to AFM consultative procedures must "faithfully represent" interests in the financial sector,[78] while those admitted to NZa consultations must conform to certain criteria for democratic representation. Healthcare interest groups, for example, must have elected boards and be accountable to their members.[79] On this basis, at AFM, big banks such as ABN AMRO and ING, and about twenty financial interest groups for bankers, accountants, and big and small investors are represented in consultative procedures.[80] At NZa, about thirty interest groups for healthcare insurers, hospitals, medical specialists, dentists, general practitioners, and the like are represented.[81]

Finally, IRA staffers sometimes decide on inclusion in an ongoing fashion without clear criteria. Many interviewed staffers and interest group lobbyists have mentioned that regulatory governance in the Netherlands is a "small world." IRA staffers and lobbyists "know whom to call" when input seems required.[82] Consumer organisations such as *Consumentenbond* 'Consumer's League', *Vereniging voor Effectenbezitters* 'Stockowners Association' (VEB), and patient groups such as the *Nederlandse Patiënten Consumenten Federatie* 'Dutch Patient Consumer Federation' (NPCF) usually are invited, but often lack the financial means, expertise, or the supposed direct interest in the decisions at hand to send delegates.[83]

During the consultative procedures, when proposed IRA decisions are discussed, a reciprocal process of representative claim-making and receiving takes place. Affected interest lobbyists must represent the material and financial interests of their employers, but as claim-makers, make creative constructions of the interests involved. IRA staffers, on their turn, as audiences evaluate these representative claims, but their reception is informed by the representative claims of the IRAS as institutions. Four representative claim-making strategies and patterns of reception can be discerned.

---

77   IRA respondent (IR) 1; IR3; Stakeholder respondent (SR) 1; SR2; SR3; SR4; SR5; SR6.
78   AFM (2007) art. 2.3.
79   NZa (2010b).
80   AFM (2019).
81   NZa (2010b).
82   IR3; IR10; IR11; IR12; IR18; IR19; SR11; SR19.
83   IR1; IR3; IR5; IR6; IR10; IR11; IR12; IR15; IR16; SR1; SR2; SR9; SR25.

REGULATION WITHOUT REPRESENTATION?

2   *Four Strategies of Representative Claim-making and Their Reception*

IRA staffers do not appreciate lobbyists all too overtly acting as lobbyists: as representatives of the direct, material interest of their corporations or professional groups.[84] Of course, lobbyists are only allowed to the table because they represent such an interest (see above), and they may certainly state a proposed IRA decision is (not) in the direct, material interest of their constituency. As a telecom lobbyist says about consultations on fiberglass regulations: "In this game, our song is: 'We always get too little.'"[85] An OPTA staffer confirms: "These are commercial parties with commercial interests. They will say so, and we know they will say so. So nobody is fooling anyone."[86] But many interviewees do not consider self-interest based lobbying a very effective strategy, even though it is very convincing as a representative claim. According to a medical specialists' lobbyist, "if you only represent naked interests, you are not going to make it."[87] An AFM staffer confirms: "If you are too obviously agitating on the basis of your own self-interest, you are automatically not going to be very effective."[88] Because IRAS and their staffers have broader interest claims, they, like lobbyists, need to translate their arguments to these broader interests.

According to interviewees, it is more effective for lobbyists to claim to represent the direct, material interests of *multiple* corporations or professional groups.[89] "When interests run parallel, we act together," says one telecom lobbyist.[90] IRAS and their staffers seem more receptive to viewpoints on proposed decisions that are shared by multiple corporations or professional groups. One healthcare insurers' lobbyist says: "The NZa is sensitive to joint solutions. When all parties together say an alternative is better, the NZa is sensitive to that."[91] An OPTA staffer reflects: "We encountered so much resistance from all market parties to a hypothesis that we reconsidered. Despite us knowing they of course have a certain interest. All parties were united there."[92] But IRA decisions are often zero-sum games: they harm certain business interests while benefiting others. Therefore, acting in concert is often no option for affected interest lobbyists.[93]

---

84   IR3;IR8; IR9; IR11; SR2; SR10; SR14; SR15; SR16; SR18.
85   SR2.
86   IR1.
87   SR15.
88   IR11.
89   IR1; IR3; IR8; IR9; IR12; IR16; IR17; SR2; SR3; SR7; SR8; SR9; SR10; SR11; SR13; SR24.
90   SR3.
91   SR24.
92   IR3.
93   IR5; IR8; SR1; SR4; SR17; SR22; SR23.

A third, more effective strategy for lobbyists, then, is to argue that proposed IRA decisions harm or benefit public interests, such as efficient marketplace competition, transparent consumer information, or the quality of networks. According to interviewees, IRAS and their staffers appreciate it when lobbyists frame their position on proposed regulatory decisions in terms of public interests.[94] One dentists' lobbyist says: "We represent the interests of dentists, of course, but we are not going to make it by that alone. So we always have to translate [our policy proposals] to the patient's perspective and demonstrate it is also in the interest of the patient."[95] One medical specialists' lobbyist says: "You always have to appeal to a societal interest, a patient interest. That is a strong card to play."[96] These broader interests, after all, are the interests the IRAS claim to represent, and form a framework in which decisions are made. "[In specific IRA proposals] sometimes the emphasis is more on affordability, sometimes on accessibility. But in the end, you want to represent all those interests," one NZa staffer says.[97] One AFM staffer says: "We consider ourselves very much the guardian of the consumer and the investor. In economic theory, we are the agent of the investing consumer who cannot obtain redress himself."[98] And one dentists' representative says about NZa: "They approach everything from the consumer interest. So when you file a proposal, you always have to emphasise the patient perspective."[99]

Yet, since lobbyists are only allowed to consultations because they represent the material interests of their employers, their claims to represent wider constituencies – the sectoral marketplace, their customer base, the public, consumers, citizens – are not entirely credible. They are, after all, not authorised by this wider constituency. Affected interest lobbyists all give their own renditions of the "consumer interest": healthcare insurers, for instance, stress the interests of policyholders, while healthcare practitioners emphasise the needs of patients. Consumer or patient organisations themselves, meanwhile, are often absent from consultations, even though they are invited. In the words of one dentist's lobbyist: "The patient himself plays no part in the entire story."[100] One Energy Chamber staffer says: "We miss their counterforce in the consultations we arrange."[101]

---

94   IR6; IR7; IR8; IR10; IR11; IR14; IR17; IR18; SR15; SR18.
95   SR18.
96   SR15.
97   IR18.
98   IR10.
99   SR18.
100   SR18.
101   IR16.

REGULATION WITHOUT REPRESENTATION? 191

A fourth strategy for lobbyists, then, is not to present themselves (only) as public or consumer interest representatives, or as corporate lobbyists, but as "experts" and "specialists." In support or as a substitute of representative claims, lobbyists put forward "hard" evidence about the effects of proposed IRA decisions. According to interviewees, IRA staffers appreciate empirical analyses and clear-cut descriptions of problems and solutions above lobbyists "preaching to the choir" or riding "hobby horses" about direct, material interests.[102] One telecom lobbyist says: "Putting forward knowledge can influence the decision-making process. (...) The more compelling you make it, the harder it is to refute."[103] An Energy Chamber staffer confirms: "If you can base your argument on statistics, that is an enormous aid."[104]

Yet despite their appreciation of lobbyists delivering factual information, IRA staffers remain aware that, for these representatives, interests are at stake. In the words of one AFM staffer: "Lobby and expertise sometimes blend into each other."[105] Lobbyists freely admit that for them, supplying expertise and representing interests are intertwined. "You argue on the basis of methods. But you do that in your role as interest representative," says a dentists' lobbyist.[106] Even in consultation procedures that are ostensibly about technical details and the "best" solution, lobbyists seek to represent constituency interests: "Here, you help to think substantively as a system expert, but you naturally also advocate your interest. It is a combination," says a lobbyist for medical specialists about NZa technical consultations.[107] One lobbyist for industrial energy consumers reflects that in regulatory governance:

> There is no such thing as value-free knowledge. Everyone works from his own perception, and those are partly coloured by the interests you represent. By whom you are paid, and by whom you are steered.[108]

IRA consultation procedures therefore are a "theatre" of representative claim-making. All participants know that for lobbyists, the material interests of corporations and professional groups are at stake. Yet, IRAS and their staffers appreciate it when lobbyists translate their arguments to broader (public or consumer) interests, or act as experts – even though they retain a healthy

---

102   IR11; IR13; cf. IR1; IR2; IR3; IR5; IR8; IR9; IR10; IR11; SR1; SR2; SR3; SR4; SR15; SR16; SR19.
103   SR2.
104   IR9.
105   IR11.
106   SR18.
107   SR15.
108   SR19.

scepticism about these representative claims. They appreciate the effort because they themselves claim to represent public interests, in an expertise-based manner.

IRA staffers nevertheless claim to have a number of strategies to try and separate useful "facts" from self-interested viewpoints. The first of these is to apply professional skills. An OPTA staffer says about information put forward by lobbyists: "There's always an interest behind it, yes. But it's kind of your job to see through that."[109] Another OPTA staffer says: "It is the core of what we do at OPTA: weighing these kinds of insights and weighing the interests behind them."[110] Applying "checks and balances" to information put forward by lobbyists is part of this professional skill. Another strategy of IRAs is to channel interest representation and "technical" deliberations into different consultative procedures. At the NZa advisory committees, lobbyists are expected to act on the basis of constituency interests, while in NZa technical consultations, they are to act as technical specialists. Yet, says one hospital's lobbyist, "everybody knows interests are represented there."[111] In the end, however, all the input from consultations is sent to the IRA board, which takes a decision – although according to many interviewees, how they do this is not always transparent.[112]

IRA staffers value the involvement of lobbyists in regulatory decision-making: not only because they view interest representation in regulation as an inherently legitimate activity, but also because it provides them with important empirical information. Consultations, moreover, create understanding and sometimes support for IRA decisions, which facilitates compliance.[113] Yet, the "over-representation" of corporate and professional lobbyists and the "under-representation" of consumer groups according to some create dangers of informational dependency and bias.[114]

Discussion and Conclusion

In this article, Saward's representative claim framework (RCF) has been employed to study representative claims about, by, and around four IRAs in the Netherlands. It has been demonstrated that these independent agencies were politically and legislatively claimed, and publicly claim themselves to

---

109   IR3.

110   IR1.

111   SR19.

112   SR10; SR11; SR15; SR16; SR17; SR22; SR23.

113   IR1; IR3; IR8; IR9; IR10; IR11; IR15; IR16; IR19; SR1; SR3; SR8; SR10; SR13; SR15; SR19.

114   SR2.

REGULATION WITHOUT REPRESENTATION? 193

represent economic and societal public interests, including the consumer interest, in marketised and liberalised domains. The IRAS reproduce these representative claims, and have over the years increasingly emphasised their purported role as consumer protectors and emancipators. And the IRAS allow for a representation of affected interests in consultative procedures – albeit with a notable absence of consumer organisations – that constitute an important part of their decision-making processes. The statement that IRAS "do not rely on any claim of representativeness"[115] is therefore refuted. IRAS embody, reproduce, and facilitate claims about the public and consumer interests they non-electorally represent on liberalised marketplaces.

What is the added value of a representative claims approach to IRAS? I will first discuss this in relation to the three dominant approaches to the position of IRAS in representative democracy. I will also consider the historical relevance of my argument. Lastly, I will discuss the question of the democratic legitimacy of IRAS from a representative claims perspective.

To study IRAS from the perspective of the representative claim framework has brought into focus, first of all, *for* and *on behalf of* whom these independent agencies were established – who their supposed *constituencies* are, and which *interests* they are claimed to represent. In the "technocratic" approach, the legitimacy of IRAS is based on their "output": the "quality" of their policy results. The representative claims approach, however, puts front and centre who the (supposed) beneficiaries are of these results. Technocratic bodies do not operate in a vacuum; their claims to output legitimacy rest on implicit and explicit claims to represent constituencies. And so their activities can be evaluated differently. How well do IRAS serve economic and societal public interests? Are their constituencies satisfied with their performance? For technocratic bodies to consider themselves representatives of public interests, moreover, may contribute to a sense of mission as well as to greater public understanding of their role.

Secondly, this focus on the public interests claimed to be represented by IRAS creates new avenues for normative critique. In the "delegation" approach, IRAS are considered mere executive bodies, agents for their political principals; the traditional fabric of representative democracy is thought to remain intact. This view underestimates that lawmakers have set up bodies beyond direct electoral control with their own claims to constituency representation. This constitutes a historical transformation of the nature of representative democracy. Whereas before, elected parliaments represented the "general interest," now adjacent regulatory bodies also independently represent public and

---

115   Maggetti (2010) 2.

consumer interests. IRAS, indeed, actively try to make people think of themselves *as* consumers. But the construction of these constituencies and the formulation of their interests is the product of a specific period: the age of the widespread liberalisation and marketisation of public domains from the 1980s to the 2000s. Do people nowadays (still) want to be portrayed and represented as consumers? And if they do, do they feel sufficiently represented by IRAS? Viewing IRAS from the perspective of the representative claim framework makes it possible to ask such questions.

Thirdly, the representative claims approach to IRAS demonstrates the representational practices inherent to the interaction between these agencies and affected interests, such as corporations and interest groups. In "relational" approaches to the legitimacy of IRAS, this interaction is often conceptualised as "interactive policy-making," "horizontal accountability," or "participatory" or "deliberative" governance. Yet participation is often performed by *representatives*, who deliberate *on behalf of* interest and constituencies, while IRAS render account to these same *representatives*. When studying IRA-regulatee interaction, it is very worthwhile to consider which representational criteria regulate access to consultative procedures, who participates on behalf of whom, which representative claims lobbyists make, and how these are received by IRAS (and vice versa). Far from a technocratic affair, regulatory governance is about interests, and the representation of these interests is a political game that should be studied as such.

Lastly: this article has adopted and applied the viewpoint of Saward that representation should not be equated with institutional mechanisms like elections or with normative values like political equality. Representation is a discursive and performative process in which a claimant asserts an entity stands or acts for a constituency. Nevertheless, Saward holds that representative claims should be considered democratically legitimate when constituencies that a claimant *intends* to represent *actually feel represented*. Could this be applied to IRAS, which in traditional conceptions of representative democracy constitute an anomaly because they are not under full electoral control? Of course, finding out whether the various public and consumer constituencies that IRAS claim to represent, actually accept this claim, would require public opinion research. Still, IRAS can contribute to the public acceptance of their non-electoral representative claims. They could, for instance, always state clearly in whose interests their decisions are made. They could make their decision-making processes more transparent, and their outcomes easier to understand. And, considering the overrepresentation of corporate and professional interests in their consultative procedures, they could make an effort to more closely involve consumer and patient groups in consultations.

REGULATION WITHOUT REPRESENTATION? 195

This would enhance the credibility of IRAs' claim to represent public and consumer interests.

List of Respondents

IRA respondent 1: OPTA staffer.
IRA respondent 2: OPTA staffer.
IRA respondent 3: OPTA staffer.
IRA respondent 4: NMa Energy Chamber staffer.
IRA respondent 5: NMa Energy Chamber staffer.
IRA respondent 6: NMa Energy Chamber staffer.
IRA respondent 7: NMa Energy Chamber staffer.
IRA respondent 8: NMa Energy Chamber staffer.
IRA respondent 9: NMa Energy Chamber staffer.
IRA respondent 10: AFM staffer.
IRA respondent 11: AFM staffer.
IRA respondent 12: AFM staffer.
IRA respondent 13: AFM staffer.
IRA respondent 14: AFM staffer.
IRA respondent 15: NZa staffer.
IRA respondent 16: NZa staffer.
IRA respondent 17: NZa staffer.
IRA respondent 18: NZa staffer.
IRA respondent 19: NZa staffer.
IRA respondent 20: NZa staffer.
Stakeholder respondent 1: telecommunications corporation representative.
Stakeholder respondent 2: telecommunications corporation representative.
Stakeholder respondent 3: telecommunications corporation representative.
Stakeholder respondent 4: telecommunications corporation representative.
Stakeholder respondent 5: telecommunications corporation representative
Stakeholder respondent 6: telecommunications corporation representative.
Stakeholder respondent 7: energy corporations representative.
Stakeholder respondent 8: energy corporations representative.
Stakeholder respondent 9: industrial energy consumers representative.
Stakeholder respondent 10: banking representative.
Stakeholder respondent 11: corporations listed at the stock exchange representative.
Stakeholder respondent 12: pension funds representative.
Stakeholder respondent 13: institutional investors representative.
Stakeholder respondent 14: stockowners representative.

Stakeholder respondent 15: medical specialists representative.

Stakeholder respondent 16: medical specialists representative.

Stakeholder respondent 17: general practitioners representative.

Stakeholder respondent 18: dentists representative.

Stakeholder respondent 19: hospitals representative.

Stakeholder respodent 20: healthcare providers for people with disabilities representative.

Stakeholder respondent 21: residential and home care organisations representative.

Stakeholder respondent 22: healthcare insurers representative.

Stakeholder respondent 23: healthcare insurers representative.

Stakeholder respondent 24: healthcare insurers representative.

Stakeholder respondent 25: patients and healthcare consumers representative.

Sources

AFM, Jaarverslag 2003, *AFM*, 2004, [accessed online 16.04.2019: <https://www.afm.nl/~/profmedia/files/afm/jaarverslag/jv-2003.pdf>].

AFM, Stichting Autoriteit Financiële Markten – Reglement ten behoeve van het Adviserend Panel van Vertegenwoordigende Organisaties, *AFM*, 2007, [accessed online 16.04.2019: <https://www.afm.nl/~/profmedia/files/afm/externe-samenwerking/huish-reglement-adviserend-panel-070415.pdf>].

AFM, Jaarverslag 2008, *AFM*, 2009, [accessed online 16.04.2019: <https://www.afm.nl/~/profmedia/files/afm/jaarverslag/jv-2008.pdf>].

AFM, Jaarverslag 2010, *AFM*, 2011, [accessed online 16.04.2019: <https://www.afm.nl/~/profmedia/files/afm/jaarverslag/jv-2010.pdf>].

AFM, Jaarverslag 2012, *AFM*, 2013, [accessed online 16.04.2019: <https://www.afm.nl/~/profmedia/files/afm/jaarverslag/2012/jaarverslag-2012.pdf>].

AFM, "Klantbelang centraal: Geef de klant wat hij nodig heeft," *AFM*, 2014, [accessed online 16.04.2019: <https://web.archive.org/web/20131115100214/http://www.afm.nl/nl/over-afm/thema/klantbelang-centraal/producten-met-toegevoegde-waarde.aspx>].

AFM, "Adviserend panel van vertegenwoordigende organisaties," *AFM*, 2019, [accessed online 16.04.2019: <https://www.afm.nl/nl-nl/over-afm/organisatie/ext-stakeholders>].

Consumer and Market Authority Establishment Act 2013. Wet van 28 februari 2013, houdende regels omtrent de instelling van de Autoriteit Consument en Markt (Instellingswet Autoriteit Consument en Markt), *Staatsblad* 102 (2013).

REGULATION WITHOUT REPRESENTATION? 197

Healthcare Market Structuring Act 2006. Wet van 7 juli 2006, houdende regels inzake marktordening, doelmatigheid en beheerste kostenontwikkeling op het gebied van de gezondheidszorg (Wet marktordening gezondheidszorg). *Staatsblad* 2006 nr. 415.

Dan, S., S. Jilke, C. Pollitt, R. van Delft, S. van de Walle, and S. van Thiel, "Effects of Privatisation and Agencification on Citizens and Citizenship: An International Comparison," *Eerste Kamer*, 27 February 2012, [accessed online at 16.04.2019: <http://www.eerstekamer.nl/id/vj45ispjadtf/document_extern/effects_of_privatisation_and/f=/vj45itou3itp.pdf>].

Second Chamber, Regels inzake instelling van een college voor post- en telecommunicatiemarkt (Wet onafhankelijke post- en telecommunicatieautoriteit). Memorie van toelichting. 25 128 nr. 3. *Kamerstukken II* (1996-1997a).

Second Chamber, Regels inzake de telecommunicatie (Telecommunicatiewet). Memorie van toelichting. 25 533 nr. 3. *Kamerstukken II* (1996-1997b).

Second Chamber, Regels met betrekking tot de productie, het transport en de levering van elektriciteit (Elektriciteitswet 19...). Memorie van toelichting. 25 621 nr. 3. *Kamerstukken II* (1997-1998).

Second Chamber, Borging van publieke belangen. Brief van de minister-president, minister van Algemene Zaken. 27 771 nr. 1. *Kamerstukken II* (2000-2001).

NMa, Jaarverslag 2008, *NMa*, 2009, [accessed online 16.04.2019: <https://www.acm.nl/nl/publicaties/publicatie/5391/NMa-Jaarverslag-2008/>].

NMa, "Organisatie," 2013a, [accessed online 16.04.2019: <http://web.archive.org/web/20130311061424/http://www.nma.nl/over_de_nma/organisatie/default.aspx>].

NMa, "Missie, visie & strategie," 2013b, [accessed online 16.04.2019: <http://web.archive.org/web/20130311055355/http://www.nma.nl/over_de_nma/missie__visie_and_strategie/default.aspx>].

NMa, Jaarverslag 2012, *NMa*, 2013c, [accessed online 16.04.2019: <http://nmajaarverslag2012.acm.nl/jaarverslag/downloads/>].

NZa, Jaarverslag 2007, *NZa* 2008, [accessed online 16.04.2019: <https://zoek.officiele bekendmakingen.nl/kst-25268-70-b4.pdf>].

NZa, Jaarverslag 2009, *NZa*, 2010, available at the author.

NZa, "Regeling Adviescommissies NZa," *NZa*, 2010b, available at the author.

NZa, "Organisatie – Nederlandse Zorgautoriteit," *NZa*, 2014a, [accessed online 16.04.2019: <https://web.archive.org/web/20140821141359/http://www.nza.nl/organisatie/overdenza/>].

NZa, "Missie – Nederlandse Zorgautoriteit," *NZa*, 2014b, [accessed online 16.04.2019: <https://web.archive.org/web/20140614154739/http://www.nza.nl/organisatie/overdenza/98050>].

OPTA, Jaarverslag 2004, *OPTA*, 2005, [accessed online 16.04.2019: <https://www.acm.nl/nl/publicaties/publicatie/8783/OPTA-Jaarverslag-2004-en-Visie-op-de-markt-2005>].

OPTA, Jaarverslag 2005, *OPTA*, 2006, [accessed online 16.04.2019: <https://www.acm.nl/nl/publicaties/publicatie/9039/OPTA-Jaarverslag-en-Marktmonitor-2005/>].

OPTA, Jaarverslag 2010, *OPTA*, 2011 [accessed online 16.04.2019: <http://optajaarverslag2010.acm.nl/jaarverslag/downloads/>].

OPTA, "OPTA is een ZBO," *OPTA*, 2013a, [accessed online 16.04.2019: http://web.archive.org/web/20121003003805/http://www.opta.nl/nl/hoe-werkt-opta/opta-is-een-zbo/>].

OPTA, "Morgen wordt vandaag bedacht," *OPTA*, 2013b, [accessed online 16.04.2019: <http://web.archive.org/web/20121003003543/http://www.opta.nl/nl/wat-doet-opta/morgen-wordt-vandaag-bedacht/>].

OPTA, "Consuwijzer," *OPTA*, 2013c, [accessed online 16.04.2019: <http://web.archive.org/web/20120530065208/http://www.opta.nl/nl/wat-doet-opta/consuwijzer/>].

Raad van State, Jaarverslag 1999, *Raad van State*, 2000, [accessed online 16.04.2019: <http://www.raadvanstate.nl/publicaties/jaarverslagen.html>].

Second Chamber, Hervorming van het toezicht op de financiële marktsector. Nota. 28 122 nr. 2. *Kamerstukken II* (2001-2002).

Second Chamber, Wijziging van de Telecommunicatiewet en enkele andere wetten in verband met de implementatie van een nieuw Europees geharmoniseerd regelgevingskader voor elektronische communicatienetwerken- en diensten en de nieuwe dienstenrichtlijn van de Commissie van de Europese Gemeenschappen. Memorie van toelichting. 28 851 nr. 3. *Kamerstukken II* (2002-2003).

Second Chamber, Visie op markttoezicht. Bijlage bij 29 200-XIII nr. 50. *Kamerstukken II* (2003-2004a).

Second Chamber, Wijziging van de Elektriciteitswet 1998 en de Gaswet ter uitvoering van richtlijn nr. 2003/54/EG, (PbEG L 176), verordening nr. 2003/55/EG (PbEG L 176), alsmede in verband met de aanscherping van het toezicht op het netbeheer (Wijziging Elektriciteitswet 1998 en Gaswet in verband met implementatie en aanscherping toezicht netbeheer). Memorie van toelichting. 29 372 nr. 3. *Kamerstukken II* (2003-2004b).

Second Chamber, Regels met betrekking tot de financiële markten en het toezicht daarop (Wet op het financieel toezicht). Memorie van toelichting. 29 708 nr. 3. *Kamerstukken II* (2003-2004c).

Second Chamber, Regels inzake marktordening, doelmatigheid en beheerste kos- tenontwikkeling op het gebied van de gezondheidszorg (Wet marktordening gezondheidszorg). Memorie van toelichting. 30 186 nr. 3. *Kamerstukken II* (2004-2005).

Telecommunications Act Revision Act 2004. Wet van 22 april 2004 tot wijziging van de Telecommunicatiewet en enkele andere wetten in verband met de implementatie van een nieuw Europees geharmoniseerd regelgevingskader voor elektronische communicatienetwerken- en diensten en de nieuwe dienstenrichtlijn van de Commissie van de Europese Gemeenschappen. *Staatsblad* 189 (2004).

Literature

Anderson, B.R.O'G., *Imagined Communities. Reflections on the Origin and Spread of Nationalism* (London, 1986).

Ankersmit, F., *Aesthetic Politics. Political Philosophy beyond Fact and Value* (Stanford, 1996).

Baldwin, R., M. Cave and M. Lodge, *Understanding Regulation. Theory, Strategy and Practice* (Oxford, 2012).

Berg, C. van den and M. Pars, '"Wij willen zichtbaar zijn". Over de legitimiteit en politieke profileringsdrang van de AFM,' in *Liberaal Reveil* 53, no. 2 (2012), 84-89.

Black, J., "Constructing and Contesting Legitimacy and Accountability in Polycentric Regulatory Regimes," in *Regulation & Governance* 2, no. 2 (2008), 137-164.

Bovens, M., "Two concepts of Accountability: Accountability as a Virtue and as a Mechanism," in *West European Politics* 33, no. 6 (2010), 946-967.

Coen, D. and M. Thatcher, "The New Governance of Markets and Non-Majoritarian Regulators," in *Governance: An International Journal of Policy, Administration, and Institutions* 18, no. 3 (2005), 329-346.

Duijkersloot, A.P.W., *Toezicht op gereguleerde markten* (Nijmegen, 2007).

Epstein, D. and S. O'Halloran, *Delegating Powers: A Transaction Costs Politics Approach to Policy Making under Separate Powers* (Cambridge, Eng., 1999).

Eulau, H. and P.D. Karps., "The Puzzle of Representation: Specifying Components of Responsiveness," in *Legislative Studies Quarterly* 2, no. 3 (1977), 233-254.

Gestel, R.A.J. van, P. Eijlander, and J.A.F. Peters, "The Regulatory Powers of Quangos in the Netherlands: Are Trojan Horses Invading our Democracy?," in *Electronic Journal of Comparative Law* 11, no. 1 (2007), 1-24, [accessed online 16.04.2019: <http://www.ejcl.org/111/art111-9.pdf>].

Gilardi, F., *Delegation in the Regulatory State. Independent Regulatory Agencies in Western Europe* (Cheltenham, 2008).

Levi-Faur, D., "Regulatory Networks and Regulatory Agencification: Towards a Single European Regulatory Space," in *Journal of European Public Policy* 18, no. 6 (2011), 810-829.

Maggetti, M., "Legitimacy and Accountability of Independent Regulatory Agencies: A Critical Review," in *Living Reviews in Democracy* 2 (2010), 1-9

Majone, G., "The regulatory state and its legitimacy problems," in *West European Politics* 22, no. 1 (1999), 1-24.

Majone, G., *Regulating Europe* (London, 1996).

Marochi, B., "Political Inclusion and Representative Claim-Making in Participatory Governance. Case Studies from Birmingham and Copenhagen," PhD Diss. (Roskilde Universitet, 2010).

Papadopoulos, Y., "Accountability and Multilevel Governance: More Accountability, Less Democracy?," in *West European Politics* 33, no. 5 (2010), 1030-1049.

Pitkin, H.F., *The Concept of Representation* (Berkeley, 1967).

Pree, J. de, "Publieke belangen, overheidsbeleid en investeringen in infrastructuur," in G. Arts, W. Dicke, and L. Hancher (eds.), *New Perspectives on Investment in Infrastructures* (Amsterdam, 2008).

Sabel, C.F. and J. Zeitlin, "Learning from Difference: The New Architecture of Experimentalist Governance in the EU," in *European Law Journal* 14, no. 3 (2008), 271-327.

Saward, M., *The Representative Claim* (Oxford, 2010).

Saward, M., "Authorisation and authenticity: representation and the unelected," in *Journal of Political Philosophy* 17, no.1 (2009), 1-22.

Saward, M., "The representative claim," in *Contemporary Political Theory* 5, no. 3 (2006), 297-318.

Saward, M., "Governance and the Transformation of Political Representation," in J. Newman (ed.), *Remaking Governance: Peoples, Politics and the Public Sphere* (Bristol, 2005), 179-186.

Severs, E. "Representation as Claims-Making. Quid Responsiveness?," in *Representation*, 46, no. 4 (2010), 411-423.

Sosay, G., "Consequences of Legitimizing Independent Regulatory Agencies in Contemporary Democracies. Theoretical Scenarios," in D. Braun and F. Gilardi (eds.), *Delegation in Contemporary Democracies* (London, 2006), 172-190.

Stellinga, B., *Dertig jaar privatisering, verzelfstandiging en marktwerking* (Amsterdam, 2012).

Strom, K., W.C. Müller, and T. Bergman (eds.), *Delegation and Accountability in Parliamentary Democracies* (Oxford, 2003).

Teulings, C., L. Bovenberg and H.P. van Dalen, *De calculus van het publieke belang* (The Hague, 2003).

Thatcher, M. and A. Stone Sweet, "Theory and Practice of Delegation to Non-Majoritarian Institutions," in *West European Politics* 25, no. 1 (2002), 1-22.

Thatcher, M., "The Third Force? Independent Regulatory Agencies and Elected Politicians in Europe," in *Governance: An International Journal of Policy, Administration, and Institutions* 18, no. 3 (2005), 347-373.

Thiel, S. van, *Quangocratization: Trends, Causes and Consequences* (ICS Dissertation Series, 2000).

Verhey, L.F.M. and N. Verheij, "De macht van de marktmeesters. Markttoezicht in constitutioneel perspectief," in *Handelingen der Nederlandsche Juristen-Vereeniging* 135, no. 1 (2005), 135-332.

Vibert, F., *The Rise of the Unelected. Democracy and the New Separation of Powers* (Cambridge, Eng., 2007).

Wetenschappelijke Raad voor het Regeringsbeleid, *Het borgen van publiek belang* (The Hague, 2000).

Wilde, P. de, "Representative Claims Analysis: Theory Meets Method," in *Journal of European Public Policy* 20, no. 2 (2013), 278-294.

Yackee, J.W. and S.W. Yackee, "A bias toward business? Assessing interest group influence on the U.S. bureaucracy," in *Journal of Politics* 68, no. 1 (2006) 128-139.

Zijlstra, S.E., *Zelfstandige bestuursorganen in een democratische rechtsstaat* (The Hague, 1997).

Index

Abbasid Empire   26-27, 30-32, 58
accessibility   3-6, 26-29, 33, 78-90
  See also leadership, models of accessible
    and distant
Adamson, John   79-80
Al-Muqtadir   27, 31-35
Al-Mu'tadid   33
Apollo   13, 67
architecture   61, 65-66, 73, 84, 88
Arch of Constantine   20, 22
Asch, Ronald G.   87-88
assembly   17, 40-41,
Association Agreement (AA)   146, 152-153,
    156, 162
audience   3, 29-32, 85, 130, 135, 139, 163,
    173-176, 178-179,
Augustus   12-14, 16-17, 20
authority   1, 17, 19, 47, 62, 66, 80, 97-98, 104,
    109-110, 112-115, 144-146
  Autoriteit Financiële Markten 'Financial
    Markets Authority' (AFM)   171, 178,
    182-184, 186, 188-191
  Independent Regulatory Authority
    (IRA)   9, 171-173, 177-195
  Nederlandse Mededingingsautoriteit
    Energiekamer 'Netherlands Competi-
    tion Authority Energy Chamber'
    (NMa Energiekamer)   178, 178n25,
    178n26, 182-187
  Nederlandse Zorgautoriteit 'Netherlands
    Healthcare Authority' (NZa)   178,
    183-186, 188-192
  Onafhankelijke Post en Telecommunicatie
    Autoriteit 'Independent Mail and
    Telecommunications Authority'
    (OPTA)   178, 178n25, 180, 182-187, 189,
    192
Avignon   58-59

Baghdad   31-32, 34
Baker, Keith Michael   2
Bandera, Stepan   150, 164-165
Bonum commune   43

Caligula   16
caliph   6, 26-28, 30-35, 58
caricature   95, 97-98, 105, 119-121
  See also political cartoon
Cassius Dio   15
ceremony   14, 31-32, 70, 85-86
Charlemagne   31
Charles II of England   87
Christianity   59, 74
Cistercian order   40-41, 44, 44n19, 51
  See also religious orders
clothing   82
  See also dress
coins   23, 23n30
Colijn, Hendrikus   7, 94, 96-121
Commodus   16-17
communal statutes   50
communicative practices   124, 127, 129, 132,
    139-140
conciliarism   38-39
Constantine   19, 23, 59
Constantinople   19
constituency   2, 126, 128, 131, 146, 173-179, 181,
    186, 190-194
  constituency construction   175-176, 178,
    181, 183-184, 187
constitution   46, 46n25, 145, 150
consumers   124, 139, 172, 180-195
contestation   144, 146, 148
Conway, Martin   128
corporate government   42-43, 51
Cossack Hetmanate   162
court culture   26-28
courtiers   11-12, 26, 29, 79, 82, 85-86, 89
Crimea   150-151, 153, 163, 166
cultural resources   175-176
custodians   45-48

Decretum   38
Deep and Comprehensive Free Trade Area
    (DCFTA)   152
delegation   31, 50-51, 171-172, 177, 193
democracy   4, 8, 94, 97-98, 109, 112, 125, 144,
    147, 149-150, 165
  crisis of   124

204   INDEX

democracy (cont.)
   direct   44, 144, 160-161
   disciplined   109-110, 118
     See also leadership, authoritative
   forms of   144-145
   parliamentary   96, 98, 104, 109, 112, 116-118, 120, 124, 128, 138
   party   128, 134
   representative   165-166, 173, 177, 193-194
   social   134
   without representation   161
diplomats   71, 83, 85
discretus/ discreti   47-48
discursive practice   2-4
Dominican order   38, 41, 44, 44n19, 50-51
   See also religious orders
Domitian   16-17
dress   27, 30, 131
   See also clothing
Duindam, Jeroen   80

Elagabalus   16
elections   16, 38, 49, 74, 125, 127, 129-130, 146-147, 149-151, 153-154, 156, 158-159, 161-162, 173-175, 194
   election fraud   146, 151, 153-154
Elton, Geoffrey   79
emperor   4-5, 11-23, 31, 39, 42, 51, 58-59, 85
Euromajdan   146-147, 152-153, 156, 159-165

favourites   26, 32, 88
Fenske, Michaela   134, 138
Forum (Augustum)   13
framing   98, 157, 163, 165
France   56, 65-68, 73-74, 116-117
Franciscan order   37, 43n17, 43-47, 49-51
   See also religious orders

general chapter   38, 40-41, 45-49
Gibbon, Edward   17
governance   28, 30, 172, 174, 194
   regulatory   177-179, 188, 191, 194

Hadrian   15, 17
Hagia Sophia   60
Hengerer, Mark   87
Hilal al-Sabi'   28, 30, 34
history of political thought   37-40

Humanism   58-60, 74
Hunt, Lynn   2

Ibn al-Furat   32, 34-35
iconography   88, 119
iconology   73
Igo, Sarah   131
institutions   3, 9, 18-20, 128, 132, 148, 171, 174, 176, 183, 188
   civic   73
   democratic   144-145, 150, 171-172, 174, 177, 179-180, 183
   political   172
   religious   38, 41-42, 44
   representative   38, 51, 145, 166
   Republican   12-13
interest groups   174-175, 187n76, 188, 194
interwar period   94, 96-98, 104-105, 136, 164
Iran   28, 33, 58

Janukovyč, Viktor   146-147, 151-152, 154, 159, 161-162
Jerusalem   57, 61
Julian the Apostate   16
Julius Caesar   12-13

king   4-5, 7, 41, 49, 51, 66-68, 73-73, 87
   See also monarch
Kučma, Leonid   147, 149-151, 154, 159, 163

Lawrence, Jon   2, 126, 139
leadership   8, 45n22, 110-114, 118-121, 140, 144-145, 149, 159, 162,
   models of accessible and distant   27-33, 35
     See also accessibility
   authoritative   8, 120
     See also democracy, disciplined
   deliberative   104, 119
   representation of   94-98, 119-121
legitimation   1, 20, 27, 60, 119, 144-146, 150, 157, 163, 165-166, 172
liberalised marketplaces   171, 173, 177, 181, 187, 193
lobbyists   179, 187, 188-194
Louis XIV   65-72
Louw, André van der   134-135

INDEX 205

Magna Mater   14
Majdan 144-167
majority
   principles   41-42
   vote   41, 47-48
   parliamentary   100, 110
Manin, Bernard   128
Marcus Aurelius   16, 18n22
Marsilius of Padua   40-43
material culture   3, 80, 88
Mergel, Thomas   2
Michelangelo   60
Middle Ages   5, 40, 61
Middle East   26
minister   45-49, 100, 103-104, 106, 108, 114,
   117-118, 136, 138, 154, 159, 180
Miskawayh   31-32
monarch   11-13, 18-19, 30, 58, 67-68, 73-74, 110,
   175
   See also king
Muhammad   27
Mu'nis   32

nation   74, 98, 109, 115, 121 149, 158, 174
nationalism   164-165
national socialists   98, 105-106, 109, 117,
   119-120
Nero   16-17
Nerva   16-17
Netherlands   94-100, 109-110, 113, 116, 119, 128,
   177-180, 188
Nizam al-Mulk   28-30

opinion polls   125, 130-131
Organisation of Ukrainian Nationalists
   (OUN)   164-165
Otpor! Movement   153-155
Ovid   68

Palaces   26-27, 31-33, 35, 56-58, 60-61, 65-73,
   84-86
papacy   42, 58-59, 61-62, 64, 74
   See also pope
parades   4, 86
Paris   46, 49, 65, 67, 72-74
parliament   1, 37-38, 41, 94-103
   Crisis of parliamentarism   94
Partij van de Arbeid (PvdA)   134-138

the people   1-2, 33-35, 94, 109-110, 124-125,
   128-133, 138, 144, 158, 166-167
   the voice of   129-130, 139-140
performance   7, 15, 80, 83, 85, 111, 139
photography   94-104, 111-113, 119
political cartoons   97, 104, 114, 119
   See also caricature
political communication   3, 124, 126, 129, 132
political culture   90, 127, 149
political discourse   181
political identity   126, 128-129, 131
political party   1-2, 94-96, 105, 134
pope   39, 42, 51, 58-66, 73-74
   See also papacy
popular culture   131
popular perceptions of political representation   8, 124, 127-128, 131, 134
popular politics   124, 126-130, 139-140
popular sovereignty   144, 162
Pora! Movement   146, 154-155
Porošenko, Petro   153, 162-164, 166-167
Potestas delegata   42
press   97, 99, 104, 129-130, 166
princely courts   78, 88
privileges   88
propaganda   56, 65-66, 74, 165
public interest   181-184, 190, 192-193

Qur'an   27-28

reception   3-4, 14, 126, 140, 173-174, 179,
   188-191
repertoire   3, 80, 83, 97, 120, 131-132, 139, 146,
   153-165
Reformation   74
religious orders   37-40
   See also Cistercian order
   See also Dominican order
   See also Franciscan order
Renaissance   56, 58, 60
representation
   aesthetic   94, 119
   mimetic   94, 119
   non-electoral   173, 175, 193-194
representative claim   2-5, 12, 20, 23, 125-126,
   131, 144-146, 172-194
   representative claim framework
   (RCF)   173-175

206 INDEX

representative government 37-41, 48
revolution
   colour revolutions 148-149, 154, 157
   Orange Revolution 146, 148-149, 151-155,
      161-162
   Revolution of Dignity 161-162, 165-166
   square revolutions 148-149, 156-157
rhetoric 56, 65, 73-74, 176
rituals 15, 26, 31, 57, 70, 85, 88
Roman Republic 12-14, 17-18
Rome 56-59, 61, 73-74
   Ara Pacis 20-21
   Palatine 13
Romulus 13
Rosanvallon, Pierre 125, 127-128
rulers 1-3, 11-20, 26-30, 33-35, 57-59, 79-82, 87
   See also king
   See also monarch
Salomon, Erich 97-104, 110-114, 120
Saward, Michael 1-2, 125-127, 173-177, 192, 194
Schmitt, Carl 79, 125
self-representation 2-5, 119, 175
Sellasie, Haile 11, 23
senatorial elite 17
space 57, 65, 68, 71, 82, 84-85, 113, 131, 148,
      159, 174
spatial organization 26, 83-85
Starkey, David 79

Statues 65, 158-159
Stedman Jones, Gareth 2
Steinmetz, Willibald 2
street politics 144, 146, 150
Suetonius 13
Symbols 60, 67-68, 73-74, 88-89, 94, 106, 110,
      116, 145, 148, 156, 158, 185

Talbot, Michael 85
Tans, Sjeng 134, 138
Television 130, 135, 138-139
Tiberius 18
Truschke, Audrey 85
Tymosenko, Julia 151-152, 154, 158, 161, 163,
      166-167

Ukraine 145-146, 150-154, 156, 158-161, 163-167
Ukrainian Insurgent Army (UPA) 164-165
Umayyad Empire 28
urban elite 74

Versailles 56, 58, 65-74
visual sources 98, 119
vizier 28, 30-35
Vondeling, Anne 134, 138
voting procedures 49-50

Weiser, Brian 87